LISPcraft

ROBERT WILENSKY

UNIVERSITY OF CALIFORNIA, BERKELEY

W • W • NORTON & COMPANY
New York   London

To my parents
Neesa and Abraham

Library of Congress Cataloging in Publication Data
Wilensky, Robert, 1951–
    LISPcraft.
    1. LISP (Computer program language)   I. Title.
    QA76.73.L23W55   1984   001.64′24   84-1473

Cover: Joseph Stella, *Brooklyn Bridge*
        Yale University Art Gallery
        Gift of Collection Société Anonyme

ISBN 0-393-95442-0

W. W. Norton & Company, Inc.,
500 Fifth Avenue, New York, N.Y. 10110
W. W. Norton & Company, Ltd.,
37 Great Russell Street, London WC1B 3NU
        6 7 8 9 0

Contents

Contents

Contents

Contents

Contents

x

Preface

1. The LISP Language

LISP is one of the oldest programming languages in active use today. The LISP language was first conceived by John McCarthy and his students in the late 1950's. The name *LISP* is an acronym for *LISt Processing,* a reference to the fundamental structure underlying most LISP programs and data. Its main use, both then and now, is in the field of artificial intelligence.

LISP is one of the few older languages to have survived the transition to the current era of computing. Since its initial inception and implementation, the LISP language has undergone considerable evolution. Many new features have been added, implementations have been dramatically improved, and interfaces markedly upgraded. Whole programming environments have been created and integrated into the language. LISP has even been given hardware support in the form of high performance LISP machines.

These developments were often in response to drawbacks in the early conception and implementations of the language. As a result, many of the reasons underlying the reluctance of some to accept LISP are no longer valid today. Nevertheless, LISP still maintains a vestige of its past reputation as an interesting but impractical language. Recent improvements in computer technology, together with the availability of some of the finest software development environments in existence, have done much to change this attitude. The LISP community currently appears to be undergoing a period of rapid expansion.

One difficulty with LISP is trying to define exactly what the LISP language is. Unlike many other languages, there is no such thing as standard LISP. Rather, LISP has evolved in a number of different directions. This has resulted in a whole family of LISP languages. While these share many basic features, they differ from one another in substantial ways. There is work today on a version of LISP called *Common LISP* that would try to set a more uniform standard for LISP programs. But no single, uniform interpretation of LISP has yet been embraced by the LISP community.

Among the most widely used dialects of LISP today are *MacLISP,* a version of LISP developed at MIT, and *INTERLISP,* developed at Bolt, Beranek and Newman and Xerox Palo Alto Research Center. Versions of these dialects currently run on various special purpose LISP machines. *Portable Standard LISP* is another dialect designed to be easily transportable across different machines. The *Scheme* dialect of LISP, invented by Sussman and Abelson at MIT, contains a rather different interpretation of a number of basic concepts than that found in most other versions of the language.

2. Scope and Aim

This text is based on a particular dialect of LISP called *Franz LISP.* Franz is probably closest to MacLISP in appearance. Franz was developed at the University of California at Berkeley and is available under Berkeley UNIX*. Insofar as it is possible, this text tries to be dialect independent. It does so mostly by specifying those points at which other LISPs are likely to deviate from the one described herein. The alternative is to create a rather flavorless version of a language strictly for pedagogic exegesis. The philosophy taken is that it is easier to learn a new dialect having mastered another than it is having learned a language for which there are no native speakers.

This text is designed to give the reader a working knowledge of Franz LISP. No formal description of the language is attempted. Rather, the text emphasizes pragmatic considerations. In addition to explaining the basic features of LISP, programming language idioms, elements of various programming styles, and system interface issues are given equal attention. It is the experience of this author that such items contribute just as much to the characteristic flavor of a programming language as do the core features of that language.

While issues of programming style are addressed, an effort has been made

---

*UNIX is a trademark of Bell Laboratories.

not to be chauvinistic. Instead, certain useful programming language styles are suggested to the reader for consideration. Comments about good and bad programming style are given throughout. These generally derive from observations of LISP programming practice rather than from stylistic prejudices.

LISP is used largely as a programming language for artificial intelligence research. However, this bias is not substantially reflected in this book. The language rather than its applications is emphasized here. After familiarizing himself with the essentials of the language, the reader may want to consult other texts that feature artificial intelligence issues more prominently.

While this document is self-contained, it does not exhaust or fully describe every aspect of Franz LISP. The reader may consult *The Franz LISP Manual* by J. K. Foderaro and K. L. Sklower for additional detail. The *Manual* is the final authority on what Franz LISP will do, except, of course, for the LISP interpreter itself.

3. Format

Programming in a computer language is a skill like any other: Proficiency does not come without practice. The best programming language text will not promote fluency in a language unless the reader uses the language as he goes along. With this in mind, this text has been designed as an interactive session with the LISP interpreter. To get the most out of this text, the reader should participate in the dialogues given below by running LISP, typing in the expressions as they appear, and noting the responses given by the LISP system.

The text should be viewed more as a travel guide than a textbook. Without the accompanying exploration, real learning is not possible. The reader should first familiarize himself with the basic features of the language as described in the initial chapter of this text. This should supply the reader with enough knowledge and safety equipment to handle any situations that are encountered by straying off the tour suggested in subsequent chapters.

The reader is encouraged to take the time to make as many side trips as possible. Not everything the reader encounters in his explorations will make sense at first. Nevertheless, a good way to get to know a country is to get off the beaten path. Do not neglect the main attractions, however. There is usually a reason that there is so much interest in them.

Bon voyage!

Acknowledgments

Richard Fateman and his students were responsible for the creation of Franz LISP. Keith Sklower, John Foderaro, and Kevin Layer made many enhancements, and directly contributed to my understanding of this system. Various members of BAIR, the Berkeley Artificial Intelligence Research Project, used Franz LISP for their research and contributed to its overall development.

James Meehan and Chris Riesbeck were of great help when I first learned LISP. The environment of the Yale Artificial Intelligence Project, created by Roger Schank, was conducive to the experimentation that learning a computer language requires.

Michael Harrison provided encouragement and valuable advice during several stages of this project. Diana Currie tested an early version of this tutorial, and was thereby responsible for numerous substantive changes. Many of the examples and exercises in this book are the direct result of her comments. She is also responsible for the title. Doug Cooper made a number of useful suggestions, and helped in my struggles with the text processing system. Paul Hansen provided some detailed corrections of a previous draft.

1

Getting Started

1.1. INTRODUCTION

In this chapter we encounter the basic elements of LISP. These include the primary data structure of LISP, called the *s-expression.* They also include the LISP *interpreter,* which constitutes the heart of any LISP system. The LISP interpreter performs computations on s-expressions through a process called *evaluation.* We examine this process, and describe how it applies to different kinds of s-expressions. Along the way, the major categories of s-expressions, called *lists* and *atoms,* are discussed.

We encounter our first LISP functions in this chapter. These are largely concerned with arithmetic computation. We also learn how to store the value of a computation for subsequent use, and how to recover from an error. By the end of this chapter, the reader will be familiar with the syntax of LISP, and be able to specify and understand complex computations.

1.2. THE LISP INTERPRETER

LISP is normally used as an *interpreter.* Think of an interpreter as a kind of glorified handheld calculator − you type in arguments and an operation to perform on them. The "calculator" does the operation and prints out an answer. To begin a session with the LISP calculator, we first need to start up a LISP process. In UNIX, this is done by issuing the command **lisp** (other operating systems may use a slightly different convention). LISP will identify itself and signal that it is ready to accept an input:

Franz Lisp, Opus 38.41
—>

The arrow is Franz LISP's signal that it is waiting for an input (of course, other LISPs will identify themselves accordingly, and may use different prompt symbols). Now we are ready to ask the LISP calculator to perform an operation for us. LISP accepts commands in a somewhat different form from most handheld calculators. First, we begin the command with a parenthesis. Next, we specify the name of an operation we would like to perform. Then we give the arguments we want to use. We finish the whole thing off with a closing parenthesis. Finally, we type a carriage return to instruct LISP to begin its computation. For example, if we want to compute "8+3" using our LISP calculator, we type the following:

—> **(plus 8 3)**
11
—>

In this example, we only typed the expression in parentheses; the arrows and the answer were output by LISP. **plus** is the name for the addition operator in this LISP; **8** and **3** are the arguments to this operator. There are lots of other operators like **plus** in LISP (a full enumeration of them can be found in the appendix). But they all work pretty much the same way. For example, if we want to multiply 8 by 3, we can type

—> **(times 8 3)**
24
—>

LISP programmers sometimes call commands like these *s-expressions,* which stands for *symbolic expressions.* This is a very general term, applying to just about anything one can say in LISP. This terminology is used because, unlike our examples so far, LISP is normally used for things other than numeric computation. However, the basic form of all symbolic expressions will be similar to what we have already seen. In fact, you have already learned most of the syntax of LISP!

For the time being, we will stick with numeric examples because they will be easier to relate to other programming experience you are likely to have had.

2

1.3. EVALUATION

The symbolic expressions given above are also called *lists*. A list is just a
sequence of objects inside a pair of parentheses. As we indicated above,
LISP assumes that the first element of the list is an operator. It assumes
that the rest of the list contains arguments to this operator. LISP applies the
operator to the arguments. This process of taking a symbolic expression, or
list, and performing a computation based on it is called *evaluation*. The
result of evaluating an s-expression is called, naturally enough, the *value* of
that expression. In our first example, we typed in the list **(plus 8 3)**; LISP
evaluated this s-expression by assuming that **plus** is an operator to be
applied to the arguments **8** and **3**. The result of this evaluation was the
value **11**. When it had finished evaluating this s-expression, LISP printed
out the resulting value on the terminal.

1.3.1. Evaluating More Complicated S-expressions

Suppose we want to compute something a bit more complicated. For example, suppose we want to know the value of "$8*(3+7)$". On a handheld calculator we would probably add 3 to 7 first, and then multiply the result by 8.
To do the equivalent computation in LISP, we would type the following
expression:

> -> **(times 8 (plus 3 7))**
> **80**
> ->

Note that this expression looks just like the last **times** we evaluated, except
that here the second argument is itself an expression. When LISP evaluates
an expression, it evaluates the arguments to the operator *before* it applies
that operator to the arguments. So when LISP tries to apply **times** to the
second argument above, it notices that this argument is itself an expression
and evaluates it. The result of this evaluation is used as the argument for
subsequent computation.   In the example above, LISP evaluates
(plus 3 7) to produce the result **10**. Then it multiplies the argument **8** times
10 to get the final result.

We see from this example that s-expressions, or lists, can contain elements
that are themselves s-expressions or lists. We can nest this construction as
much as we like, that is, put lists inside lists inside lists, and so on. LISP
will evaluate every expression according to one simple rule:

The LISP Evaluation Rule: *Look at the outermost list first. Evaluate each of
its arguments. Use the results as arguments to the outermost operator.*

3

In this manner, we can use LISP to compute expressions of arbitrary complexity. For example, to compute "$(8+3)*(4+(9*2))$", we would type

> **-> (times (plus 8 3) (plus 4 (times 9 2)))**
> **242**
> **->**

While this expression looks complicated, it is easy to see what it means to LISP. In accordance with the rule just given, LISP first tries to evaluate the entire expression. That is, it tries to apply **times** to its two arguments. Since each of these arguments is itself a list, LISP has to evaluate each one before it can perform the multiplication.

The first argument is **(plus 8 3)**. Evaluating this is simple — LISP merely applies **plus** to **8** and **3** and gets **11**. However, the second argument is **(plus 4 (times 9 2))**. This itself contains an argument that is a list, namely, **(times 9 2)**. Thus to evaluate the second argument of the entire expression, LISP must first evaluate its complex argument. This evaluation is itself straightforward — LISP applies **times** to **9** and **2** and gets **18**. Now the expression that contains this multiplication can be evaluated. The other argument in this expression is **4**, so LISP applies **plus** to **4** and **18** and gets **22**.

LISP has now completed the evaluation of the two arguments of the entire expression. The outermost expression is now ready to be evaluated. The result of the evaluation of the first argument was **11**, so LISP applies **times** to **11** and **22** and gets **242**. This result is then printed out on the terminal.

LISP will not be bothered by such nesting. But you might be. Although they are perfectly legal, it becomes difficult to read heavily nested s-expressions. Writing them often leads to errors involving *unbalanced parentheses* (an old joke among LISP hackers is that LISP really stands for "Lots of Irritating Single Parentheses"). There are ways around this problem, involving the use of good indentation and editors that help you write LISP. These help, but nevertheless, most people consider it to be bad programming style to use many deeply nested s-expressions.

LISP Evaluates Everything

In these examples, we said that LISP evaluates complex arguments in order to apply an operator. Actually, LISP tries to evaluate *all* its arguments, even simple ones like **8** and **3**. But what does it mean to evaluate a number? The answer, in LISP, is that numbers evaluate to themselves.

That is, any time LISP tries to evaluate **8**, the answer is always **8**; when it tries to evaluate **3**, the answer is always **3**.

This is just a convention. It makes LISP more uniform, because we can say that LISP expressions evaluate their arguments without having to make exceptions for numbers and other things we are going to see later on. One way in which this uniformity is manifest is that we can ask LISP directly to evaluate an **8** or a **3**. That is, we can type the following:

```
-> 8
8
-> 3
3
->
```

In sum, numbers are really s-expressions too. They are just very simple ones that always evaluate to themselves.

Expressions Always Return a Value

Another general rule about LISP that has been true so far is that expressions always return a value. When we evaluate the innermost argument of a complicated expression, the result is a value that is used by the next stage of our computation. Eventually, a value is returned from the evaluation of the whole expression. LISP prints this value back to the user.

1.4. ARGUMENTS TO FUNCTIONS

Our examples above all contain two arguments. There is nothing sacred about two, however. For example, **add1** is a LISP operator that takes a number and adds 1 to it, as in

```
-> (add1 8)
9
->
```

Some LISP operators, such as **plus**, can take a variable number of arguments. For example, we can do the following in LISP:

```
-> (plus 7 8 9)
24
->
```

Since we do not normally talk about operators when more than two arguments are involved, we should more properly call things like **plus** *functions.*
We will use this terminology from now on.

The function **plus** is somewhat unusual in that it will handle any number of
arguments. Most LISP functions require a fixed number of arguments. For
example, look what happens if we supply the incorrect number of arguments
to **add1**:

> —> **(add1 8 9)**
> **Error: incorrect number of args to add1**
> **<1>:**

LISP caught our error and printed out a message. However, the familiar
—> prompt is gone, replaced by a mysterious <1>:. This is LISP's way of
communicating with us after an error. The <1>: is simply a new prompt;
we can follow it with any s-expression, and LISP will evaluate it just as
before. Try a few examples if you like. If we were debugging a real program, this would give us the opportunity to debug the program interactively.
We will discuss LISP debugging facilities in detail later on. However, we
will not bother with this for now. Instead, we would simply like LISP to
forget the error ever happened and put us back where we were. To do this,
type the following expression:

> **<1>: (reset)**

> **[Return to top level]**
> —>

The s-expression evaluated in this example, **(reset),** is simply a list of one
element. Evaluating such an s-expression is equivalent to executing a function of no arguments. Executing this particular LISP function causes LISP
to print the message in brackets and go back to where we came from. As
we can see, the place where we were is called the *top level* of LISP. Think of
the top level as the place where LISP has finished all pending evaluations
and is waiting for new input from the user. Whenever you get into trouble
because of an error and wish to get back to the top level, you can execute
the **reset** function.

Note: Different LISPs will use different prompt conventions upon
encountering an error. They will also use functions other than **reset** to continue after an error. While the details may be different, the basic format is
apt to be the same.

reset is different from the other functions we have seen in that it does not return a value. In fact, it never returns at all. Instead, it causes LISP to start over again. *This sort of function is highly atypical.* Unless otherwise noted, we can assume that all LISP functions will return a value.

LISP is somewhat unusual in that virtually everything gets done by executing a function. In fact, there is really no more to LISP than that. All the complexity of LISP comes from the particular functions LISP provides and the details of how various types of functions are treated by the interpreter.

1.5. ATOMS AND BINDING

So far, we have seen how to perform arbitrarily complex numerical computations in LISP. But we have not seen any way to store the results of such computations. We need something to fill the role played by variables in other programming languages. LISP provides a similar service through the use of *atoms*. Atoms look like variables, although atoms have other uses as well. Examples of atoms are **foo**, **baruch**, and **long-variable-name13**. Just as one can assign a value to a variable in most programming languages, one can *bind* a value to an atom in LISP.

Binding is just another name for assigning a value, as far as we are concerned. However, while most programming languages provide a special notation for assignment, e. g., an assignment arrow or an equal sign, LISP does no such thing. Instead, LISP uses its routine workhorse, the function. LISP has a special function which binds the value of one of its arguments to the other argument. This function goes under the rather peculiar name of **setq**. For example, to accomplish the equivalent of "x ← 5" in LISP, we do the following:

> −> **(setq x 5)**
> **5**
> −>

It does not look like much has happened. But we can now query LISP about the value of **x**:

> −> **x**
> **5**
> −>

The use of **setq** has caused LISP to remember a value for **x**. Another way of saying this is that atoms are also s-expressions that LISP tries to evaluate when we type them in. The value of an atom in LISP is the value bound to that atom by some previous operation.

We can use atoms wherever we expect an s-expression to appear. For example, having previously bound a value to **x**, we can do the following:

> -> **(plus x 8)**
> **13**
> -> **x**
> **5**
> ->

Note that using an atom as an argument to a function does not ordinarily change its value, unless that function is something specially designed for that purpose, like **setq**.

What would the value of an atom be if there were no previous operation? Let us find out by asking LISP to evaluate some previously unmentioned atom:

> -> **money**
> **Error: Unbound Variable: money**
> **<1>:**

Franz LISP considers this to be an error. Let us issue a **reset** so we can go on.

But there appears to be an inconsistency here. We said before that LISP tries to evaluate arguments before applying a function. When we evaluate a **setq**, the atom whose value we are changing may not be defined. If LISP treated **setq** like any other function, then should not LISP try to evaluate its first argument, and thereby cause an error? For example, if we type in **(setq x 5)**, should not LISP try to evaluate the argument **x**, and generate an error because **x** is undefined?

In fact, it should. The only reason this does not happen is because LISP treats **setq** differently from the other functions we have seen so far. In particular, **setq** does not cause its first argument to be evaluated (the second argument is subject to normal treatment). For example, we can type

> -> **(setq x (plus 4 5))**
> **9**
> -> **x**
> **9**
> ->

Here LISP evaluated the expression constituting the second argument. Then it bound **x** to the result of this evaluation.

8

LISP's special treatment of **setq** might seem like a hack at first glance. However, later on we will see a more systematic treatment of functions that will make this exception seem more reasonable.

Note that when we bound **x** to a value using **setq**, LISP also printed out that value. That is, the expression **(setq x 5)** returned the value **5** *in addition to binding* **x** *to* **5**. This is important in that we can use the value returned by **setq** to continue the computation. Consider the following example:

> $->$ **(plus 2 (setq x (times 3 4)))**
> **14**
> $->$ **x**
> **12**
> $->$

This may look strange at first, but let us apply our rule of LISP evaluation: LISP tries to evaluate arguments first, so first it evaluates **2** to **2**. The second argument then gets evaluated. This is a **setq**, so to evaluate it, LISP only evaluates its second argument. This causes the **times** function to be applied to **3** and **4**, and the value **12** is computed. Then **setq** is applied to **x** and **12**. **setq** sets **x** to **12** and also returns **12** as its value. **plus** is now applied to **2** and **12**, and the answer **14** returned. Since **x** was changed in the process, we can query LISP for its value afterwards.

This sort of construct is not too desirable from a programming-style vantage point. We have caused a side-effect (i. e., changing the value of an atom) right in the middle of an expression, and this can be confusing. So even though this is legal, it should be used with caution. Later on we will see some techniques that will help us structure our code to avoid such expressions.

Numbers and Functions Are Atoms

LISP uses the term **atom** to refer to just about any expression it cannot take apart, in contrast to a list. In particular, numbers are considered to be atoms too. Of course, one cannot bind different values to numbers like we can to ordinary atoms. To pay homage to this distinction, items like **foo** and **x** are sometimes called *symbols,* or *literal atoms.*

The symbols that we use to denote functions in LISP, e. g., **times**, **plus**, and **add1**, do not constitute a separate class of object. Rather, these are literal atoms, just like **x**, **y**, and **foo**. The only difference is that members of the former group are known to LISP as denoting some function, while those of the latter are not. For example, watch what happens when I try to use the

9

atom **bodily** where LISP expects a function name:

> -> (bodily 1 2)
> **Error: eval: Undefined function bodily**
> **<1>:**

LISP objected to this because it does not know about any function named
bodily. We can issue a **(reset)** here to go on.

Other than the fact that they denote functions built into LISP, there is nothing at all special about the symbols **plus**, **times**, etc. For example, I can
bind values to these symbols just as I can to less prominent atoms:

> -> (setq plus 17)
> 17
> -> plus
> 17
> -> (plus 3 6)
> 9
> ->

Here I bind **plus** to the value **17**. This operation has absolutely no effect
whatsoever on **plus**'s role as a function name.

Thus literal atoms serve the dual roles of function identifiers and variables
in LISP. And it is possible to use symbols for both roles simultaneously, as
the above example demonstrates. However, doing so is usually bad programming practice. Expressions such as **(setq plus 17)** tend to be confusing. The programmer is probably better off picking a name that is not
already serving another purpose.

1.6. LEAVING LISP

If at any point you should wish to terminate your current session with the
LISP interpreter, most LISPs have some function that will do so. In Franz
LISP, such a function is called **exit**. This is a function of no arguments
which terminates the current LISP process. Control is returned to the
parent process (probably the shell). Thus:

> -> (exit)
> %

exit kills the current LISP process, so if you want to play with LISP some
more, you will have to create a fresh process, as we did in the beginning of

this chapter. Of course, this fresh process will not know about any of the things you did in your previous session, for better or for worse. For example, if we **setq** the values of some atoms in one session and then **exit**ed LISP, the next LISP process we create will be oblivious to these bindings:

> **−> (setq x 4)**
> **4**
> **−> (exit)**
> **% lisp**
> **Franz Lisp, Opus 38.67**
> **−> x**
> **Error: Unbound Variable: x**
> **<1>:**

To leave LISP temporarily, you can use the general UNIX job control facilities. That is, you can type **CTRL-z**, which suspends the current process. The UNIX command **fg** can then be used to reinstate the process later on. Of course, such UNIX facilities are extremely system dependent.

If you are unfamiliar with these UNIX features, you can use one of the fancier functions described in the later chapter on system functions. For example, the function **shell**, of no arguments, creates a shell subprocess. When this subprocess is terminated, control is returned to LISP:

> **−> (setq x 5)**
> **5**
> **−> (shell)**
> **% pwd**
> **/na/bair/wilensky/cs182/lisp**
> **% exit**
> **% 0**
> **−> x**
> **5**
> **−>**

The use of the **shell** function is not recommended, however, as you are apt to forget that you have a LISP process around, and end up cluttering up the system with unnecessary processes.

1.7. SUMMARY

We have encountered the following types of LISP objects:

(1) *s-expressions,* which encompass everything we have seen, including both lists and atoms,

(2) *lists,* which are sequences of s-expressions inside matching parentheses,

and

(3) *atoms,* which are s-expressions that LISP treats as whole things. There are two kinds of atoms, *numbers* and *literal atoms* (also called *symbols).* The latter fill the roles of both variables and function names.

We communicate with a LISP *interpreter,* which tries to *evaluate* each s-expression we type in. After evaluation, the interpreter prints the value it computed. We refer to this aspect of the LISP system with which we communicate directly as the *top level* of LISP.

Evaluation is done according to the following rules:

(1) Numbers evaluate to themselves.

(2) Symbols evaluate to the last value bound to them.

(3) Lists are evaluated by interpreting the first element as a function name, and the rest of the list as arguments to that function. The arguments are (usually) evaluated, and the function applied to them. The value returned by the function is the value of the list.

We have seen the following functions:

(1) Arithmetic functions like **plus, add1**, and **times**. Some of these accept any number of arguments, and some, a fixed number. They all cause all their arguments to be evaluated.

(2) **setq**, which *binds* its first argument, which should be an atom, to the value of its second argument.

(3) The systems functions **reset**, **exit**, and **shell**. All are functions of no arguments.

reset starts LISP over again after an error.

exit terminates the current LISP process.

shell creates a shell subprocess which returns to LISP upon termination.

Exercises

(1)   Write s-expressions to compute each of the following:

(a) $3^2 + 4^2$

(b) $(3*17) + (4*19)$

(c) $12^3 + 1^3 - (9^3 + 10^3)$

Most LISPs will recognize more than one name for the same function. For example, Franz LISP recognizes **add** and **sum** as identical to the function **plus**. The function **+** is similar, except it only works on small integers. Note that **+** is not a special operator or syntactic feature of LISP, but merely an atom with a short, unusual name. Similarly, the LISP function **times** can also be called **product** or ***** (the latter only applies to small integers); **difference** goes by the name **diff** and **−** (again, this is restricted to small integers); **/** is a version of **quotient** that works on small integers. For example, "8*(3+7)" can be expressed as **(* 8 (+ 3 7))** as well as **(times 8 (plus 3 7))**. You may use any combination of these names in answering these problems.

(2)   All the numbers we have encountered in this chapter have been whole numbers, also called *fixed point numbers*. LISP allows *floating point numbers* as well. Floating point numbers are designated using decimal points or scientific notation. For example, **18.3**, **0.07**, and **6.02252E23** are all floating point numbers. The same functions that we discussed in this chapter also apply to floating point numbers.

Familiarize yourself with floating point numbers by doing some computations on them using the functions we encountered in this chapter.

(3)   Write an s-expression that computes the average of the following numbers: 83, 83, 85, 91, 97. Note that the result of a computation on integers will generally be an integer, so your answer to this problem will be truncated to get a whole number. However, if at least one of the arguments to a function is a floating point number, LISP will produce a floating point result. Use this feature to produce a more accurate answer to this problem.

(4)   The function **sqrt** returns the square root of the value of its argument. Use this function to write LISP s-expressions that find the roots of the equation $x^2 - 11x - 1302 = 0$.

(5)   Compute 1!, 2!, 3!, etc., efficiently by storing the latest result as the value of an atom (recall that n! = n(n−1)(n−2)...1).

(6)   Find the largest floating point number your LISP can handle.

(7)   Does LISP distinguish between upper and lower case atom names? Try binding values to atoms with names like **foo**, **FOO**, and **Foo** to see if these are the same or different. Determine whether function names like **plus** and **setq** are also sensitive to case.

2

Symbolic Computation

2.1. INTRODUCTION

So far, we have treated LISP as if it were a sort of interactive FORTRAN or PASCAL, doing arithmetic operations and storing some results by binding them to atoms. Of course, LISP was not designed particularly for these operations, but for *symbolic operations*. Symbolic operations are rather abstract manipulations of LISP data structures. Because they are so abstract, symbolic operations might seem a bit meaningless at first. Not to worry. Later on we will apply them in useful ways.

In this chapter we introduce the fundamental symbolic operations of LISP. These are primarily methods of putting s-expressions together and taking them apart. In the process of exploring symbolic computation, we examine the structure of lists more closely. We learn about some pervasive LISP concepts such as the *empty list,* and how to prevent evaluation of s-expressions when it is necessary to do so.

2.2. MORE ON LISTS

The basic symbolic operations involve tearing apart lists, and putting lists together. Before we look at these, let us familiarize ourselves with lists a bit more. Consider the list **(a b c)**. This is a list of three elements, namely, the atoms **a**, **b**, and **c** (we generally refer to the number of elements in a list as its *length,* so we might call this a list of length three). Now consider the following list: **(a (b c) d)**. How many elements does this list have? The answer is, also three. The first element is the atom **a**, the second the list **(b c)**, and the third the atom **d**. It just so happens that the second element of this list is itself a list. But the original list is still a list of length three.

As we can observe from these examples, we need to be careful not to confuse the various "levels" within a list whose elements are also lists. LISP distinguishs the elements of a list from the elements of its elements. Thus the atom **b** is *not* an element of the list **(a (b c) d)**, while the list **(b c)** *is* the second element of this list. When we refer to "the next element of a list", we are referring to the next item at the same level; this may be either an atom or a list, depending upon the particular datum. So the next element of the list **(a (b c) d)** after the element **a** is the list **(b c)**; the next element after this one is the atom **d**. The embedded list **(b c)** has two elements, the atoms **b** and **c**, and there is no next element after **c** in this list.

Let us consider some more "tricky" examples to get the hang of things. Consider the list **(((x)))**. What is the length of this list? You are right if you answered one. This is a list of one element, namely, the list **((x))**. This in turn is also a list of one element, the list **(x)**, which is also a list of one element, the atom **x**.

What about the list **((a b))**? Also a list of length one. It contains only one element, the list **(a b)**. This element, of course, is a list of length two. This example demonstrates that lists can contain elements that themselves have more elements than the list that contains them.

Note that the LISP objects **((a b c))** and **(a b c)** are very different. The first is a list of one element, the list **(a b c)**. The latter is a list of three elements, the atoms **a**, **b**, and **c**. Now consider the lists **(a)** and **(a a)**. These are also quite different. The first is a list of one element, and the second a list of two elements, both of which happen to be the same atom. The lists **(a b)** and **(b a)** are both the same length, but they are different lists because their elements appear in different orders.

In sum, lists must look alike to be equivalent lists. That is, they must have exactly the same elements in the same order to be considered the same.

2.3. TAKING THINGS LITERALLY

We are just about ready to begin some symbolic operations. Symbolic operations will appear just like arithmetic functions, or any other LISP function for that matter. We will specify a symbolic operator or function in the beginning of a list, and its arguments will be found in the rest of the list. LISP will apply the function to its arguments as before. The only difference here is that the arguments, and resulting value, will be general s-expressions (i. e., lists or atoms) rather than numbers.

But there is a problem. Whenever we have previously entered a list into LISP, LISP tried to evaluate it. For example, if we type the list **(plus 2 3)**, LISP evaluates this by applying **plus** to **2** and **3**. However, if we want to perform symbolic operations on lists, somehow we will have to get them to be arguments to functions without them first being evaluated. To see why this is a problem, consider what would happen if we just typed **(a b c)** directly to the LISP interpreter. In fact, let us try this:

>   -> **(a b c)**
>   **Error: eval: Undefined function a**
>   **<1>: (reset)**
>
>   **[Return to top level]**
>   ->

What happened? LISP tried to interpret the first element of the list as a function, and the rest of the list as its arguments. But LISP does not know about any function called **a**, so it gave us an error message.

A similar thing would happen if we tried to supply the list **(a b c)** as an argument to some function. LISP will eventually try to evaluate the list, and will give an error message when it tries to interpret the first element as a function.

The problem is that we want LISP to take the list **(a b c)** literally, rather than evaluate it. That is, we would like some way of overcoming LISP's tendency to evaluate everything we give it. This is done in LISP, as you may have guessed by now, through the use of a special function. This function is called **quote**. **quote** is a function of one argument, which is *not* evaluated. **quote** simply returns this argument as its value.

For example, let us type **(quote (a b c))** directly to LISP and see what happens:

>   -> **(quote (a b c))**
>   **(a b c)**
>   ->

LISP evaluates this list as it would any other. It considers the first element to be a function and the rest to be arguments. In this case, because the function is **quote**, LISP does not evaluate the argument, but merely applies **quote** to it. **quote** returns the argument as its result.

quote may appear to be a rather uninteresting function, since it does nothing. But in fact, the need to prevent LISP from evaluating something arises so often that a special syntax is provided for **quote**ing expressions. Rather than writing the cumbersome **(quote (a b c))**, LISP allows you to write **'(a b c)**. That is, we preface the s-expression with the ''single quote'' or ''apostrophe'' character (be sure not to use the similar looking ''backquote'' character `, as this has a rather different interpretation).

This is just syntactic sugar — the two expressions are identical as far as LISP is concerned.

We can apply **quote** harmlessly to anything. For example:

```
-> '(a b c)
(a b c)
-> 'a
a
-> '6
6
->
```

The last example might strike you as superfluous. It is. **6** would evaluate to **6** anyway, so putting in the **quote**, while legal, is wasteful and should be avoided.

Let us use **quote** in a more useful example:

```
-> (setq x '(a b c))
(a b c)
-> x
(a b c)
->
```

Here we bind to the atom **x** the value **(a b c)**. Remember, **setq** causes only its second argument to be evaluated. Since this is quoted, the argument evaluates to the list **(a b c)**. This list is supplied as an argument to **setq**, which then binds it to the first argument. We could now use this value as an argument for a subsequent symbolic computation.

LISP Values Are S-expressions

Note that values in LISP are arbitrary s-expressions. That is, they are exactly the same sort of object that we ask the LISP interpreter to evaluate for us. This may take a little getting used to at first, since values and programs look identical in LISP. For example, I could bind an atom to a value that looks just like an s-expression I would normally ask the interpreter to evaluate:

> **—> (setq x '(plus 3 4))**
> **(plus 3 4)**
> **—>**

Here I bound **x** to the value **(plus 3 4)**. LISP did not evaluate this value, because **quote** prevented it from doing so. Instead, it treated **(plus 3 4)** just like it were any random data object. I might just as well have typed **(how are you)** as far as this example is concerned.

This example illustrates that expressions that contain functions like **plus** or **setq** have a special meaning to LISP only when they are evaluated. Otherwise, they are inert data objects with the same status of any other LISP s-expression.

We can bind atoms to other atoms as well. For example:

> **—> (setq x 'y)**
> **y**
> **—> x**
> **y**
> **—> (setq a 'a)**
> **a**
> **—> a**
> **a**

In the first example, we bind **x** to **y**, and in the second, we bind **a** to **a**. (there is nothing wrong with binding an atom to itself, although there are not too many cases where we have a good reason to do this).

As is the case for lists, the atomic values that I bound to these atoms are themselves real live LISP s-expressions. For example, the **y** that was bound to **x** above is a real LISP atom, and could have a value bound to it as well. And, if we had a LISP function that changed, not the value of its argument, as **setq** does, but the value of its value, then I could change the value of the atom **y** indirectly by going through **x**.

In fact, the function **set** does just this. **set** is like **setq**, except it causes its first argument (as well as its second) to be evaluated. It then binds the value of the second argument to the *value* of the first. For example, suppose **x** had **y** bound to it as above. Then we could do the following:

```
-> x
y
-> (set x 'z)
z
-> y
z
-> x
y
```

set causes both its arguments to be evaluated, so **x** is evaluated to **y** and **'z** to **z**. These are passed to **set**, which then binds the value of the first to the second, i. e., **y** is given the value **z**. We then check this by asking LISP to evaluate **y**. LISP obligingly returns **z**.

But what happened to **x**? We check this at the end and find that it is still bound to **y**. The call to **set** did not affect **x** at all.

If this example strikes you as a little confusing, you are in good company. Although it is perfectly legal and sometimes necessary, such uses of LISP are relatively rare and always a bit hairy. We almost always know the actual atom we want to bind, so there is no need to have the extra level of indirection. In practice, most calls to **set** would look like the following:

```
-> (set 'x '(a b c))
(a b c)
-> x
(a b c)
->
```

Here we want to bind the literal atom **x** to something. Therefore, we quote **x**, and **set** causes this argument to evaluate to **x**.

Since this construction occurs so frequently, LISP allows a special shorthand for it, namely, **setq**. **setq** is named for **set quote** since it combines these two functions into a more practical package. Now that we know this, we will rarely see **set** again. It is important that you understand the above examples, though, so you understand how LISP works.

20

2.4. car AND cdr

Now that we know how to use **quote**, we are ready to do some symbolic operations on lists. As mentioned above, symbolic operations on lists consist primarily of taking lists apart and building them up. Let us consider taking lists apart first. LISP provides two basic functions for this, called **car** and **cdr** (the latter is usually pronounced "could-er"). These names have to do with the machine upon which LISP was first implemented and, unfortunately, now have no mnemonic value.

Both **car** and **cdr** are functions of one argument, which should be a list. **car** returns the first element of this list. **cdr** returns the list with its first element missing, that is, the list that results from taking the argument and removing its first element. **car** and **cdr** always cause their argument to be evaluated. For example:

>   -> (car '(a b c))
>   a
>   -> (cdr '(a b c))
>   (b c)

In both cases, the argument evaluates to the list **(a b c)**. **car** returns the first element of this list, the atom **a**. **cdr** returns the list that results from removing the first element, namely, the list **(b c)**.

CAR and CDR are Non-destructive

car and **cdr** do not actually change the lists on which they operate. Consider the following evaluations:

>   -> (setq x '(a b c))
>   (a b c)
>   -> x
>   (a b c)
>   -> (car x)
>   a
>   -> x
>   (a b c)
>   -> (cdr x)
>   (b c)
>   -> x
>   (a b c)
>   ->

21

Since these functions cause their argument to be evaluated, **(car x)** results in **car** being applied to **(a b c)**. But this does not change the value bound to **x** in the slightest. Similarly for **cdr**.

Thus when we say that **cdr** returns a list with its first element removed, we are speaking figuratively. **cdr** does not really remove an element from anyone's list; it merely returns as its value a list that looks like the list one would get from crossing off the first element of the list supplied as the argument to **cdr**.

Let us consider some more examples:

> -> (cdr '(a b))
> **(b)**
> -> (car (cdr '(a b)))
> **b**

Taking **cdr** of the list **(a b)** returns the list **(b)**, the list that results from scratching out the first element of **(a b)**. Remember, this is a completely different creature from the atom **b**. To get at the second element of the original list, we have to compose two functions, as in the second example. Let us see why this works. To evaluate the second expression, LISP first evaluates the argument. The argument in this case is a call to the function **cdr**. To evaluate this call, LISP first evaluates this function's argument. This is **'(a b)**, which evaluates to **(a b)**. LISP then applies **cdr** to this value, and **cdr** returns **(b)**. Then **car** is applied to this result. **car** always returns the first element of its argument, in this case, **b**.

Parentheses Are Important

A few "extra" parentheses are very important to LISP, even if they may not seem so significant to us humans. For example, what would you suppose the **car** of **((a b))** would be? Try to determine this from what you have learned so far. Now let us ask LISP to see if you are right:

> -> (car '((a b)))
> **(a b)**

You get one brownie point if you got this answer and not **a**. This answer can be seen to be correct if we consider the structure of the list **((a b))**. This is a list of one element, the list **(a b)**. **car** always returns the first *element* of a list, not the first *atom* it can find. The first *element* of the list **((a b))** is the list **(a b)**, so **car** returns this as its value.

What function could I apply to **((a b))** to return the atom **a**? Since **car** of this list returns **(a b)**, and since the first element of this value is the atom **a**, then the **car** of the **car** of **((a b))** should get us what we want. Let us try this and see:

>   −> **(car (car '((a b))))**
>   **a**
>   −>

Now let us consider taking the **cdr** of **((a b) (c d))**. What value should this return? Choose your answer, and now let us test it:

>   −> **(cdr '((a b) (c d)))**
>   **((c d))**
>   −>

Go to the head of the class if you chose this value, and not **(c d)**. Why is this answer correct? Because **((a b) (c d))** is a list of two elements, the list **(a b)** and the list **(c d)**. **cdr** returns the list that results from crossing off the first *element* of a list. If we cross off the first element of **((a b) (c d))**, we are left with the list of one element **((c d))**, which is the value **cdr** returns.

This might be clearer if you consider taking the **cdr** of a list like **((a b) (c d) (e f))**. This is a list of three elements, the lists **(a b)**, **(c d)**, and **(e f)**. **cdr** removes the first element, and therefore should return a list consisting of the other two:

>   −> **(cdr '((a b) (c d) (e f)))**
>   **((c d) (e f))**
>   −>

How could we get the list **(c d)** from the list **((a b) (c d))**? **cdr** of this list returns **((c d))**, a list whose first element is the list we seek. Since the first element of a list is returned by **car**, it should suffice to take the **car** of the **cdr** of the original list:

>   −> **(car (cdr '((a b) (c d))))**
>   **(c d)**
>   −>

What if we composed these functions in the opposite order? That is, instead of taking the **car** of the **cdr**, suppose we took the **cdr** of the **car**. Well, the **car** of **((a b) (c d))** should be its first element, namely, the list **(a b)**, and the **cdr** of this list should be the list **(b)**. Let us check:

```
-> (cdr (car '((a b) (c d))))
(b)
->
```

What would happen if we tried executing **(cdr (car '(a b)))**? You are right if you think this would be a mistake. Since **(car '(a b))** evaluates to **a**, taking **cdr** of this value amounts to taking **cdr** of an atom. But **car** and **cdr** were meant to apply only to lists, so this would be an error. (Note: Some LISPs use **car** and **cdr** of an atom for implementation-dependent hacks. Even in such LISPs, however, it is a bad idea to write code that depends heavily on being able to take the **car** or **cdr** of an atom, as the code is likely to be obtuse and difficult to transport to other LISP systems.)

Something like this example might be valid if we have a more complicated list, though. For example

```
-> (cdr (car '((a b c) (d e f))))
(b c)
-> (car (car '((a b c) (d e f))))
a
-> (car (cdr '((a b c) (d e f))))
(d e f)
-> (car (car (cdr '((a b c) (d e f)))))
d
-> (cdr (car (cdr '((a b c) (d e f)))))
(e f)
-> (car (cdr (car (cdr '((a b c) (d e f))))))
e
->
```

You should go through each of these examples and be sure you understand why it returns what it does.

2.5. cadr, ETC.

As you no doubt have noticed, code containing long strings of **cars** and **cdrs**, like the ones in the examples above, is hard to follow. Most LISP programmers consider this bad programming style and try writing their code to avoid such long sequences. However, since the need to do this sort of computation sometimes occurs, LISP provides a slightly more convenient way of composing **cars** and **cdrs**. This is done by providing a built-in function corresponding to each possible sequence of **cars** and **cdrs**. For example, **cadr** is a LISP function equivalent to taking the **car** of the **cdr**:

```
-> (car (cdr '((a b c) (d e f))))
(d e f)
-> (cadr '((a b c) (d e f)))
(d e f)
->
```

Franz LISP allows you to use functions whose names contain a sequence of as many **a**'s and **d**'s as you like. For example, **(cadadr x)** is equivalent to **(car (cdr (car (cdr x))))**, and **(caddaar x)** is equivalent to **(car (cdr (cdr (car (car x)))))**. Thus, the following two lines of code compute the same thing:

```
-> (car (cdr (car (cdr '((a b c) (d e f))))))
e
-> (cadadr '((a b c) (d e f)))
e
->
```

While the second item above is terser (and more efficient) than the first, it is no less cryptic. Good LISP programmers use these functions sparingly as well.

Finally, just to reinforce the point that programs and data are the same sort of stuff in LISP, consider the following computation:

```
-> (car '(cdr '(a b c)))
cdr
->
```

What is going on here? The argument to **car** evaluates to the list **(cdr '(a b c))**. This happens to be a valid s-expression for evaluation, but LISP could not care less about that in this context. The argument has already been evaluated, and LISP just passes along the result. **car** treats the resulting value like any old list, and returns its first element, which happens to be the atom **cdr**.

The example is tricky only because the value of the argument to **car** looks like something that would ordinarily be evaluated. The **quote** prevents it from being evaluated in this example, though, so the value acts just like any other piece of passive data. Take away the first **quote**, and the expression would have a radically different meaning:

```
-> (car (cdr '(a b c)))
b
->
```

Here the evaluation of the argument to **car** causes the s-expression containing the **cdr** to be evaluated also. This returns **(b c)**, the first element of which is returned by the **car**.

Programs and data are made out of the same stuff in LISP. A **quote** here or there may be all that determines whether something will be treated as one or the other.

2.6. THE EMPTY LIST

Note that when we take the **cdr** of a list, the resulting value is always one element shorter than the argument. **(cdr '(a b c))** returns **(b c)**, a list of length two, and **(cdr '(b c))** returns **(c)**, a list of length one. But what would **(cdr '(c))** return? If we followed this logic, we would expect something like ( ), a list of length zero. Let us try it and see:

```
-> (cdr '(c))
nil
->
```

Relax. LISP really did compute a list of length zero. However, rather than print out a list of length zero as ( ), LISP always prints this out as the atom **nil**.

nil means the empty list in LISP. To see that this is really the same thing as ( ), the list of no elements, let us type '( ) directly into LISP and see what happens:

```
-> '( )
nil
->
```

LISP evaluated this expression to ( ), and then printed out this value. But since LISP always prints out the empty list as **nil**, we get the result shown above.

Actually, we did not need to quote the empty list. This is because, by convention, the empty list always evaluates to itself. So we have

```
-> ( )
nil
-> nil
nil
->
```

nil serves several important functions in LISP. In fact, it is so important that LISP will not let you change its value. That is, trying to **setq nil** to something will cause an error.

2.7. cons

Just as **car** and **cdr** take lists apart, **cons** builds lists up. **cons** is a function of two arguments. The second argument should always evaluate to a list. **cons** evaluates both its arguments, and then returns as its value the list obtained by taking the second argument and sticking the first one in front of it. For example:

```
-> (cons 'a '(b c))
(a b c)
->
```

cons constructed a new list by taking the value of the second argument, **(b c)**, and inserting the value of the first argument, **a**, as its first element. **cons** returns the new, composite list **(a b c)** as its value.

A good way to think of **cons** is as a sort of inverse function of **car** and **cdr**. **cons** will always produce a list whose **car** is the first argument to the **cons**, and whose **cdr** is the second argument. Thus

```
-> (setq x (cons 'a '(b c)))
(a b c)
-> (car x)
a
-> (cdr x)
(b c)
->
```

Here we save the value **cons** produces, and then take **car** and **cdr** of this value. The results are the same as the values of the original arguments to **cons**.

A few other examples will help to give you the feel of this:

27

```
-> (cons 'a '(b))
(a b)
->
```

Here we simply **cons** the atom **a** onto a list of length one and get a list of length two.

What would happen if we **cons** the list **(a b)** onto the list **(c d)**? Decide your answer, and now let us check:

```
-> (cons '(a b) '(c d))
((a b) c d)
->
```

The answer is not **(a b c d)** because **cons** blindly sticks its first argument into the front of the list that is its second argument, without caring whether its first argument is an atom or a list. How can we get the list **(a b c d)** starting with the list **(c d)**? This would require two **cons**'s, as follows:

```
-> (cons 'a (cons 'b '(c d)))
(a b c d)
->
```

The innermost **cons** returns **(b c d)**, and the outermost one prefixes **a** to this value.

What if I start with a list of two elements, like **(a b)**, and want to put each of its elements in the front of the list **(c d)** to produce **(a b c d)**? Then I would have to use some sequence **cars** and **cdrs** to access each element of the first list, and then **cons** them onto the second. For example, if **x** were bound to **(a b)**, I could access **b** by getting the value of **x**, and taking the **car** of its **cdr**; I could **cons** this value onto the list **(c d)** to get **(b c d)**. Then I could access **a** by taking the **car** of the value of **x**, and produce the desired result by **cons**ing this value onto the value built up so far. Thus we have the following:

```
-> (setq x '(a b))
(a b)
-> (cons (car x) (cons (cadr x) '(c d)))
(a b c d)
->
```

The second s-expression is a typical LISP construct. Make sure you understand what it is doing. In essence, it uses **car** and **cdr** to tear apart an s-expression, and **cons** to stick the pieces back together.

What happens when we **cons** something onto the empty list? For example, suppose I **cons a** onto **nil**. Since **nil** represents the list of no elements, i. e., ( ), **cons** should make a list whose only element is **a**, i. e., the list **(a)**. Let us try and see:

> —> **(cons 'a nil)**
> **(a)**
> —>

CONS is Non-destructive

As is the case for **car** and **cdr**, **cons** does not change its arguments. Consider the following:

> —> **(setq x 'a)**
> **a**
> —> **(setq y '(b c))**
> **(b c)**
> —> **(cons x y)**
> **(a b c)**
> —> **x**
> **a**
> —> **y**
> **(b c)**
> —>

Thus **cons** builds a list out of its arguments, but does not change them in any way.

CONSing Requires Storage and Is Expensive

car and **cdr** do not have to create anything because they return as their value a piece of a structure that is already there. For example, **cdr** of **(a b c)** returns **(b c)**, which is actually a piece of the longer list. However, unlike **car** and **cdr**, **cons** has to return a list that is not there to begin with, and thus must create something new.

But this creation must require some new storage. Where does this storage come from? The answer is that LISP dynamically allocates storage for lists as the need arises (e. g., in response to calls to **cons**). When it runs out of room, LISP garbage-collects unused **cons** cells, as they are called, and reuses them. Since garbage collection is very expensive, the effective average cost of using **cons** is quite high. For example, an efficient LISP implementation may execute a **car** as a single machine instruction, taking, say, a microsecond. But the effective cost of a single **cons**, when garbage collection is considered, might be a millisecond.

Unfortunately, one cannot avoid **cons**ing up lists altogether. But remember that functions that build lists tend to be much more expensive than comparable functions that just manipulate existing lists. Use the former frugally.

2.8. LIST CONSTRUCTION FUNCTIONS

We can use **cons** to build up arbitrarily complicated s-expressions from scratch. For example, to get the lists **(a b c)** and **(a (b c) d)**, we would do the following:

```
-> (cons 'a (cons 'b (cons 'c nil)))
(a b c)
-> (cons 'a (cons (cons 'b (cons 'c nil)) (cons 'd nil)))
(a (b c) d)
->
```

Since this is cumbersome, LISP provides us with some more convenient list-building tools. **list** is a function that takes any number of arguments, evaluates them, and builds a new list containing each value as an element. **append** is a function that takes any number of arguments, which should all evaluate to lists, and creates a new list by sticking all the elements of these lists together. So

```
-> (list 'a 'b 'c)
(a b c)
-> (list 'a '(b c) 'd)
(a (b c) d)
-> (append '(a b) '(c d) '(e f))
(a b c d e f)
->
```

LISP contains many other more specialized functions to help construct lists. As you become more proficient in LISP, you will want to consult Appendix A to see what other list construction functions may be pertinent to your needs.

At this point, you may be wondering what all this symbolic manipulation could possibly have to do with anything. Why should anyone care that we can take lists of meaningless symbols, and produce yet longer lists of meaningless symbols, even if we can do it elegantly? Of course, in a real application, our symbols might not be quite so meaningless. For example, instead of random **a**'s and **b**'s, the elements of a list might correspond to the words of an English sentence, and another list might denote some sort of analysis of this sentence. Values bound to atoms may represent repositories of information that are useful in making such an analysis.

Unfortunately, at this point we can only be suggestive, as we have not yet built up enough machinery to solve any "real world" problems you are likely to have. We will enrich our repertoire in the next few chapters to remedy this situation. For a little while, though, we will have to be satisfied with some rather abstract-looking computations.

2.9. SUMMARY

In this chapter we have encountered the basic elements of symbolic computation:

(1)   **quote** is used to prevent the interpreter from evaluating an s-expression. **(quote (x y z))** can be abbreviated as **'(x y z)**.

(2)   **car** is a function of one argument, which should evaluate to a list. **car** returns the first element of this list as its value.

(3)   **cdr** is a function of one argument, which should evaluate to a list. **cdr** returns the rest of this list after removing its first element.

(4)   There are a set of functions called **cadr**, **caar**, **cadar**, etc. Each function is equivalent to some sequence of **car**s and **cdr**s, with each **a** indicating a **car** and each **d** indicating a **cdr**.

(5)   **cons** is a function of two arguments, of which the second should evaluate to a list. **cons** returns a list whose value looks like the list one would get by inserting the value of the first argument at the front of the value of the second argument.

(6)   **list** and **append** are list-building functions. They both take any number of arguments, all of which are evaluated. **list** returns a list whose elements are the values of its arguments; **append** returns a list whose elements are the elements of the values of its arguments, which should all be lists.

(7)   **nil** is the empty list, the list of no elements. **nil** is identical to **( )**, although LISP always prints out the empty list as **nil**. By convention, the empty list always evaluates to itself.

(8)   **set** is an infrequently used function that evaluates both its arguments, and then binds the value of the first to the value of the second.

Exercises

(1)   Find the sequences of **car**s and **cdr**s that return **x** when applied to the following s-expressions:

   (a)   **(a b x d)**

   (b)   **(a (b (x d)))**

   (c)   **(((a (b (x) d))))**

(2)   Construct the lists used in Exercise 1 using only atoms and calls to **cons**.

(3)   The function **length** returns the length of the value of its argument, e. g., **(length '(a b c))** returns **3**. Use **length** to check your assessment of the lengths of the lists in Exercise 1.

(4)   Bind **x** to the value **(a b c)**. Use this to produce the list **(a b c a b c)**.

(5)   Write the expression ''**(a)** using **quote** rather than '. What data type is the expression '**a**?

(6)   Bind **x** to the value **y**. Now, without mentioning **y** explicitly, bind the value **(1 2 3)** to **y**.

(7)   What is the difference between the following s-expressions:

   (a)   **(car (setq x '(a b c)))**

   (b)   **(car '(setq x '(a b c)))**

(8)   Evaluating **(caadadr '(a '(b (c))))** returns the value **b**. So does evaluating **(caadr (cadr '(a '(b (c)))))**. If I evaluate the second part of this expression, i. e., **(cadr '(a '(b (c))))**, I get '**(b (c))**. But evaluating **(caadr '(b (c)))** returns **c**. Explain this.

3

Defining Our Own Functions

3.1. INTRODUCTION

We now have the machinery to construct some heavy-duty expressions. However, it is a futile exercise to write down a complex s-expression, evaluate it once, and never use it again. Rather, we would prefer to do what is done in all programming languages: Write a stored program that takes a few inputs, and produces some output, and which we can use repeatedly.

In this chapter, we describe LISP's facility for allowing the user to create stored programs. This is done in LISP by allowing the user to create his own functions. We examine LISP's function calling scheme in some detail, with particular attention paid to the treatment of program variables. In passing, we also introduce some LISP conveniences. These include *superparentheses,* which make it easier for the user to write well-formed expressions, and a means to save function definitions in files for future use.

3.2. USER-DEFINED FUNCTIONS

In LISP, we achieve the equivalent of a stored program by creating a new function. User-defined functions will be used just like the functions that come with LISP. That is, once a function is defined, we can put it in the beginning of a list, in front of a few arguments, and LISP will apply the

33

function to those arguments. For example, suppose **addthree** were a function I defined that takes one argument, and adds three to it. Then I could type expressions like the following:

```
-> (addthree 7)
10
-> (setq x (addthree 19))
22
->
```

and so on. I could use this function in LISP wherever I could use those functions that were native to LISP. In effect, I have extended LISP by adding a new function to its repertoire.

All we need to know is how to create a new function. Well, how do we do anything in LISP? We have some function tailored to that need. So to define new functions, we have a LISP function that produces new functions. Such a function is called **defun**, for "define function". **defun** takes as its arguments the name of the function to be defined, a list of formal parameters (which should all be literal atoms), and some bodies of code (which are just s-expressions). **defun** does not evaluate any of these arguments; rather, it merely associates the formal parameter list and bodies of code with the function name for future reference.

Let us take as an example the simple function we mentioned above, **addthree**. Here is how we can use **defun** to create this function:

```
-> (defun addthree (x) (plus x 3))
addthree
->
```

The name of the function is **addthree**, so that appears first in the definition. Then comes the formal parameter list. We intend for **addthree** to be a function of only one argument (namely, the value to which we wish to add three), so the list only contains one atom. I picked the uninspired name **x** here. Finally, we have the single body of code that constitutes the function. In this case, the body is an s-expression that adds three to the atom **x**. Note that the call to **defun** returned as its value the name of the function it defined. We do not normally use functions like **defun** for the value they compute, but rather for their side-effects (in this case, creating a new function). Nevertheless, **defun** is an ordinary LISP function, and obediently returns some value.

Having used **defun** in this manner to create **addthree**, we can now use **addthree** as advertised above. Thus we have

```
-> (addthree 11)
14
->
```

To evaluate an expression that contains a user-defined function such as this one, LISP gets the formal parameter list associated with that function name by the call to **defun** that defined the function. Then it binds the atoms in the formal parameter list to the values of the actual arguments. In the case of **addthree**, the only element of the formal parameter list is **x**; thus when **addthree** was called with the argument **11** above, **x** was bound to **11**.

Next, LISP retrieves the bodies of code associated with the function name by the previous call to **defun**, and evaluates them. In the case of **addthree**, there is only one body, **(plus x 3)**. Since **x** was previously bound to **11**, this piece of code evaluates to **14**. This value is returned as the value of the call to **addthree.**

More generally, a call to **defun** looks like this:

> **(defun fname (v1 v2 ... vn)**
> **(...body of code 1...)**
> **(...body of code 2...) ...)**

The formal parameters, **v1** to **vn** in this example, are just a (possibly empty) list of atoms. Each body of code is just any old s-expression.

If I defined **fname** this way, then I could call **fname** as follows:

> **(fname arg1 arg2 ... argn)**

LISP would evaluate this call in the following manner:

(1)   First, it would evaluate all the arguments, **arg1** to **argn**.

(2)   Then each formal parameter in the function definition is bound to the value of the corresponding argument. **v1** would be bound to the value of **arg1**, **v2** to the value of **arg2**, and so on. If **v1** had some value before the function is called, LISP kindly saves this for later.

(3)   Next, LISP evaluates each body of code in turn, from left to right. The value of the last body is returned as the value of the call to **fname.** Also, the previous values of the formal parameters are restored (if a formal parameter was unbound before the call, it will still be unbound at its completion).

35

Normally, the bodies of code will contain references to the formal parameters of the function. So a good way to think about a function call to a user-defined function is as follows: *Evaluating a function is like evaluating its bodies of code with the formal parameters replaced by the values of the corresponding actual arguments.*

Let us trace through the evaluation of (**addthree 11**) in greater detail:

(1)   LISP evaluates arguments first. In this case, it merely evaluates the single argument, **11**, which evaluates to itself.

(2)   Then we bind formal parameters. Here the single formal parameter, **x**, is bound to the value of the single argument, **11**. If **x** already has some value, LISP remembers it.

(3)   Next, LISP does the real work. It evaluates the bodies; in this case, there is only one, (**plus x 3**). This evaluates to **14**, because **x** is bound to **11**. **14** is returned as the value of the call to **addthree**. Before LISP goes on, it restores **x** to whatever value it had before we made this call.

Saving and restoring the values of formal parameters ensures that a call to a function does not cause any unexpected side-effects. For example, even though the definition of **addthree** uses a formal argument called **x**, calling **addthree** will not cause the value of **x** to change outside of that function:

```
-> (setq x '(a b c))
(a b c)
-> (addthree 7)
10
-> x
(a b c)
```

The value of **x** outside of **addthree** would not be changed even if **addthree** explicitly changed its value, say, by calling **setq**.

Let us do another simple example. Suppose we want to write a LISP function that takes two values and averages them. Our function will therefore require a formal parameter list containing two atoms, one for each value, and its body will add these values together and then divide by two:

```
-> (defun average (x y) (quotient (plus x y) 2))
average
```

```
-> (average 7 21)
14
-> (average 9 32)
20
->
```

When we call the function **average**, say, by evaluating **(average 7 21)**, LISP evaluates the arguments, and binds them to the corresponding formal parameters. In this case, **x** gets bound to **7** and **y** to **21**. Then LISP evaluates the body, and returns the resulting value as the value of the call to **average**. Any previous bindings of **x** and **y** are saved prior to the call and restored upon completion.

Note that the arguments to the functions we define are evaluated, so we can call a user-defined function and supply it with arbitrary s-expressions as arguments:

```
-> (average (times 3 4) (quotient 48 3))
14
->
```

User-defined functions can call other user-defined functions as well. For example, I can define a function **squared** that multiplies its argument by itself:

```
-> (defun squared (x) (times x x))
squared
->
```

Now I can use **squared** to compute the length of the hypotenuse of a right triangle from the length of its sides (recall that this length is the square root of the sum of the squares of the sides):

```
-> (defun hyp (x y) (sqrt (plus (squared x) (squared y))))
hyp
-> (hyp 3 4)
5.0
->
```

Even though my two user-defined functions happened to use the same atom as a formal parameter, LISP does not get confused. Changes to the value of a formal parameter are local to a function. Thus when I evaluate **(hyp 3 4)**, **x** gets bound to **3** and **y** to **4**, and any previous values of these atoms are saved. When the s-expression **(squared y)** within the function body of **hyp** gets evaluated, the formal parameter of **squared** gets bound to

the value of **y**, which is currently **4**. The formal parameter of **squared** is
x, so the old value of **x** (currently bound to **3**) is saved, and **x** is bound to
4. The s-expression **(times x x)** is then evaluated, and returns **16**. We are
now ready to leave **squared**, so the formal parameter **x** is restored to its previous value, **3**. From the point of view of **hyp**, this is just as if the value of
x had never changed. Of course, when **hyp** finishes, both **x** and **y** will be
restored to whatever previous values they may have had at the top level. So
from the point of view of the top level of LISP, this is just as if the values
of neither atoms had been played with.

Because LISP always saves and restores the bindings of formal parameters
upon entering and leaving a function call, you may use the same atom as a
parameter in as many definitions as you like. You need not fear that a
parameter name will clash with a parameter name in another function, even
if the functions call each other intimately.

Let us look at some user-defined functions that do some symbolic computation. For example, if you do not like the order of arguments that **cons**
requires, you can define your own function that accepts arguments in the
opposite order:

```
-> (defun xcons (l e) (cons e l))
xcons
-> (xcons '(b c) 'a)
(a b c)
->
```

In this example, I used **l** and **e** as formal parameters, intending these names
to be mnemonic for "list" and "element", respectively.

Now let us write a function that expects as input a list of two elements, and
returns as its value a list of the list of each element:

```
-> (defun list-of-lists (x)
      (list (list (car x)) (list (cadr x))))
list-of-lists
-> (list-of-lists '(a b))
((a) (b))
-> (list-of-lists '(1 2))
((1) (2))
->
```

Note that I entered the definition of this function on two separate lines. In
general, LISP will allow you as many lines as you need to enter an s-
expression.

3.3. FREE VARIABLES

Scope

The following is a good way to think about the saving and restoring of the values of formal parameters. When we enter a function in which some atom is a formal parameter, changes to the binding of that atom will last only for the duration of that function call. When we leave, the previous value is restored. In a sense, then, entering a function narrows the *scope* of the atoms that serve as formal parameters. That is, the scope of any changes to the values of these atoms is limited to the code that gets evaluated during the call to the function; code outside that range will not be affected.

If, during the call to a function, another function is entered that uses the same atom as a formal parameter, the scope of the atom is narrowed again. Thus, each time we enter a function, the scope of its formal parameters is narrowed to the duration of that function call; each time we leave a function, the scope is broadened to its previous range.

Atoms that are bound at the top level are sometimes called *global variables,* to indicate that their scope is as wide as can be, and that changes to them will be widely felt. Many programmers feel that global variables should be used with great care for this reason.

In contrast, the scope of an atom used as a formal parameter in a function is restricted to the duration of a call to that function. Even if the code of a user-defined function explicitly changes the values of its formal parameters, when the function returns, these atoms will be re-bound to their previous values. However, if a function twiddles with the value of some atom that is *not* a parameter, the change will *not* be confined to that function. For example, the following function first binds the atom **sum** to the sum of its arguments, and then returns their average:

```
-> (defun sum-average (x y)
     (setq sum (plus x y))
     (quotient sum 2))
sum-average
-> (sum-average 29 13)
21
```

```
-> sum
42
-> (sum-average 7 93)
50
-> sum
100
->
```

If **sum** had some value before the first call to **sum-average**, that value would have been lost.

An atom whose value is accessed or changed within a function, but which is not a parameter of that function, is called a *free variable* with respect to that function. For example, **sum** is *free* within **sum-average**. Atoms that are not free within a function (i. e., formal parameters), are said to be *bound* variables.

There is nothing special you really need to know about free variables, except to use them with care. The repercussions of a change to a free variable are not confined to a specific function, and are therefore difficult to anticipate. Some programmers use special spelling conventions when naming free variables, for example, always beginning their names with !, or some such, just so they will be more careful about manipulating them. Eternal vigilance is the price of free variables.

There is one important issue that arises as a consequence of the existence of free variables. Above we saw that when we changed the binding of an atom that was free in some function, we changed the binding of that atom on the top level. That is, changing **sum** within **sum-average** resulted in the value of **sum** being changed when we got back to the top level. However, we also noted above that calling a function narrows the scope of its formal parameters. So suppose a variable were free in one function, but bound in another. Suppose further that the latter function calls the former. According to our ground rules, when the first function is called, the scope of the atom should be narrowed; then when the second function is called, references to variables free in that function should pertain only to this narrow scope; the values of these atoms on the top level should remain unchanged.

Let us make up an example to check this out. First, let us create a function that calls **sum-average** and which uses the atom **sum** as a formal parameter:

```
-> (defun test (sum x y) (sum-average x y) sum)
test
->
```

If **sum—average** changes the value of **sum** only within the call to **test**, then **test** will return the value of the average computed; when we return to the top level of LISP, the value of **sum** should be unchanged. On the other hand, if **sum—average** changes the value of **sum** bound at the top level, and not the value of **sum** within **test**, then **test** will return the value we pass it for **sum**.

First, let us bind something to the value of the **sum** at the top level:

> —> (setq sum '(a b c))
> (a b c)
> —>

Now let us call **test** and see what happens:

> —> (test 0 55 65)
> 120
> —> sum
> (a b c)
> —>

test had no effect on the value of **sum** bound at the top level. Instead, the value of **sum** inside **test** was changed, as evidenced by the value **test** returned.

All this means that, when a function contains a free variable, you cannot really tell what variable will be accessed just by looking at that function's definition. Instead, we need to know which function calls this function at runtime. If we call **sum—average** at the top level, then references to the value of **sum** will refer to the value bound to **sum** on the top level. If **sum—average** is called by some function in which **sum** is bound, then the value of **sum** will be changed only within the scope of the calling function, and **sum** will not be changed at the top level.

Since you need to know the runtime calling sequence to determine the scope of the value of a free variable, this sort of regimen is called *dynamic scoping*. Dynamic scoping is often contrasted with *lexical scoping* (also called *static scoping*). Lexical scoping means that you can determine the scope of a variable just by looking at the code in which it is defined. We cannot do this in LISP, because the reference depends upon who called whom, and this may vary at runtime.

There are versions of LISP that use static scoping (notably, Sussman's SCHEME), but we shall not be concerned with them here.

3.4. SUPERPARENTHESES

When writing LISP functions, it is often a good idea to use spacing and indentation to make the structure of the code more apparent. Even so, having all those parentheses around is sometimes confusing. For example, when I typed in **list—of—lists** above, I had to count the number of parentheses I needed at the end to be sure I had closed off the function properly. Since this can be a pain, LISP provides a convenience called *superparentheses*. Superparentheses are denoted by square brackets, [and]. A right superparenthesis will close off as many open ordinary left parentheses as there are. However, it will stop as soon as it runs into a left superparenthesis. For example, I could have written **list—of—lists** as follows:

```
-> (defun list-of-lists (x)
      (list (list (car x)) (list (cadr x]
list-of-lists
->
```

Some people prefer to use superparentheses to demarcate significant structures in one's code. For example, superparentheses are a nice way to highlight the bodies of a function definition. Here is the function **sum—average** given above, this time using superparentheses:

```
-> (defun sum-average (x y)
      [setq sum (plus x y)]
      [quotient sum 2] )
sum-average
->
```

Some LISP programmers prefer not to use superparentheses, claiming that they will only help mask errors in your code. Instead, they prefer using an editor that graphically matches parentheses as you type. While such an editor is certainly a boon, judicious use of superparentheses will make some code more readable. Be careful not to use these too liberally, though, or they will become of little value.

3.5. SAVING FUNCTIONS IN FILES

By now some of the LISP expressions we are playing with have become awkward to type in at the keyboard. Besides, you now know enough to write some useful functions of your own that you may want to keep around for your next session with LISP. Rather than typing these functions in from scratch each time, LISP allows you to put your functions in a file, and then read them in. This way, you can use your favorite editor to enter and edit these functions, and load them in quickly each time you run LISP.

To make use of this facility, use an editor to create a file and put some LISP function definitions in it. Franz LISP prefers that the file name end with a .l. Then the next time you run LISP, you can read in this file by using the function **load** (other LISPs may use different functions to do essentially the same task). For example, suppose I put the definitions given above for **average** and **sum–average** in the file **utilities.l**. If I then want to use these functions during a subsequent session with LISP, I could do the following:

> −> **(load 'utilities)**
> **[load utilities.l]**
> **t**
> −>

LISP knows to look for the file name **utilities.l**. The functions that were in this file are now defined.

load goes through a file and reads and evaluates each expression in it just as if you typed it in yourself. You could put any LISP s-expressions in such a file and they will be evaluated. But you will generally only want to put in things like calls to **defun** and **setq**, which have some lasting effects.

The function **include** is similar to **load**, except that it does not evaluate its argument.

3.5.1. Automatic Initialization

Most LISPs also allow some loading to go on automatically. Each time Franz LISP is run, it checks your home directory for a file named **.lisprc**. If it finds one, its contents are loaded. You can place your frequently used function definitions and **setq**s, etc., in this file, so your working environment will be ready for you each time you begin a session with the interpreter.

3.6. SUMMARY

(1) We can create our own functions using the function **defun**. Once they are created, our own functions can be used just as if they came built into LISP.

(2)   Changes to the bindings of formal parameters of a function are local to a call to that function. However, changes to *free variables,* i. e., atoms occurring within a function definition but which are not formal parameters, are not local to the function call.

Atoms bound at the top level of LISP are called *global variables.*

(3)   LISP uses *dynamic scoping,* meaning that references to the value of an atom will refer to the value of the most recently introduced formal parameter of that name.

(4)   We can use *superparentheses,* [and], to demarcate pieces of code and to avoid having to count closing parentheses.

(5)   The functions **load** and **include** can be used to read in files just as if their contents were typed in to the interpreter. **load** evaluates its argument, while **include** does not. LISP automatically loads the file **.lisprc** if it finds one in the home directory.

Exercises

(1)   Define a function that computes the area of a circle given its radius.

(2)   Given that yearly interest rates are 10%, write a function that computes the monthly payment on a loan of a given amount.

(3)   Write a version of the answer to Exercise 2 in which the interest rate is a free variable. Test your function by using it for different interest rates.

(4)   The *Euclidean distance* between two points (x_1, y_1) and (x_2, y_2) is defined as $\sqrt{(x_1-x_2)^2+(y_1-y_2)^2}$. Suppose we represent a point (x,y) as a two-element list. Write a function that takes two such lists as arguments, and returns the Euclidean distance between the points they represent.

(5)   If you are distressed that the names **car** and **cdr** are non-mnemonic, you are now in a position to do something about it. Define functions **head** and **tail** that behave exactly like **car** and **cdr**, respectively.

(6)   Write a function **switch** that accepts a two-element list and returns a list with these elements in the opposite order. E. g., **(switch '(a b))** returns **(b a)**.

(7)   In the following definition, **basis** is a free variable used to adjust values:

(defun normalize (v) (quotient v basis))

Suppose we also had the following function:

(defun n−percentage (a b basis) (quotient a (normalize b)))

If **basis** has the value **100.0** on the top level, what value will be computed by the expression **(n−percentage 50.0 100.0 125.0)**? Why?

© 1977 United Feature Syndicate. Inc

4

Predicates, Conditionals, and Logical Operators

4.1. INTRODUCTION

To gainfully employ the functions we have encountered, we need to be able to arrange them into the LISP equivalent of programs. In particular, we would like to do something other than write "straight-line code" (code with no branching). To do so, we need some kind of conditional (i. e., "if...then...else..." type statement). In addition, we must have some way of testing s-expressions for various properties.

In this chapter we introduce LISP *predicates,* which are functions that test for various conditions. These predicates can be combined into more complicated tests using other functions called *logical operators.* We also discuss the basic LISP mechanisms for altering flow of control. Together with predicates and logical operators, the LISP flow of control mechanisms allow us to write arbitrary computations in LISP.

4.2. LISP PREDICATES

To alter the flow of control in any language, we must first have some way of testing a value for a particular property. Of course, we will do this in LISP by having special functions that test for different things. Such a function is called a *predicate*. This is a term borrowed from logic. Predicates are just tests, that is, functions that return true or false. In LISP, false is indicated by **nil**, and true by any value other than **nil**.

As a convention, LISP often returns the atom **t** to mean true. **t** is special in that, like **nil**, it evaluates to itself and its value cannot be changed. However, **t** is generally not distinguished from other non-**nil** values. That is, most LISP functions will check to see that a value is either **nil** or non-**nil**; **t** is merely a convenient way of returning something other than **nil**.

One useful predicate in LISP tells whether or not an s-expression is an atom. This function, naturally enough, is called **atom**. So

> −> **(atom 'a)**
> **t**
> −> **(atom 8)**
> **t**
> −> **(atom '(a b c))**
> **nil**
> −> **(atom (car '(a b c)))**
> **t**
> −> **(atom (cdr '(a b c)))**
> **nil**
> −>

Similarly, the function **listp** determines whether something is a list (many LISP predicate names end in **p**, for "predicate").

> −> **(listp 'a)**
> **nil**
> −> **(listp 8)**
> **nil**
> −> **(listp '(a b c))**
> **t**
> −> **(listp (car '(a b c)))**
> **nil**
> −> **(listp (cdr '(a b c)))**
> **t**
> −>

Is **nil** an atom or a list? This would appear to be an ambiguous case. We said above that **nil** is atom, but **nil** is also ( ), the empty list, and surely, this must be a list. Fortunately, we can appeal to the ultimate arbiter of such disputes, the LISP interpreter:

```
-> (atom nil)
t
->
```

So **atom** claims that **nil** is an atom. What does **listp** think?

```
-> (listp nil)
t
->
```

listp also claims rights to **nil**. So **nil** seems to be treated as both an atom and a list, as far as these functions are concerned.

Actually, **nil** is a special case. It is often necessary to distinguish **nil** from other s-expressions, so LISP has a special predicate just for this purpose:

```
-> (null nil)
t
-> (null 'a)
nil
-> (null '(a b c))
nil
-> (null ( ))
t
->
```

null returns **t** if its argument evaluates to **nil**, and returns **nil** otherwise.

There is also a predicate called **dtpr** that returns true for every list other than **nil**, in case we want an easy way of determining if something is a non-**nil** list. We will talk more about this predicate when we discuss LISP internals in Chapter 15.

(Note — Other LISPs may use a slightly different set of predicates to distinguish among the cases just described. However, all LISPs need to make these distinctions one way or another.)

Another useful predicate is **equal**, which tests if two s-expressions look alike. For example:

```
-> (equal 'a 'b)
nil
-> (equal 'a 'a)
t
```

```
-> (equal '(a b c) '(a b c))
t
-> (equal '(a b c) '(a (b) c))
nil
->
```

There are lots of arithmetic predicates as well. For example, **numbp** tests to see if its argument is a number. Thus we have

```
-> (numbp 6)
t
-> (numbp 'a)
nil
->
```

zerop, **oddp**, **evenp**, **lessp**, and **greaterp** all do about what you would expect.

A more interesting LISP predicate is **member**. The second argument to member should always be a list. **member** checks to see if the first argument appears in the second argument. If so, **member** returns the part of the list at which the match first occurs. If not, **member** returns **nil**:

```
-> (member 'b '(a b c))
(b c)
-> (member 'x '(a b c))
nil
-> (member 'y '(x (y) z))
nil
-> (member '(a b) '(a b c))
nil
-> (member '(a b) '((x y) foo a b (a b) (c d) (a b)))
((a b) (c d) (a b))
->
```

Why doesn't **member** just return **t**, like the other predicates we have seen? Remember, LISP distinguishes only between **nil** and non-**nil** as far as true and false are concerned. Thus a value like **(b c)**, which is returned in the first example above, would be considered true, just as **t** would. However, the value **(b c)** is likely to be more informative. For example, if I want to know if a value occurs twice in a list, returning **t** would not help. But returning the rest of the list after the match would. In general, LISP tries to return something informative as the result of a predicate.

Note also that **(member 'y '(x (y) z))** returns **nil**. **member** only checks to see if the first argument is literally an element of the second. In this example, **y** is not an element of **(x (y) z)** (although it is an element of one of its members). We could write a LISP function that checked for "anywhere membership", but **member** happens not to do this.

There are plenty more predicates that come with LISP, but these will do for now. Again, you will want to stare at Appendix A when you have mastered the basics to see what else is available.

Of course, we could use **defun** to define arbitrary predicates of our own. For example, if we want a predicate that determines if the **car** of a list is an atom, we could do the following:

```
-> (defun car-atomp (x) (atom (car x)))
car-atomp
-> (car-atomp '(a b c))
t
-> (car-atomp '((a) (b) (c)))
nil
->
```

Actually, **car-atomp** is not exactly what we want. It blindly takes the **car** of its argument, and thus if we happen to pass it an argument that is not a list, **car-atomp** will cause an error. In such cases, we would rather that **car-atomp** simply return **nil**.

What we would like to do here is to test to see if our argument is a list, and take its **car** *only* if this were the case. However, as yet, we have no way of writing such a function. We have seen how to use a predicate to determine whether some condition holds, but so far we have not seen any way to evaluate something conditionally, based on the outcome of a test. To do so, we need to introduce a new construct.

4.3. CONDITIONALS

Now we are ready to use predicates to make a choice. To do so, we need some equivalent of a conditional branch. Once again, LISP provides this facility through the use of a function. In this case, the function's name is **cond**, for conditional. **cond** is similar to an "if...then...else..." statement, but is a bit more general. A **cond** can have any number of arguments, which are sometimes called **cond** clauses . Each **cond** clause consists of a series of s-expressions. The first element of a **cond** clause is treated as a condition to be tested for; the rest of the clause consists of things to do should the condition prevail.

To evaluate a **cond** clause, LISP first evaluates its condition, i. e., the first element of the clause. *It evaluates the rest of the expressions in the clause only if the condition evaluates to true.*

For example, if I want to be sure that something is a list before I take its car, I could do the following:

(cond ((listp x) (car x)))

This is a **cond** of one clause, the s-expression **((listp x) (car x))**. The first element of this clause, **(listp x)**, is the condition of this clause. If this evaluates to true, only then will LISP evaluate the elements in the rest of the clause; in this case, there is only one additional element in the clause, the expression **(car x)**.

Let us bind **x** to something and see how this works:

```
-> (setq x '(a b c))
(a b c)
-> (cond ((listp x) (car x)))
a
-> (setq x 'y)
y
-> (cond ((listp x) (car x)))
nil
->
```

Like any other LISP function, **cond** returns a value. As we can see in this example, when the test in the **cond** clause panned out, LISP evaluated the next expression. It also returned the value of that expression as the value of the **cond**. When the test failed, the **cond** returned **nil**.

While the above example is perfectly legal, it does not make much sense to evaluate a **cond** on the top level of LISP. Rather, **cond**s are meant to be used inside function definitions, where the values they encounter will vary from application to application. For example, we can use **cond** to write a better version of the function **car–atomp**, which we tried to write in the previous section. Recall that **car–atomp** is supposed to return true only if the **car** of its argument is an atom. Above we noted that we had no way to ensure that we only take the **car** of an expression when it is legitimate to do so, i. e., when the expression is a list. However, with **cond**, it is easy to assure such conditional evaluation:

```
-> (defun car-atomp (x) (cond ((listp x) (atom (car x)))))
car-atomp
-> (car-atomp '(a b c))
t
-> (car-atomp 'z)
nil
->
```

Here we use **cond** to determine if it is safe to take the **car** of the argument. If it is not, the **cond** simply returns **nil**, which is returned as the value of the function. Otherwise, the **cond** returns the value of **(atom (car x))**, whatever that happens to be.

4.3.1. More Complex CONDs

In this example, **cond** has the effect of an "if...then..." statement: We evaluate the latter part only if the former part tells us to. However, it is possible to use **cond** to make some more discriminations. In particular, **cond** allows us to specify as many **cond** clauses as we like. LISP will evaluate the test in the front of each one until it finds a test that returns true. Then it will evaluate the rest of that **cond** clause as above. If there are additional **cond** clauses after the one that is evaluated, they will all be ignored.

For example, suppose I want to write a function that behaves as follows: If it is passed a list, it **cons**es the atom **a** onto the front of it; if it is passed a number, it adds **7** to it; otherwise, it just returns **nil**. We can construct this function using a **cond** with two clauses:

```
-> (defun cond-example1 (x)
   (cond
       ((listp x) (cons 'a x))
       ((numbp x) (plus 7 x)) ) )
cond-example1
-> (cond-example1 '(b c))
(a b c)
-> (cond-example1 9)
16
-> (cond-example1 'z)
nil
->
```

Note that I indented the **cond** clauses to better reveal the structure of the function. This is good programming practice in general.

When we use **cond–example1**, the condition of the first **cond** clause is evaluated first. This will return true whenever the argument is a list. In this case, **a** is **cons**ed onto the front of the list. The resulting value is returned as the value of the **cond**, the other **cond** clause being ignored. However, if the argument is not a list, the condition of the first **cond** clause returns false, and the rest of that clause is ignored. The condition of the next **cond** clause is evaluated. This will return true whenever the argument is a number, in which case **7** is added to that number and the resulting value returned. If the conditions of both **cond** clauses evaluate to **nil**, we fall off the end of the **cond**, which then returns **nil**.

Thus far, each of our examples of **cond** clauses had only one expression to evaluate should its condition return true. However, LISP will allow any number of s-expressions after the condition of the clause. If that clause is reached and its condition evaluates to true, each expression after the condition is evaluated in order. The value of the last expression is returned as the value of the **cond**. For example, here is another version of the function we just wrote. Unlike the previous example, this one has the side-effect of setting the global variable **flag** to the value **list** or **number**, depending on its argument:

```
-> (defun cond-example2 (x)
     (cond
         [(listp x) (setq flag 'list) (cons 'a x)]
         [(numbp x) (setq flag 'number) (plus 7 x)] ) )
cond-example2
-> (cond-example2 '(b c))
(a b c)
-> flag
list
-> (cond-example2 9)
16
-> flag
number
->
```

cond–example2 looks just like **cond–example1**, except that here each **cond** clause has an additional expression in it. In addition, I used super-parentheses here to highlight the **cond** clauses, a practice many LISP programmers advocate. When the condition in either clause pans out, all the s-expressions following the condition are evaluated. In the case of each **cond** clause in **cond–example2**, the new expression causes the atom **flag** to be bound to a value before the expression producing the value of the **cond** is evaluated. Thus **cond–example2** always returns the same value as **cond–example1**, but in addition produces the side-effect of changing the binding of **flag**.

Note that **cond—example2** may not do exactly what we want. For example, if I call **cond—example2** with an argument that is a number, say, it will bind **flag** to **number**. But if I call **cond—example2** again with the argument **'z**, neither clause is evaluated and **flag** will not be reset. Instead of this behavior, we might prefer to bind **flag** to some other value, say **neither**, in the instance in which neither **cond** clause is used. Thus we would like a kind of catchall **cond** clause that always gets used if the other **cond** clauses are of no avail.

A standard way to do this is to begin a **cond** clause with the atom **t**. **t** always evaluates to **t**, which is non-**nil**, so any **cond** clause that begins with **t** will always be used if it is reached. For example, we can correct the problem with **cond—example2** as follows:

```
-> (defun cond-example3 (x)
     (cond
        [(listp x) (setq flag 'list) (cons 'a x)]
        [(numbp x) (setq flag 'number) (plus 7 x)]
        [t (setq flag 'neither) nil] ) )
cond-example3
-> (cond-example3 '(b c))
(a b c)
-> flag
list
-> (cond-example3 'z)
nil
-> flag
neither
->
```

cond—example3 has three **cond** clauses, of which the last begins with **t**. If neither of the first two clauses is used, the third one will be. This results in setting the value of **flag** to **neither**. Since we do not want to return this value as the value of the **cond**, we put another element in this clause. This is the value **nil**, which is the value we want **cond** to return in this instance.

4.3.2. The General Form of COND

We have now seen **cond** in all its glory. We can write out this general form as follows:

```
(cond (exp11 exp12 exp13 ... )
      (exp21 exp22 exp23 ... )
      (exp31 exp32 exp33 ... )
        .
        .
        .
      (expn1 expn2 expn3 ...))
```

Each list of expressions (e. g., **(exp11 exp12 exp13 ...)**) is one **cond** clause.

In general, to evaluate a **cond**, LISP examines the first **cond** clause. LISP takes the first element of this clause, and evaluates it. If it returns true (i. e., non-**nil**), LISP will continue down that clause, evaluating each expression, until it comes to the end. Then LISP returns the value of the last expression it evaluates as the value of the **cond**. The rest of the **cond** is ignored. On the other hand, if the first element of the clause evaluates to false, LISP ignores the rest of the elements of that clause. It finds the next **cond** clause and repeats the whole procedure. Eventually, either some **cond** clause will pay off, or LISP will run off the end of the **cond**. If this happens, the **cond** evaluates to **nil**.

In the general case above, LISP would first evaluate **exp11**. If it returns true, LISP continues by evaluating **exp12** and then **exp13**, and so on, until it reaches the last expression of the clause. When it finishes evaluating this expression, it returns its value as the value of the **cond**. On the other hand, if **exp11** evaluates to **nil**, LISP skips the rest of its **cond** clause. Then it evaluates **exp21**. LISP repeats this procedure until one expression turns out to be true, or until it runs out of them.

There is one fine point about **cond** that is useful to know. It is perfectly legal to have a **cond** clause with only one expression in it. In this case, the expression still serves as the condition of the clause. However, if the condition evaluates to true, LISP will return the value of the condition as the value of the **cond**. For example, suppose I want **cond—example** to both bind **flag** to **neither** *and* return **neither** as its value, in the case where it is passed neither a number nor a list. I could accomplish this as follows:

```
-> (defun cond-example4 (x)
     (cond
        [(listp x) (setq flag 'list) (cons 'a x)]
        [(numbp x) (setq flag 'number) (plus 7 x)]
        [(setq flag 'neither)] ) )
cond-example4
```

55

```
-> (cond-example4 '(b c))
(a b c)
-> flag
list
-> (cond-example4 'z)
neither
-> flag
neither
->
```

The last **cond** clause here consists of only one expression, **(setq flag 'neither)**. Since this expression is in the condition position, if we reach this clause, the expression will be evaluated. It will always return a non-**nil** value (namely, the value **neither**), so this value will be returned as the value of the **cond**.

Some LISP programmers avoid this feature of **cond**, claiming that it makes code less transparent. For example, they would put a **t** in the beginning of the third **cond** clause above. The resulting **cond** has exactly the same effect, but its logical structure is more apparent.

One way to conceptualize a **cond** is as a generalized "if...then...else...". I will write out the general form of **cond** below, with capitalized English words annotating the expressions they precede:

```
(cond ( IF exp THEN DO exp ALSO DO exp ... )
      ( ELSE IF exp THEN DO exp ALSO DO exp ... )
      ( ELSE IF exp THEN DO exp ALSO DO exp ... )
              .
              .
              .
      ( ELSE IF exp THEN DO exp ALSO DO exp ... ) )
```

While **cond** allows any number of clauses with any number of expressions to be evaluated, in practice, most useful **cond**s are relatively simple. For example, here is a handy function that uses **cond** in order to **cons** an element onto a list only if that element is not already in that list. We call this function **enter**:

```
-> (defun enter (e l)
     (cond
         [(member e l) l]
         [t (cons e l)] ) )
enter
```

```
-> (enter 'b '(a b c))
(a b c)
-> (enter 'b '(x y z))
(b x y z)
->
```

enter uses **member** to first check if the list bound to l contains the element bound to **e**. If so, then the list is simply returned. Otherwise, the value bound to **e** is **cons**ed onto l and the resulting list is returned as the value of **enter**.

In this example, **cond** is used as an "if...then...else" construct. This probably represents the prototypical use of **cond** in actual programming situations.

4.4. LOGICAL OPERATORS

Suppose we want to check if an s-expression evaluates to an even number between 50 and 100. We can use the predicates **evenp**, **greaterp**, and **lessp** to check the various parts of this condition, and compose them using a **cond**. For example, the following function would do the job:

```
-> (defun even-50-100 (x)
      (cond ((numbp x)
            (cond ((evenp x)
                  (cond ((greaterp x 49)
                        (lessp x 101]
even-50-100
-> (even-50-100 17)
nil
-> (even-50-100 88)
t
-> (even-50-100 89)
nil
-> (even-50-100 102)
nil
-> (even-50-100 '(a b c))
nil
->
```

Needless to say, the function works, but it is just about impossible to read. In general, it is bad practice to imbed a **cond** within another **cond** for reasons of readability. However, with what we have at our disposal, we would have no other choice.

Fortunately, LISP, like most programming languages, provides an easier way to compose predicates. This is through the use of *logical operators.* Logical operators take truth values as arguments, and return truth values as results. The most commonly used logical operators are **and**, **or**, and **not**.

not is the simplest, returning **t** if its argument evaluates to false, and **nil** if it evaluates to true. For example, if we want to check to see if the value of **x** is not an atom, we could do the following:

> **−> (not (atom x))**

This will return true exactly when **(atom x)** returns false.

(Note − Since true and false are non-**nil** and **nil**, respectively, **not** has exactly the same behavior as **null**. These are really two different names for the same function, provided to help make programs more readable. You should use **null** if you conceptualize its argument as a (possibly empty) list, and **not** if you conceptualize its argument as a truth value.)

and and **or** each take any number of arguments, which are evaluated one after the other. In the case of **and**, the evaluation goes on until some argument evaluates to **nil**, in which case **and** returns **nil**; if it reaches the end without any argument returning **nil**, **and** returns the value of its last argument (which by now would be guaranteed to be non-**nil**). For example, to determine if **x** were both even and less than 100, we could type

> **(and (evenp x) (lessp x 100))**

or works similarly, stopping before the end only if some argument evaluates to true. If any does, **or** returns the value of that argument; otherwise it returns **nil**.

For example, if we want to know if the value of **x** is either a number or **nil**, we could write

> **(or (null x) (numbp x))**

This expression would return true if either of the predicates within it return true.

4.4.1. Using AND and OR for Flow of Control

Since **or** and **and** are guaranteed to stop evaluating their arguments as soon as they know what the result is going to be, they are useful for flow of control as well as for their logical value. For example, suppose we want to know if the first element of the list l is a number. If we just do a **(numbp (car l))**, this would cause an error if l evaluates to an atom. But we can check for this first:

(and (listp l) (numbp (car l)))

Since **and** evaluates the first argument before looking at the second, the expression above will never take the **car** of l unless the first condition is true, i. e., unless l is a list, in which case the **car** should be safe.

In this example, we used **and** instead of **cond** to effect a conditional evaluation. Using **cond** for this purpose would be only slightly less elegant:

(cond ((listp l) (numbp (car l))))

However, as we saw at the beginning of this section, **cond** becomes awkward if the composition is more complex. Let us use logical operators to write a version of **even−50−100** and compare it to the one above that uses **cond**:

```
->  (defun even-50-100 (x)
       (and (numbp x) (evenp x) (greaterp x 49) (lessp x 101)))
even-50-100
->
```

Clearly, using **and** is much simpler and more expressive for this purpose.

4.5. SUMMARY

(1) *Predicates* are functions that check to see if a certain condition prevails. LISP uses **nil** to mean "false" and non-**nil** to mean "true". The special atom **t**, which always evaluates to itself, is used as a convenient way to return a non-**nil** value.

(2) Some commonly used LISP predicates are **atom**, **listp**, **null**, **numbp**, **equal**, **evenp**, **oddp**, **greaterp**, **lessp**, **zerop**, and **member**.

(3) Predicates can be conveniently composed into more complex predicates using *logical operators*. The most common logical operators are **not**, **and**, and **or**. **and** and **or** cease evaluation when they have determined a result; hence they are useful for flow of control as well as for their logical properties.

(4)   Predicates are commonly used inside **cond**s, which allow conditional evaluation of s-expressions. A **cond** consists of any number of **cond** clauses, each of which consists of a condition and a series of things to do. LISP evaluates each condition until it finds one that prevails; then it evaluates the rest of the expressions in that **cond** clause, returning the value of the last one as the value of the **cond**.

Exercises

(1)   What values do the following expressions return?

(a) **(not (atom '(a b c)))**

(b) **(member '(y) '(x y z))**

(c) **(and (setq x 4) (not (numbp x)) (setq x 5))**

(d) **(or (setq x 4) (not (numbp x)) (setq x 5))**

(e) **(equal ( ) 'nil)**

(2)   Write a LISP predicate that determines if its argument is an odd number greater than a million.

(3)   Write a LISP predicate **multiple–member** that returns true if the value of its first argument occurs at least twice in the value of its second.

(4)   Write a LISP function that averages its two arguments, first checking to see that they are numbers; if they are not, have the function return **0**.

(5)   Write a LISP function that checks to see if two numbers are sufficiently close to one another to be counted as identical for some purpose. "Sufficiently close" will mean that the two numbers are within the value of **tolerance** of one another, where **tolerance** is a global variable.

5

Recursion

5.1. INTRODUCTION—RECURSION VERSUS ITERATION

The functions we have written so far have been rather simple. They all compose built-in LISP functions or previously written user-defined functions, possibly using **cond** to influence flow of control. However, we have not written any more interesting functions because doing so requires some notion of repetition. For example, we cannot currently write a function that does something to each element of a list of arbitrary length, because we have no way to express such an indefinite notion. What we need is some LISP construct that enables us to do something an indefinite number of times, each time varying the objects that we manipulate.

We could accomplish this aim by introducing some LISP constructs designed specifically to promote indefinite repetition. The explicit use of constructs for repetition is usually called *iteration,* and will be discussed in the next chapter. However, none of this is really necessary to do what we want. Instead, we can accomplish the equivalent of indefinite repetition through the use of *recursion.* A function is said to be *recursive* if it refers to itself in its definition. In this chapter we will see how relatively simple recursive functions can be designed to perform relatively complex computations.

Most of the examples of recursive functions given in this chapter could also be implemented using the iterative methods shown in the next chapter.

However, older versions of LISP tended not to support iteration very much at all, and programmers were encouraged to use recursive techniques instead. In fact, some LISP "purists" frown on the introduction of iteration to LISP. This position has generally softened today, and most LISPs and LISP programmers include both recursive and iterative techniques in their repertoire. I introduce recursion first to demonstrate its power and elegance, and because many LISP programmers still favor it. But the reader should decide for himself which techniques constitute better programming.

For those readers familiar with recursion, this chapter should present no difficulties. However, recursion does take a bit of getting used to. Those readers who are not familiar with recursion should not be discouraged by any initial difficulties they may experience. These are common and will dissipate with practice.

5.2. THE FUNDAMENTALS OF RECURSION

Writing recursive functions is simple once you get the hang of it. The basic idea is to use the function we are defining in its own definition. The trick is to make sure that the function checks first for some appropriate termination condition, so it will know when to stop.

For example, suppose we wanted to write our own version of **member**. Remember, **member** checks to see if an element is contained in a list. One way to think about this function is as follows:

> First, check if the first element of the list is the element in question; if so, we are done.
> Otherwise, peel off the first element, and repeat the process. Be sure to check that there is some list left before continuing.

In LISP, we could state this as follows:

```
(defun our-member (e l)  ; our own version of member
    (cond
        [(null l) nil]              ; any list left?
        [(equal e (car l)) l]       ; make the test
        [t (our-member e (cdr l))] ) )  ; do recursive step
```

Note that I commented some of the lines of **our-member** using the LISP comment character ; (semicolon). LISP simply ignores the rest of a line after a semicolon (other LISPs may use other comment characters).

The first **cond** clause of **our-member** ensures that we exit the function when l is bound to the empty list. If not, the next **cond** clause checks to see if the value of **e** is the same as the first element of **l**. It returns **l** in this case (recall that **member** is supposed to return the rest of the list from the point of the match). These two **cond** clauses represent the "basic" situations of this recursion. These are the situations in which our function has encountered some condition that allows it to return a value.

If neither of these situations is the case, the final **cond** clause is used. This clause calls the function **our–member** again. This part of the definition constitutes the characteristic "recursive step" of the function. Note that this time **our–member** is passed **e** and **(cdr l)**. **(cdr l)** contains one less element than **l**. So in effect, we are asking **our–member** to do a slightly easier job this time.

Having the recursive step do a simpler task is a crucial aspect of all recursive functions. If we call a function recursively on a problem that is just as hard as the original problem, the computation will never terminate. But if the problem gets simpler each time, the recursion will inevitably reach a "basic" situation. For example, in the case of **our–member**, each time the recursive step is taken, **our–member** gets passed a shorter list. This cannot go on indefinitely. **our–member** will eventually be called with **l** bound to **nil**. Its first **cond** clause will catch this and cause the process to terminate.

Let us trace through a call to **our–member** to see how it works. Suppose we evaluate the expression **(our–member 'b '(a b c))**. As with any other function call, the formal parameters get bound to the values of the actual arguments, so in this case, **e** gets bound to **b** and **l** gets bound to **(a b c)**. Next, we evaluate the function body. **l** is not **nil**, so the first **cond** clause is not used; the **car** of **l** is not **equal** to **b**, so the second **cond** clause is not used either. The final **cond** clause begins with **t**, so it is used. This calls the function **our–member** again. LISP does not handle this call differently than it would any other function call. It evaluates the actual arguments, and binds to the resulting values the formal parameters of the function called. So **e** evaluates to **b**, and **(cdr l)** to **(b c)**. The parameters of **our–member**, **e** and **l**, are bound to these values, respectively. Of course, LISP saves the previous values of these parameters, as it would in any function call. It will restore them upon completion of the function call.

At this point we have entered **our–member** again with **e** bound to **b** and **l** bound to **(b c)**. **l** is still not **nil**, so that clause is ignored. However, the **car** of **l** is **equal** to **b**, so the condition of the second **cond** clause is met. We have now reached a "basic" situation, and we begin our climb back up the recursion ladder. LISP evaluates the rest of the expressions of this **cond** clause, in this case, the lone expression **l**. It returns this value as the value of the **cond**. Since **l** is currently bound to **(b c)**, this value is returned from the **cond** and, subsequently, as the value of the most recent call to **our—member**. This most recent call to **our—member** occurred in the final **cond** clause of the previous call to **our—member**. We have now finished evaluating that **cond** clause. It returns the value returned by its call to **our—member**, namely, the list **(b c)**. This value is returned as the value of the **cond**, and thereby, as the value of the original call to **our—member**.

Even in this simple example, tracing through a recursive function call is a bit confusing. However, all recursive functions conform to a simple regimen. A recursive function first checks to see if it has reached some "basic" situation. A "basic" situation is one in which the function either computes some desired element or runs out of things to try. If it has not encountered such a situation, then the function calls itself on a slightly simpler version of the same problem. Since the problem to which the function is applied gets simpler each time, the function will eventually encounter a basic situation. Thus the computation will terminate eventually.

Note that our definition of **our—member** has a slight bug in it. Can you find it? **our—member** first checks for **nil**, and then, if **l** is non-**nil**, tries to take its **car**. This would result in an error if a user mistakenly used a non-**nil** atom as the second argument. A good way to fix this bug is to change the call to **null** to a call to **atom**. Since **nil** is an atom, using **atom** will catch all the cases that using **null** would catch; in addition it would prevent a hard error if an atom were supplied as the second argument.

5.3. RECURSION AND PARAMETER BINDINGS

Since LISP saves and restores the bindings of formal parameters each time it enters and leaves any function, having a function call itself does not result in that function's bindings getting confused. We did not exploit this feature in our previous example, but it is a crucial part of recursion. For example, suppose we want to write a function that computes n!. Recall that n! is defined as $n(n-1)(n-2)...1$, so that $3! = 3*2*1 = 6$, $5! = 5*4*3*2*1 = 120$, etc. By convention, 0! is defined as 1. If we observe that n! is equal to $n(n-1)!$, the recursive version of this function becomes rather trivial:

```
-> (defun factorial (n)
      (cond [(zerop n) 1]
            [t (times n (factorial (sub1 n)))] ) )
factorial
-> (factorial 3)
6
```

```
-> (factorial 6)
720
->
```

factorial first checks to see if the value of its parameter **n** is **0**. If so, it returns **1**. This is the basic situation of this recursion. If **factorial** has not reached a basic situation, it calls **factorial** again, this time asking it to compute the factorial of **n**−1. As is always the case for a recursive step, this computation constitutes an application of the recursive function to a simpler version of the original problem.

When this simple computation is complete, **factorial** multiplies the result by **n** to obtain the factorial of **n**. For this process to work, LISP must ensure the integrity of the value of **n** within a given call to **factorial**. Each call to **factorial** temporarily changes the value of **n**, but must change it back to the way it found it so that the previous call to **factorial** can compute the right value. However, LISP deals with the formal parameter bindings of all functions in just this manner. Therefore, evaluating calls to recursive functions does not present a special problem to the LISP interpreter.

5.4. A COMMON RECURSIVE BUG

Introducing recursion in LISP also introduces a new source of potential problems. For example, consider what happens if we call **factorial** with a negative number, or with some non-integer value. Each time **factorial** is called, its argument is decremented by one. But a negative or non-integer argument will never become 0 in this process. Thus LISP will foolishly call **factorial** over and over again until it computes a number whose magnitude is too large for the machine to handle, or until it runs out of room to nest more recursive calls. Either way, the program runs for a long time and then blows up. For example:

```
-> (factorial −1)
Error: NAMESTACK OVERFLOW
<1>:
```

LISP called **factorial** so many times that it ran out of room to stack the binding of the formal parameter. Some internal stack used to implement function calls bumped into a wall, and LISP had to abort the computation.

We could patch **factorial** to prevent this particular error from happening. However, in the course of writing and debugging a recursive function, such travesties are bound to occur. When your program causes a **NAMESTACK OVERFLOW** error, you almost certainly have an improper

termination condition in a recursive function definition (other LISP implementations may give you a slightly different error message).

If your function is doing some particularly complex computation, it may
take quite a while for an error to occur. If you get suspicious and are tired
of waiting, most operating systems and associated LISPs will allow you to
interrupt the computation. In Franz, you can always interrupt LISP by typing the UNIX interrupt character (usually either RUBOUT or CTRL-c). For
example, here I interrupt an errant call to **factorial** by typing CTRL-c, the
interrupt character that I use:

>   **−> (factorial 0.1)**
> **Interrupt:^C**
> **Break nil**
> **<1>:**

LISP shows the interrupt and then behaves just as if an error occurred. We
can **reset** here, or use some of the debugging techniques described in a later
chapter.

5.5. MORE COMPLEX RECURSION

A more elegant use of recursion appears in the definition of the function
subst. This is a function of three arguments; the first is substituted for the
second in the third, i. e., **(subst x y z)** substitutes the value of **x** for the
value of **y** wherever it appears in the value of **z**. Unlike **member**, **subst**
does its work on all levels, not just at the top one. For example,
(subst 'a 'b '((a b c) b c (d c b a))) returns **((a a c) a c (d c a a))**.

To write this function using recursion, think of it this way: We want to
build a new list whose **car** is the old **car** with the substitution already done,
and whose **cdr** is the old **cdr** with the substitution already done. Thus our
basic recursive step in **subst** will be to apply **subst** to the **car** and **cdr** of the
old list, and **cons** the results together. Thus **subst** will have a line of code
that looks like this:

      (cons (subst x y (car z)) (subst x y (cdr z)))

where **x**, **y**, and **z** are the arguments to **subst**. That is, we want to perform
the same substitution in each part of the original list, and then paste the two
parts back together.

For this magic to work, **subst** will have to first check to see if the value of
z is the same as the value of **y**, the value it is to get rid of. If so, **subst** will

return the value of **x**. If not, **subst** should make sure that the value of **z** is a list, so it can continue the recursive step. Now we are ready to write the whole function:

```
(defun subst (x y z)
    (cond
        [(equal y z) x]        ; can we make the substitution?
        [(atom z) z]           ; if we reach bottom, just return
        [(cons (subst x y (car z)) (subst x y (cdr z)))] ) )
                               ; do the recursive step
```

Note that the last clause in this **cond** has only the one expression in it, since this expression both computes the value that we want and is guaranteed to be non-**nil**.

The first two clauses of the **cond** detect the basic situations of this recursion. That is, we do not search any further if we have encountered something we want to substitute; similarly, we cannot search any further if we encounter an atom. As in all instances of recursion, we must check for these terminating conditions first before we take the recursive step.

The recursion used to write **subst** is basically no different from the previous versions of recursion we have seen. In the previous cases, we were not interested in looking inside each element of a list to an arbitrary depth, so we only recursed down the **cdr**, so to speak. In this example, we are interested in looking inside each element to an arbitrary level, so we have to recurse both down the **car** as well as down the **cdr**.

In general, we can think of the "single recursion" technique of the previous examples as a method for marching down the elements of a list (sometimes called "**cdr**ing down a list", for obvious reasons). In these cases, we do not care to examine the constituents of these elements. We can think of the "double recursion" used in **subst** as a technique for **cdr**ing down a list *and* simultaneously examining the contents of each element of that list.

Incidentally, this version of **subst** will get rid of the entire third argument if it matches the second, i. e., **(subst 'a 'b 'b)** will return a. Doing so is probably a matter of taste, although a slightly more complicated version of **subst** can be written to avoid this.

As an exercise, let us trace through a call of **(subst 'a 'b '(c b a))** to see what happens. Be forewarned that tracing through a call to a recursive function is confusing. The power of recursion comes from *not* having to consider explicitly all the various details of the flow of control when we write the code. Instead, we just specify the basic structure of the problem and let

LISP take care of the rest. Thus the definition of **subst** is quite simple, but the computation it performs is quite complex. We will look at that computation here to get a better understanding of how recursion works. However, it is important to realize that one need not (in fact, better not) be concerned about all these details when one is programming.

When we first enter **subst**, its parameters get bound as shown in Figure 5.1.

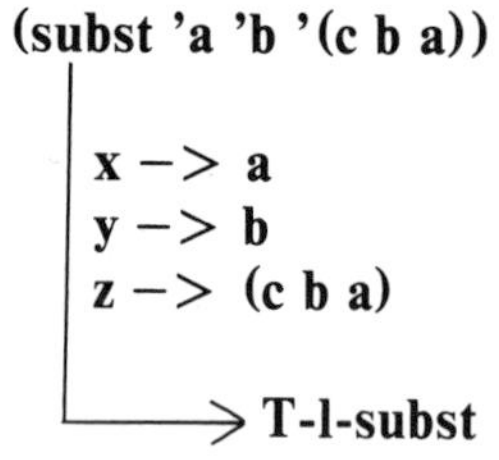

(subst 'a 'b '(c b a))

> x -> a
> y -> b
> z -> (c b a)
>
> ⟶ T-l-subst

Figure 5.1: The initial function call is made.

Typing in the given s-expression causes **subst** to be called with its parameters bound as shown. Since we will have need to refer to a number of different calls to **subst** in this exposition, I have adopted a naming convention for them. I will call the initial call to **subst** "T-l-subst", for "top level call to **subst**". There are two recursive calls to **subst** within **subst**. I will refer to one as "car-subst" and the other as "cdr-subst". I will use a number to indicate how many times each of these calls has been made.

The initial call to **subst** causes its last **cond** clause to be evaluated. **subst** is called again, resulting in the situation shown in Figure 5.2.

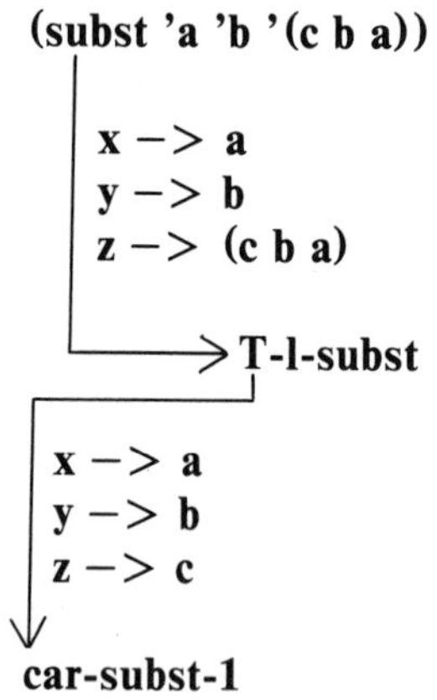

(subst 'a 'b '(c b a))

> x -> a
> y -> b
> z -> (c b a)
>
> ⟶ T-l-subst

> x -> a
> y -> b
> z -> c

car-subst-1

Figure 5.2: The first recursive step is taken.

68

Note that we have not yet exited from the initial call to **subst**. LISP saved the previous values of **x**, **y**, and **z** so that evaluation of "T-l-subst" can continue when "car-subst-1" is finished. "car-subst-1" actually finishes right away: **b** is not **equal** to **c** but it is an atom, so "car-subst-1" returns **c**.

The value **c** computed by "car-subst-1" is returned to "T-l-subst", i. e., the original call to **subst**. Back there, we were evaluating the first argument of a **cons**, and now it is the second argument's turn. This is again a call to **subst**. We now have the situation depicted in Figure 5.3.

(subst 'a 'b '(c b a))

$$x \rightarrow a$$
$$y \rightarrow b$$
$$z \rightarrow (c\ b\ a)$$

→ **T-l-subst**

$$x \rightarrow a \qquad\qquad x \rightarrow a$$
$$y \rightarrow b \qquad\qquad y \rightarrow b$$
$$z \rightarrow c \qquad\qquad z \rightarrow (b\ a)$$

                              c

*car-subst-1   **cdr-subst-1**

Figure 5.3: The first recursive step finishes; another begins.

In this figure I use the asterisk to indicate that the call to **subst** termed "car-subst-1" has been completed. The value it returned to "T-l-subst" is also shown.

In the execution of "cdr-subst-1", the third **cond** clause is again reached, causing yet another call to **subst**. This is shown in Figure 5.4.

At this point, there are three pending calls, "T-l-subst", "cdr-subst-1", and "car-subst-2". Note that the initial list passed to **subst** contains only atoms, so we will not travel down any of its elements. That is, all "car-subst" calls will return immediately, so our example does not really exploit the full power of the recursion built into **subst**.

Thus "car-subst-2" also finishes right away, returning **a**. This step does the actual substitution for which the whole function is designed. The other calls to **subst** simply build up a new list to house the substituted version of the argument.

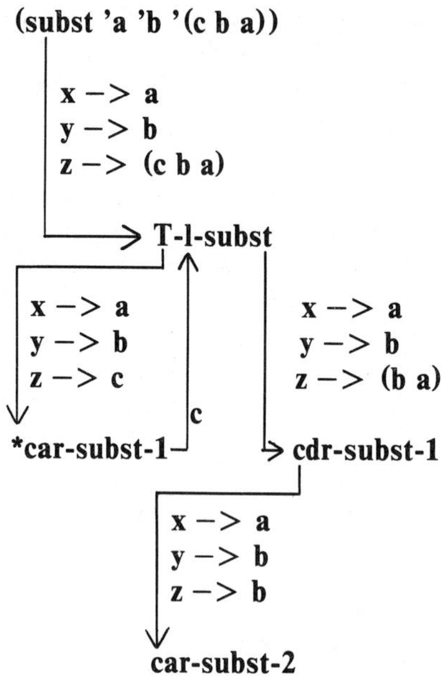

(subst 'a 'b '(c b a))

    x -> a
    y -> b
    z -> (c b a)

                        T-l-subst

    x -> a   x -> a
    y -> b   y -> b
    z -> c   z -> (b a)

                 c
*car-subst-1┘   cdr-subst-1

             x -> a
             y -> b
             z -> b

             car-subst-2

Figure 5.4: A recursive step within a recursive step.

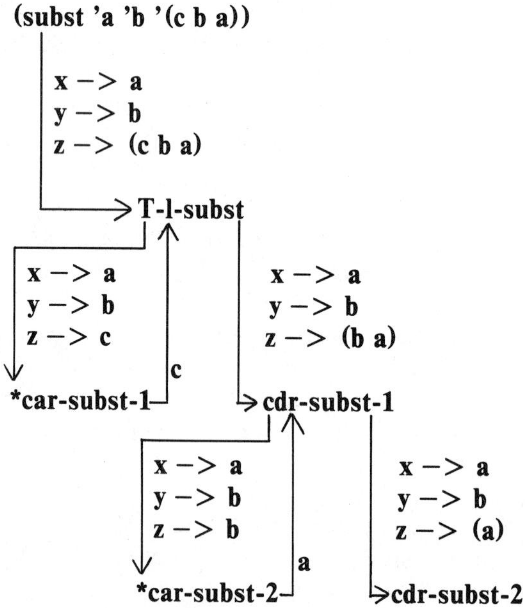

(subst 'a 'b '(c b a))

    x -> a
    y -> b
    z -> (c b a)

                      T-l-subst

    x -> a   x -> a
    y -> b   y -> b
    z -> c   z -> (b a)

                 c
*car-subst-1┘   cdr-subst-1

             x -> a   x -> a
             y -> b   y -> b
             z -> b   z -> (a)

                         a
            *car-subst-2┘   cdr-subst-2

Figure 5.5: A substitution is made and recursion continues.

Now we enter **subst** yet again, resulting in the configuration shown in Figure 5.5.

Next we reach the third **cond** clause again, and make a call to "car-subst-3", which immediately returns **a**. This is returned to "cdr-subst-2", which now calls "cdr-subst-3". The resulting state of affairs is shown in Figure 5.6.

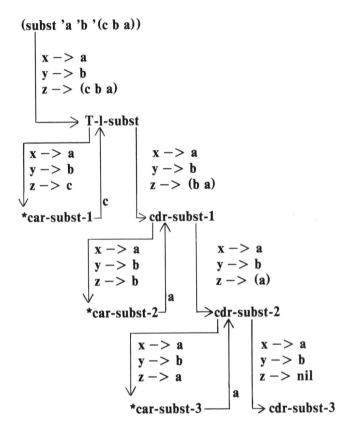

Figure 5.6: The final rung of the recursion is reached.

"cdr-subst-3" returns **nil** right away. We now return to "cdr-subst-2", which is in the middle of executing a **cons**. The other argument to this call to **cons** was already computed to be **a** by "car-subst-3", so "cdr-subst-2" returns **(a)** to "cdr-subst-1". This call was also in the middle of computing a **cons**. The first argument to this call to **cons** was computed to be **a** by "car-subst-2", so "cdr-subst-1" returns **(a a)**. "cdr-subst-1" was called by "T-1-subst", which was also in the middle of computing a **cons**. The first argument to this call to **cons** was computed to be **c** by "subst-car-1". So "T-1-subst" can now run to completion, returning **(c a a)**.

We summarize the overall flow of the computation in Figure 5.7.

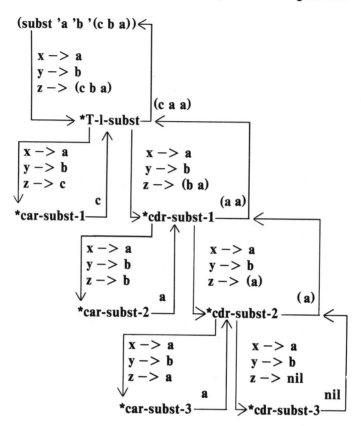

Figure 5.7: The recursive computation is complete.

Fortunately, it is harder to follow the flow of control through recursive functions than it is to write them. It is important to go through the exercise once, though, so that you understand what is actually going on.

Note that a function need not call itself directly for it to be recursive. For example, if function **a** calls function **b**, and function **b** calls **a** again, this is also considered to be a form of recursion. Thus a recursive function is one whose execution will result in another call to that function before the initial call is complete. It makes no difference whether or not there is an intervening series of function calls.

5.6. SUMMARY

(1) *Recursion* is a method for doing indefinite repetition that does not require any additional LISP constructs. Recursion involves having a function call itself during its execution. Because of LISP's normal tendencies to remember which function called which and to save and restore parameter bindings during function calls, having a function call itself does not require any special machinery.

(2) The general form of a recursive function is as follows: First, check for "basic" situations. Then take the recursive step. A common error in writing a recursive function is an improper check for the "basic" situations. In this case, a call to the function is liable to cause a long computation ending in an error.

(3) Much of the time, recursion is used to **cdr** down a list. We can use *double recursion* to both **cdr** down a list and recursively examine the contents of each of the list's elements.

Exercises

(1) Write a recursive function **power–of–two** that computes the nth power of 2. E. g., **(power–of–two 8)** returns **256**.

(2) Write a recursive function **count–atoms** that counts the number of atoms that appear at all levels of an s-expression. For example, **(count–atoms '(a (b c) (d (e) f)))** returns **6**.

(3) Write a recursive function **remove** that removes all occurrences of an element from a list. For example, **(remove 'b '(a b c b d))** returns **(a c d)**.

(4) Use recursion to write your own version of the LISP function **assoc**. **assoc** "looks up" a value in a list of lists, and returns the first list it finds whose first element matches the desired value. For example, **(assoc 'y '((x a) (y b) (z c)))** returns **(y b)**.

(5) A common mistake involving recursion takes the following form. Suppose we want to write a function **if** that uses an "if...then...else" format. We might try to do this as follows:

```
-> (defun if (condition then-action else-action)
       (cond (condition then-action) (t else-action)))
if
-> (if (< 4 5) 'yes 'no)
yes
-> (if (> 4 5) 'yes 'no)
no
->
```

if seems to work. But what might happen if we use **if** inside a recursive definition? For example, suppose we wrote **factorial** in terms of **if**:

```
-> (defun factorial (n)
       (if (zerop n) 1 (times n (factorial (sub1 n)))))
factorial
->
```

What would happen if we used this version of factorial? Why? Fortunately, Franz LISP has a built-in function called **if** that does just what we want.

6

Iteration in LISP

6.1. INTRODUCTION

While many LISP aficionados prefer recursion, iteration has some useful applications. In iterative code, indefinite repetition is designated by explicit instructions to do something repeatedly. To accommodate iteration, LISP has several built-in functions that enable the user to write an explicit loop. In this chapter we discuss these functions, and give iterative alternatives to the recursive functions of the preceding chapter.

6.2. prog

The most general LISP iteration function is called **prog** (short for "program"). **prog** lets you write code that looks more like traditional programming language constructs, with statements, branches, and so on. As is the case with **cond**, **prog** is generally used within function definitions. For example, here is a **prog** that is used to define the function **ln**, which returns the number of items in a list (**ln** has the same effect as the built-in function **length**):

```
-> (defun ln (l)
     (prog (sum)
        (setq sum 0)
      again
        (cond [(atom l) (return sum)] )
        (setq sum (add1 sum))
        (setq l (cdr l))
        (go again)))
ln
-> (ln '(a b c))
3
-> (ln 3)
0
-> (ln '(a (b c)))
2
->
```

The first argument in a **prog** is always a list of *local variables*. Local variables are initialized to **nil** upon entering a **prog**, and are rebound to their previous values when the **prog** is finished. In this case, there is only one local variable, the atom **sum**.

The next element of the **prog** is a call to **setq**. LISP will just evaluate this expression. In fact, after the initial list of local variables, LISP will start evaluating the remaining non-atomic s-expressions in the **prog**, one after the other.

However, the next s-expression in this **prog** is an atom, namely, the atom **again**. (This is the next expression in the **prog**, although I indented it differently to make it stand out.) **progs** just ignore atoms when they appear; we will see their significance in a minute.

The next s-expression in the **prog** is a **cond** of one clause. This clause contains a reference to the function **return**. To interpret a **return**, LISP evaluates its argument and exits from the **prog**; the value of the **prog** will be the value of the argument to **return**. In this case, if the **return** is executed, the **prog** will return the value of **sum**. It is legal to use **return** only inside of a **prog**, as we are doing in this example.

If the **cond** clause does not pan out and the call to **return** is not evaluated, we just continue evaluating the s-expressions in the **prog**. The next couple of s-expressions change the bindings of the atoms **sum** and **l**, respectively. Then we encounter a call to the function **go**. LISP looks at the argument to **go**, which is not evaluated, and looks in the **prog** for an atom of this name. In this case, LISP looks in the **prog** for an atom named **again**. LISP resumes evaluating the expressions in the **prog** starting at the expression immediately after the atom designated by **go**. In our example, the computation would continue with a reevaluation of the **cond**. Like **return**, it is only legal to call the function **go** from inside a **prog**.

Suppose we applied the function **ln** to an argument, as in **(ln '(a b c))**. It would behave as follows: First, the formal parameter **l** would be bound to the actual argument **(a b c)**. Then we enter the **prog**. Since **sum** is declared to be local to the **prog**, the previous value of **sum** is saved, and **sum** is initialized to **nil**. Then **sum** is explicitly bound to the value **0**. Next, we test to see if **l** is bound to an atom. It is not, so we go on. We bind **sum** to **1** (i. e., its old value plus 1), and **l** to **(b c)** (the **cdr** of its old value). We then jump to the expression immediately following the atom **again**, i. e., the call to **cond**. **l** is still not an atom, so we bind **sum** to **2** and **l** to **(c)**. We jump to the **cond** again; the condition is still not met; we bind **sum** to **3** and **l** to **nil**, and jump to the **cond** once more. This time, **l** is an atom, so the **return** gets evaluated. We leave the **prog**, returning the value **3**, and rebind the atom **sum** to any previous value it may have had. The value of the **prog** is returned as the value of the call to **ln**.

6.2.1. The General PROG

The structure of a general **prog** is as follows:

> (**prog** (- *local variables* -) *exp1 exp2 ... expn*)

The first argument to **prog** is a (possibly empty) list of local variables. Then come any number of s-expressions. When LISP enters a **prog,** it goes through the following steps:

(1)   It stacks any previous value bound to one of the local variables and rebinds the variables to **nil**.

(2)   Then it examines the first s-expression. If it is an atom, it ignores it for now. If it is list, it evaluates it.

(3)   What happens next depends on the expression just evaluated:

(a) If the expression includes something of the form (**go** *symbol*), LISP looks for an atom among the **prog**'s s-expressions by the name *symbol*. It continues execution by evaluating the s-expression immediately following that atom (not finding such an atom is an error).

(b) If the expression includes the form (**return** *s-exp*), LISP evaluates the s-expression *s-exp,* and exits the **prog** returning the value of this s-expression as the value of the **prog**.

(c) If neither a **go** nor a **return** transfers control, **prog** evaluates the next s-expression in the list. If there is no next s-expression, because we have reached the end of the list of expressions in the **prog,** we exit the **prog** with value **nil.**

(4)   The old values for the local variables are restored.

As an illustration, let us rewrite **member** iteratively using **prog**:

```
(defun iterative—member (e l)
   (prog ()
      label1
      (cond [(atom l) (return nil)]
            [(equal e (car l)) (return l)]
            [t (setq l (cdr l)) (go label1)] ) ) )
```

I did not need any local variables here, so I just supplied an empty list. Next, I inserted a label where I wish to loop back later on. Then comes a **cond** to do the work. The **cond** first checks to see if there is any list left to search, and if so, checks if it begins with the desired object. If not, it chops off the first element of this list and jumps back to the beginning.

Note that, as is the case for the formal parameters of any function call, changing the value of l does not change the actual argument passed, so no harm is done to the calling code. That is, if **x** were bound to **(a b c)**, and **(iterative—member 'b x)** were evaluated, the value of **x** would remain **(a b c)**, even though the value of l would change several times during execution.

There are usually several ways to write essentially the same code using **prog**. For example, I could just as well have written the following:

```
(defun another—iterative—member (e l)
   (prog ()
      label1
      (cond [(atom l) (return nil)]
            [(equal e (car l)) (return l)])
      (setq l (cdr l))
      (go label1)))
```

I prefer this version because it has somewhat less nesting. Incidentally, it is good programming style not to bury a **go** or a **return** too deeply within a

prog. In fact, some LISPs cannot handle calls to these functions if they occur too far from the surface of the **prog**.

6.3. ITERATION VERSUS RECURSION

Here is another example of iteration. The function **reverse** takes one argument, a list, and returns a list with the same elements but in the reverse order, i. e., **(reverse '(a b c))** returns **(c b a)**. To do this iteratively, we use a local variable to help build up the reversed list as we **cdr** down the original:

```
(defun iterative-reverse (l)
    (prog (temp)
       loop
       (cond [(null l) (return temp)])
       (setq temp (cons (car l) temp))
       (setq l (cdr l))
       (go loop)))
```

We build up **temp** as we peel off each element of l, and return the value of **temp** when we are finished. Note that if l were bound to **nil** initially, **iterative-reverse** would return the value of **temp**. This is what we want, because **prog** variables are initialized to **nil** upon entry.

A recursive version of **reverse** is a bit tricky. We could write a function that reversed the **cdr** of the list, and then stuck the **car** on the end. The problem with this is that, in LISP, it is harder to add an element to the end of a list than to the beginning. In fact, with what we know so far, we would have to rebuild the whole list each time, and that would require a lot of **cons**es! (Think about how to do this if you are not sure why this is so.)

A more efficient way to use recursion would be to have a function that was called with a partially reversed list and with part of the original list. This function would move one element from the original list to the beginning of the partially reversed list, and then call itself again with these arguments. Eventually the original list would become **nil**, and the recursion would terminate. Such a version of **reverse** would look like this:

```
(defun reverse-2 (original revdlist)
    (cond [(null original) revdlist]
       [t (reverse-2 (cdr original)
                      (cons (car original) revdlist)) ] ))
```

The only problem here is that **reverse—2** is a function of two arguments, and we really want **reverse** to be a function of a single argument, the list to be reversed. The way to accomplish this is to create another function, of one argument, which calls **reverse—2** passing along its argument and a second argument of **nil**:

(defun recursive—reverse (l) (reverse—2 l nil))

For my part, the iterative version of **reverse** is more transparent than the recursive version, even though the former has an explicit jump in it.

In addition, iteration is often more efficient than recursion. For example, the iterative versions of **reverse** do not require entering a function over and over again, as does the recursive version. The overhead of calling a function may be considerable, in both time and storage, so the iterative version is liable to require fewer resources. Some LISP interpreters are smart enough to minimize the overhead of certain types of recursive calls so that their efficiency is comparable to that of iterative methods. But in many cases on many LISPs, iteration will be more efficient than recursion.

6.4. OTHER ITERATIVE FORMS

There are a number of simpler variants of **prog**. These are useful when you do not need to alter flow of control, but merely wish to execute some expressions one after the other.

One such function is **prog1**. **prog1** takes any number of s-expressions, evaluates them in order, and returns the value of the first one. For example, **prog1** is useful for simulating the popping of a stack, where you return the first element of a list and set that list to its **cdr**. Thus

(prog1 (car stack) (setq stack (cdr stack)))

returns the first element of the list **stack,** without having to first save this element temporarily as the value of a variable.

prog2 is just like **prog1**, except that it always returns the value of its second s-expression (**prog2** exists primarily for historical reasons). **progn** is similar, returning the last expression it evaluates.

A similar form of sequential execution has been incorporated into other aspects of LISP. As we discussed previously, LISP allows multiple bodies of code in function definitions, which are evaluated one after another. At one point, LISP did not have this facility, so these simpler forms of **prog** were very useful. They are used less frequently now that LISP supports functions with multiple bodies of code.

6.4.1. More Structured Iteration

There are some LISP forms that allow iteration without explicit **gos**, if you prefer "goto-less" programming. These are fairly widespread today, but not particularly standardized. For example, Franz has a form called **do** which is similar to a **while** statement in other languages. It has the following general format:

(**do** *((v1 val1 rep1) (v2 val2 rep2) ...) test-form exp1 exp2 ...)*

The clause right after the **do** is a (possibly empty) list of forms that initialize the values of variables. First, all the *vali* are evaluated; then each *vi* is set to the value of the corresponding *vali* (the old values of the *vi* are saved and restored when the **do** is finished). Since all the *vali* are evaluated first, no *vi* is changed until after all the *vali* have been evaluated. The *repi* are ignored for the time being.

Next, *test-form* is examined. If it is non-**nil**, then its **car** is evaluated. If this evaluates to non-**nil**, then the rest of the forms in *test-form* are evaluated in order, and the last one is returned as the value of the **do**. Otherwise, the *expi* are evaluated in order; if *test-form* is **nil**, then the **do** returns with the value **nil**. Otherwise, the *repi* are evaluated and the values of the *vi* are bound to these values. This process is then repeated starting with the examination of the *test-form*.

For example, the following function reverses a list using **do**:

```
-> (defun do-rev (l)
      (do  ((x l (cdr x))  (res nil (cons (car x) res)))
           ((null x) res) ))
do-rev
-> (do-rev '(a b c))
(c b a)
```

Here the **do** initially binds **x** to the value of **l** and **res** to **nil**. Each subsequent pass through the **do** binds **x** to successive **cdr**s of this list, and **cons**es the leading element of **x** onto **res**. The test terminates the **do** when there is no more list, and causes the value of **res** to be returned. There are no *expi* in this particular example.

There is a simpler version of **do** which only allows one variable. It has the following general form:

> (**do** *v val rep test exp1 exp2 ...*)

This works as follows: *v* is bound to the value of *val;* then *test* is evaluated, and if it is non-**nil**, **do** returns with value **nil**. Otherwise, the *expi* are evaluated in order. Then *v* is bound to the value of *rep* and the process continues from the examination of the test.

The functions **go** and **return** are legal within a **do**; **do** just allows you to implement explicit iteration without them.

Another idea related to iteration is called *function mapping*. We talk about this concept in Chapter 8. There are also some rather non-standard flow-of-control functions in LISP, which are discussed in Chapter 16.

6.5. SUMMARY

(1)   *Iteration* refers to the implementation of indefinite repetition by explicit instruction. LISP has several built-in forms that accommodate iteration, the most general of which is **prog**.

(2)   The **prog** function allows the user to declare local variables, to branch to explicit labels, and to exit directly from any point in the **prog**. Branching and exiting are accomplished with the functions **go** and **return**, respectively. Both these functions are legal only in a **prog**.

(3)   Less elaborate forms of iteration are effected using the functions **prog1**, **prog2**, and **progn**. These do not allow the use of **go** or **return**, just the evaluation of a number of expressions.

(4)   The function **do** allows a more structured form of iteration that does not involve explicit branching.

(5)   Many functions can be programmed using either recursive or iterative techniques. In many cases, the choice is a matter of style. However, sometimes iteration is more efficient than recursion.

Exercises

(1)   Write iterative versions of the functions **factorial, power–of–two, remove**, and **assoc**, which were defined in the last chapter.

(2)   Write an iterative version of the function **make–assoc–list**, which makes a list of the sort **assoc** uses out of two lists of items to be paired with one another. For example, **(make–assoc–list '(a b c d) '(1 2 3 4))** returns **((a 1) (b 2) (c 3) (d 4))**.

3)   Write a function **sub–splice** which is like **subst**, but which "splices in" its first argument for the second. For example, **(sub–splice '(1 2) 'b '(a b c))** returns **(a 1 2 3)**; **(sub–splice '(1 2) 'b '(a (b c) d))** returns **(a (1 2 c) d)**. Decide which is simpler, a recursive or iterative version of this function. Implement the simpler version.

(4)   Write a LISP function that computes *perfect numbers*. A perfect number is defined as a number whose proper divisors sum to that number. For example, 6 is a perfect number because the sum of the proper divisors of 6, namely, 1, 2, and 3, is equal to 6; 28 is a perfect number because the proper divisors of 28 are 1, 2, 4, 7, and 14, which add up to 28. You may write this as a function that finds all perfect numbers between a range of two numbers supplied as arguments.

5)   Suppose we represented a *matrix* in LISP as a list of lists. For example, **((a b) (c d))** would represent a 2x2 matrix whose first row contains the elements **a** and **b**, and whose second row has the elements **c** and **d**. Write a function that takes a matrix as input, and outputs its transpose. For example, **(transpose '((a b) (c d)))** should return **((a c) (b d))**.

(6)   Write a function **intersect** that computes the *set intersection* of two lists. The set intersection of two lists is the list of elements that occur in both lists. For example, **(intersect '(a b b c d) '(c a b b))** returns **(a b c)**. Note that we ignore the order of elements in a list as far as set intersection is concerned. In addition, an element should appear only once in the result, even if it appears repeatedly in the arguments.

(7)   Do all recursive functions have an iterative, non-recursive version? Consider the functions **subst** and **count–atoms** described in the last chapter.

7

Property Lists

7.1. INTRODUCTION

So far, we have treated atoms just like they are variables in other programming languages, even though we claimed that they are different. One
important difference is that atoms can have something called *properties.*
Think of the properties of an atom as being like the properties of a real
world object. For example, a chair can have a color, a weight, a height, and
so on. A given chair might be blue, weigh 40 pounds, and be 3 feet tall.
To describe an object, then, we need *property names,* like **color**, **weight** and
height, and *property values,* like **blue**, **40** pounds and **3** feet.

Properties of atoms in LISP are based on this idea. In this chapter we
describe the LISP notion of properties, and introduce property manipulation
functions. Then we give some programming examples to illustrate their
utility. Finally, we use properties to help demonstrate how different atoms
are from ordinary programming language variables.

7.2. THE BASICS

An atom can have any number of property names, each of which can have
its own value. We can assign properties to atoms using the function
putprop. **putprop** takes three arguments, an atom, a property value, and a

property name. It changes the value of that property of that atom to the specified value. For example, to indicate that **chair3** is the color blue, we can say:

> -> **(putprop 'chair3 'blue 'color)**
> **blue**
> ->

Note that **putprop** returns the property value as its value.

defprop is a function almost exactly like **putprop**, except that it does not evaluate its arguments. So

> -> **(defprop chair3 John owner)**
> **John**
> ->

makes **John** the **owner** of **chair3**. (Note — in some LISPs, **defprop** returns the first argument rather than the second.)

We can now access these stored values using the function **get**. **get** takes two arguments, which should evaluate to an atom and a property name. For example, to retrieve some of the property values of **chair3** that we stored using **putprop** and **defprop**, we can do the following:

> -> **(get 'chair3 'owner)**
> **John**
> -> **(get 'chair3 'color)**
> **blue**
> ->

LISP maintains all the properties and associated values together on a *property list* associated with each atom. You can think of these property lists as a simple kind of data base: **putprop** inserts into this data base and **get** queries it.

If there is no property corresponding to the one you specify when you do a **get**, **get** will return **nil**. Note that **get** will *not* distinguish between a property whose value is **nil**, and a nonexistent property:

> -> **(defprop chair3 nil animate)**
> **nil**
> -> **(get 'chair3 'animate)**
> **nil**

85

```
-> (get 'chair3 'manufacturer)
nil
->
```

Here we define the **animate** property of **chair3** to be **nil**. When we retrieve this value, we get **nil** back. However, we get exactly the same answer when we do a **get** on a property name we have never mentioned before. The former case is likely to indicate that some feature is known not to be present (in this case, the chair is not an animate thing), while the latter is likely to be indicative of not knowing something (in this case, who the manufacturer is). As a programmer, you should be careful to distinguish between these situations if the distinction is meaningful within the context of your program.

7.3. AN EXAMPLE

As an example of the use of property lists, consider the problem of maintaining a data base of information about the books in our library. For each book, I might want to use property lists to store its title, author, and publisher. I might use the global variable **Library** to hold the list of all the books I know about. Then I can write a utility function to add a new book to the data base:

```
-> (defun add-book (bookref title author publisher)
     (putprop bookref title 'title)
     (putprop bookref author 'author)
     (putprop bookref publisher 'publisher)
     (setq Library (cons bookref Library))
     bookref)
add-book
->
```

bookref will be bound to the atom used to represent a book, e. g., **book1**, **book2**, etc. **add-book** just sticks its arguments on the property list of this atom and adds that atom to the library. For example:

```
-> (setq Library nil)
nil
-> (add-book 'book1
        '(War and Peace)
        '(Leo Tolstoy)
        '(Frumpdeedump Press))
book1
```

```
-> (add-book 'book2
           '(Artificial Intelligence)
           '(Patrick Winston)
           '(Addison-Wesley))
book2
-> (add-book 'book3
           '(Data Structure Techniques)
           '(Tim Standish)
           '(Addison-Wesley))
book3
-> Library
(book1 book2 book3)
->
```

We can also define some functions that access this data base. For example, here is a function that retrieves items from the data base that have a certain characteristic:

```
-> (defun retrieve-by (property value)
     (prog (l result)
        (setq l Library)
        loop
        (cond [(null l) (return result)]
              [(equal (get (car l) property) value)
                 (setq result (cons (car l) result))] )
        (setq l (cdr l))
        (go loop)))
retrieve-by
-> (retrieve-by 'author '(Leo Tolstoy))
(book1)
-> (retrieve-by 'publisher '(Addison-Wesley))
(book3 book2)
->
```

I might introduce any number of other properties to complete my library system. For example, I could use a property **status** to indicate whether the books were checked out or are on the shelf, another to indicate who has borrowed it if it is checked out, etc. I might also write functions to remove books from the data base, or for any other library "bookkeeping" that I needed.

7.4. THE SIGNIFICANCE OF PROPERTY LISTS

In the early days, people seemed to take the analogy between LISP properties and properties of real world objects rather seriously. Some people in artificial intelligence, for example, thought that using property lists in this manner might be a good way to represent the real world inside the machine. While there is some merit in this approach, representing real properties of real objects turned out to be more complicated than the naive version of properties that comes with LISP. The upshot of all this is that today people use properties as just another LISP programming language feature. Most AI researchers, for example, will use property lists to implement more complex theories, but do not attribute theoretical significance to property lists per se.

7.5. PROPERTY LISTS AND THE UNIQUENESS OF ATOMS

The following example illustrates an important fact about LISP. Suppose we had the following session with the LISP interpreter:

```
-> (setq v 4)
4
-> (defprop v black color)
black
-> (prog (v) (setq v 9) (return v))
9
-> v
4
-> (prog (v) (defprop v red color) (return (get 'v 'color)))
red
-> (get 'v 'color)
???
```

When we enter the **prog** and declare **v** to be local, changes to the value of **v** will only last as long as we are in the **prog**. When we return to the top level of LISP, **v** is back to its previous value. However, what do you suppose happens to the old value of a property if we change it inside a **prog**? If you executed these lines of code, you have found that the last one returned **red**, not **black**! A change to a property is *not* local to a function definition or **prog**, even if the atom is a formal parameter or a local variable!

This seeming inconsistency is based on the following distinction. An atom in LISP may have different values bound to it at different times, but each atom is a unique object. When you use an atom as a formal parameter or a local variable, you are still using the same atom; you are merely instructing LISP to manipulate that atom's value in a certain way. Thus the atom **v** inside a **prog** is the same atom **v** as on the top level, and is the same atom **v** as appears elsewhere in your code. If you change a property of this atom **v**, you have changed a property of the atom **v**, period.

Some people do not like this feature of LISP because it is so totally global, i. e., a change in some obscure part of a program can affect the behavior of the rest of the program. However, if you think of property lists as a data base, this may not seem so terrible.

7.6. DISEMBODIED PROPERTY LISTS

It is sometimes useful to use the idea of a property list even if you do not have an atom around. For example, if you want to associate some data with some keys, and then look up the data by key, property lists are handy. But these keys and data may have nothing to do logically with properties of an atom. Thus I may want to assert that John owns a Mercedes, Bill a Ford, and Mary a Porsche, using something like **putprop**. Then I could ask what kind of car one of them has using something like **get**. But these assertions are not logically the properties of any preexisting atom.

To allow functions like **putprop** and **get** to be applied to such uses, some LISPs have introduced *disembodied property lists.* These are property lists that are not necessarily associated with an atom. **putprop** and **get** will manipulate disembodied property lists just like ordinary property lists. But they operate on the lists directly, not on an atom with which the list is associated.

Disembodied property lists have one additional feature. They have an odd number of elements. When you hand a disembodied property list to **putprop** or **get**, it simply ignores the first element. This first element is useful if you want to include some sort of identifying information in the beginning of the list.

For example, I can use **get** on a disembodied property list to implement the automobile example given above:

>   -> (get '(nil John Mercedes Bill Ford Mary Porsche) 'Bill)
>   Ford
>   ->

Here I began the disembodied property list with **nil**, since I do not want to mark it in any special way. Of course, in an actual example, we would normally store the disembodied property list in some more permanent location.

Note that **putprop** will actually change the disembodied property list it works on. For this reason, use of disembodied property lists is not recommended for amateurs. Read Chapter 15 on LISP internals to more fully understand the implications of this feature.

We will not have much use for disembodied property lists ourselves in any case. But they are used in Franz to help implement vectors, for example. This is described in a Chapter 18.

7.7. SUMMARY

(1) Every LISP atom can have any number of *properties*. Each property has a *property name* and a *property value*. The set of property name and value associations for a particular atom is called its *property list*.

(2) We can create or change a property of an atom using the function **putprop**. **putprop** takes three arguments, which are all evaluated. It interprets them as atom name, property name, and property value, respectively, and sets the given property name of the atom to the given property value. **defprop** is just like **putprop** except that it does not evaluate its arguments.

(3) We can access the property of an atom using the function **get**. **get** takes two arguments, which are evaluated. **get** interprets the first as the name of an atom and the second as a property name. It returns the value of that property name of that atom, or **nil** if there is no such property.

(4) Changes to property lists are totally global. They are not saved or restored by entering function calls or **prog**s.

(5) A *disembodied property list* is one that is not necessarily attached to an atom. It contains an odd number of elements. LISP ignores the first element while doing **get**s and **putprop**s. The user may use the first element for his own convenience. Disembodied property lists are passed directly to **get** and **putprop**.

Exercises

(1) Use property lists to represent information about the cost and model numbers of a set of different makes of automobiles. For example, you might include that a Mercedes 380SL costs $45,000, a BMW 320i, $15,000, a Plymouth Volare, $8,000, and a Toyota Tercel, $6,000.

Now write a function that, given a list of cars as input, returns the model of the least expensive car.

(2)   A common use of property lists is to "mark" atoms for various purposes. For example, we can use "marking" to speed up the set intersection function we wrote as an exercise in the last chapter (recall that set intersection takes two lists, and returns the elements that they have in common). The idea is to go through one list of elements and "mark" them by putting something on their property lists. For example, we can set the **mark** property of each atom to **t**. Then we can go through the second list, and collect only those elements whose **mark** property is **t**, and return these as the set intersection.

This function is fast because it requires running through each list only once, while the version you wrote at the end of the last chapter had to run through one list once for every element of the other list.

Write a version of set intersect that uses property lists as described above. Remember that we want elements to appear only once in the answer, no matter how many times they appear in the input.

If you are not careful, your version of this function may leave marks on atoms when it is finished. Then subsequent calls may mistake these old marks for current markings and give the wrong answer. Be sure that your version of set intersection does not behave this way.

Note that this hopped up version of set intersection is intrinsically more limited than the previous version. What is this limitation?

(3)   We can implement a sort of virtual property list using a technique known as *inheritance*. For example, suppose we stated that a canary was a bird, and that a bird has wings. We would like to able to ask the question "Does a canary have wings?" and get a positive answer. One way to do this is to store these facts as properties. For example, we can assert **(defprop bird t wings)**, meaning that birds have wings, and **(defprop canary bird isa)**, meaning that a canary is a bird. This latter assertion is sometimes called an "isa—link".

We now need a special function **inherit—get**. **inherit—get** will get two arguments, just like **get**. It will try to do a **get** first, and if this succeeds, will return the value **get** returns. However, if **get** fails, **inherit—get** will use **get** to get the **isa** property of its first argument. If it finds one, **inherit—get** will examine the resulting value to see if it has the desired information. **inherit—get** will keep on going up this "isa hierarchy" until it finds the property requested or it runs out of isa-links.

For example, suppose we evaluated (**inherit–get** 'canary 'wings). **inherit–get** will first try a **get** of the **wings** property of **canary**. When this returns **nil**, **inherit–get** will do a **get** of the **isa** property of **canary**. This returns **bird**. **inherit–get** then does a **get** of the **wings** property of **bird**, and gets the answer **t**. **inherit–get** returns this as its result.

In general, **inherit–get** may go through any number of iterations before it fails or finds an answer. For example, if we evaluated (**inherit–get** 'canary 'alive), we would first check **canary**, and then **bird** for an **alive** property. These both fail, so we check the **isa** property of **bird** and find that it **isa animal**. This may not have the desired information either, so we move up the hierarchy again. The **isa** property of **animal** might be **living–thing**, which should carry the target information.

Write a version of **inherit–get** that works as described.

8

Functions as Arguments: EVAL, APPLY, and Mapping Functions

8.1. INTRODUCTION

Property lists are one way in which LISP begins to look less like other programming languages. Another way in which LISP differs from many other languages is in the flexible way in which functions can be used. So far, we have applied functions to arguments in a rather rigid manner. We have put functions in the beginning of lists, filled out the lists with arguments, and let the interpreter evaluate these expressions. However, LISP allows us to exercise more control over how functions are applied.

In particular, LISP functions may be passed to other functions as arguments, and used within the functions to which they are passed as those functions see fit. In this chapter we examine a number of ways in which LISP functions may be used as arguments to other functions. We show how the user may apply functions to arguments directly, gaining more control over the function application process. Similarly, we show how the user may control the evaluation of s-expressions. We also introduce *mapping functions,* which allow the user to apply a function repeatedly to a series of different sets of arguments.

8.2. FUNCTIONS AS ARGUMENTS

Suppose I want to write a function that determines the sum of the first **n** integers. I could write a straightforward version of this function as follows:

```
-> (defun sum-of-ints (n)
       (prog (result)
           (setq result 0)
           loop
           (cond [(zerop n) (return result)])
           (setq result (plus n result))
           (setq n (sub1 n))
           (go loop)))
sum-of-ints
-> (sum-of-ints 5)
15
-> (sum-of-ints 10)
55
->
```

However, suppose I now want to write a function that computes the sum of the *squares* of the first **n** integers. With what we have seen so far, I would have to write a function that would be completely distinct from the one I just wrote. And if I want to write a function that computes the sum of the cubes of the integers, or the sum of their square roots, I would have to write distinct functions for each case. This is annoying, since the logic of computing the sum of the squares, etc., is almost identical to computing the sum of the integers, and I would like to take advantage of the similarity.

To do so, I would have to be able to write a function **sum-loop** that computes the sum of an arbitrary function of the first **n** integers. **sum-loop** looks almost identical to **sum-of-ints**, except that instead of just adding **n** to **result**, **sum-loop** would first compute an arbitrary function of **n**. This arbitrary function would be supplied as an argument to **sum-loop**. For example, to compute the sum of the squares of the integers, I would supply **sum-loop** with the function **squared**; to compute the sum of the square roots, I would supply it with the function **sqrt**. It would be **sum-loop**'s job to apply this function to **n** and then add the result to the running sum. Thus **sum-loop** would look something like the following:

```
-> (defun sum-loop (func n)
      (prog (result)
          (setq result 0)
          loop
          (cond [(zerop n) (return result)])
          (setq result (plus (func n) result))
          (setq n (sub1 n))
          (go loop)))
```

Here **func** is meant to be a *function argument.* For example, to compute the sum of the square roots of the first 10 integers, I would type **(sum-loop 'sqrt 10)**. **func** would get bound to the function **sqrt**, and **sum-loop** would use this function in the computation.

However, **sum-loop** has an important bug in it. Can you find it? Look at the piece of code that purports to apply the function argument to **n**. What it actually says is to apply the function **func** to **n**. If **func** happens to have a function definition, LISP will use this definition to evaluate the s-expression **(func n)**, just as it would any s-expression whose form is a list beginning with an atom. For example, if I had previously defined **func** to compute cube roots, applying **func** to **n** will always compute the cube root of **n**, regardless of what value I bind to **func** when I call **sum-loop**.

This confusion results because we have made the function we want to apply the *value* of **func**. But LISP looks at an atom's function definition, not its value, when determining how to interpret an s-expression.

To write a proper version of **sum-loop**, we need some way of applying a function to an argument ourselves. That is, we would like to take an atom whose value is a function, and apply that value to an argument. Right now, the only way we know how to apply functions to arguments is by putting the actual function name and arguments in a list and asking the interpreter to evaluate it. This will only work if we know in advance what the function is. This will not be the case if the function is supplied as an argument.

8.3. apply

To rectify this situation, LISP provides a set of functions that apply functions under user control. One such function is called **apply**. **apply** takes two arguments, which are both evaluated. The first argument should evaluate to a function, and the second, to a list of arguments to that function. For example, let us use **apply** to apply the function **cons** to the arguments **a** and **(b c)**. We do this by supplying **apply** with one argument that evaluates to the function **cons**, and another argument that evaluates to the list of arguments to **cons**, in this case **(a (b c))**:

> —> (apply 'cons '(a (b c)))
> (a b c)

Note that **apply** evaluates its arguments, but then applies the first directly to elements of the second. The above expression is equivalent to evaluating **(cons 'a '(b c))**; you do not have to quote the arguments within the list of arguments to **apply**. In fact, you had better not, because **apply** passes these arguments unevaluated to the user-supplied function. Also, the second argument to **apply** should always be a *list* of arguments. For example, to use **apply** to apply **car** to the list **(a b c)**, I would have to type the following:

> —> (apply 'car '((a b c)))
> a
> —>

The second argument here is **((a b c))**, the list of the single argument to **car**.

It is fairly pointless to use **apply** on the top level of LISP, where the normal process of interpretation allows a simpler syntax. However, we could use **apply** to complete **sum—loop**:

> —> (defun sum—loop (func n)
>   (prog (result)
>   (setq result 0)
>   loop
>   (cond [(zerop n) (return result)])
>   (setq result (plus (apply func (list n)) result))
>   (setq n (sub1 n))
>   (go loop)))
> sum—loop
> —>

This function definition is identical to the previous, buggy version of **sum—loop**, except for one new piece of code. This code, **(apply func (list n))**, applies whatever function is bound to **func** to the argument **n** (recall that **apply** requires a *list* of arguments, so we needed to put the value of **n** in a list to conform to this condition). Now that we have gone through all this trouble, let us play with **sum—loop** a bit:

```
-> (sum-loop 'sqrt 5)
8.382332347441762
-> (sum-loop 'sqrt 10)
22.4682781862041
-> (defun squared (x) (times x x))
squared
-> (sum-loop 'squared 5)
55
-> (sum-loop 'squared 15)
1240
-> (defun cubed (x) (times x x x))
cubed
-> (sum-loop 'cubed 5)
225
-> (sum-loop 'cubed 15)
14400
->
```

Take a moment to appreciate the power of this simple function. By taking advantage of the ability to pass functions as arguments, we have been able to separate out the control structure of a process from other aspects of the computation. The result is a simple procedure that can be used for many potential applications, each one requiring only the specification of an appropriate function argument.

Note that a function being passed to another function as an argument may refer to some free variables. These may interact with variables in the calling function in undesirable ways. The problem of preventing such interaction is sometimes called the *functional argument* or *funarg* problem. We will not discuss this problem further here. Instead, in Chapter 12 we show how it can be resolved by a device called a *closure*.

Most LISPs have a few functions that are alternative versions of **apply**. For example, Franz LISP has a function called **funcall**. This works like **apply**, except that **funcall** expects the arguments to its function argument to appear one right after another directly after the function argument, rather than in a list. For example, to **apply cons** to the arguments **a** and **(b c)**, we would type **(apply 'cons '(a (b c)))**. But to use **funcall** to do exactly the same thing, we would type **(funcall 'cons 'a '(b c))**.

funcall accepts as many arguments as its function argument requires.

For example, if we wrote **sum-loop** with **funcall** instead of **apply**, it would look like this:

```
-> (defun sum-loop (func n)
      (prog (result)
         (setq result 0)
         loop
         (cond [(zerop n) (return result)])
         (setq result (plus (funcall func n) result))
         (setq n (sub1 n))
         (go loop)))
sum-loop
->
```

This appears to be a bit simpler than using **apply**, since we did not have to put the argument in a list. Why bother to use **apply** at all, then? Well, **apply** is a bit older and more universal than **funcall**, which is actually the internal function that the Franz LISP interpreter uses to evaluate lists. You should feel free to use whichever is better suited to your programming situation, however.

By the way, there is one minor point involving **sum-loop** that you should know about. If you tried the original, buggy version of **sum-loop**, you might have found that it actually works. This is because of a seldom used feature of some LISPs. In some LISPs, including Franz, the interpreter will try to use the *value* of an atom as a function if the atom has no function definition. For example, it is legal in Franz to do the following:

```
-> (setq x 'cons)
cons
-> (x 'a '( b c))
(a b c)
->
```

Here **x** has no function definition, so LISP checks its value. Its value happens to be the function **cons**, so LISP applies this function to the arguments in the expression.

In general, it is a bad idea to depend on this feature. If later on you give **x** a definition, this code will work quite differently. Hence it is much safer to use **apply** or **funcall**.

8.4. eval

In our examples of the use of **sum-loop**, we had to define the functions **squared** and **cubed**. We could not just pass **sum-loop** expressions like **(times n n)**, because these are not functions, as **apply** requires, but merely s-expressions. However, we might want a version of **sum—loop** that accepts such expressions as arguments, and evaluates them as **n** marches through different values. To do this, we would need a way to evaluate an s-expression ourselves. **apply** does not help directly, since it knows how to apply a function to arguments, not how to evaluate entire s-expressions.

Fortunately, LISP provides a function that does just what we want. This function is called **eval**. **eval** takes one argument, which is evaluated. It should evaluate to a legitimate s-expression. *LISP then evaluates this value again.*

For example, consider the following:

```
-> (setq x '(cons 'a '(b c)))
(cons 'a '(b c))
-> (eval x)
(a b c)
->
```

Here I set **x** to the value **(cons 'a '(b c))**. When I evaluate the call to **eval**, **x** is evaluated, returning its bound value. Then **eval** evaluates this expression, just as if I typed it into the interpreter directly.

As another example, consider the following:

```
-> (setq a 'b)
b
-> (setq b 'c)
c
-> a
b
-> b
c
-> (eval a)
c
->
```

To evaluate **(eval a)**, LISP first evaluates the argument. This produces the value **b**. So **b** is passed to **eval**. **eval** now evaluates this value, just as if we typed it in for the top level of LISP to interpret. Since the value of **b** is **c**, the latter value is returned by **eval**.

We can also use eval to execute a piece of code we create on the fly. For example, consider the following:

```
-> (eval (cons 'plus '(2 3)))
5
->
```

Here the argument to **eval** evaluates to the list **(plus 2 3)**. This is then passed to **eval**. **eval** treats its argument the same way the LISP interpreter would if we typed it in, so it returns the result **5**.

This particular usage of **eval** reveals a significant fact about LISP. Since the data to LISP, s-expressions, are of the same form as expressions of the language itself, it is perfectly possible to have LISP programs that write code as they run, and then execute this code later on. The example above is a rather trivial instance of this, but this feature can be exploited in much more dramatic ways.

Let us return to our attempt to write a version of **sum—loop** that accepts expressions as arguments. With **eval** at our disposal, this can be done as follows:

```
-> (defun exp-sum-loop (exp n)
      (prog (result)
         (setq result 0)
         loop
         (cond [(zerop n) (return result)])
         (setq result (plus (eval exp) result))
         (setq n (sub1 n))
         (go loop)))
exp-sum-loop
-> (exp-sum-loop '(times n n) 10)
385
-> (exp-sum-loop '(times n n n) 10)
3025
->
```

exp—sum—loop simply uses **eval** to evaluate its argument each time it goes through the loop.

exp—sum—loop is not a wonderful example of programming style, however. In order for the expression we supply as an argument to evaluate properly within **exp—sum—loop**, it must use as a variable the same atom that happens to be used as the formal parameter to **exp—sum—loop**. That is, we must always pass as arguments to **exp—sum—loop** expressions that are functions of the atom **n**, because **exp—sum—loop** happens to use **n** as a formal parameter. Thus the caller of the function **exp—sum—loop** must know something about the details of the implementation of that function. And whenever the

100

success of a function depends heavily on the implementation of the functions it calls, this is usually asking for trouble.

8.4.1. Context Problems with EVAL

In fact, **eval** should be used with care in general. Whenever we evaluate an s-expression using **eval**, we are liable to evaluate it in some context in which the s-expression has a different meaning than we intended. For example, suppose LISP came with no function **set**, just **setq** (recall that **set** changes the binding of the *value* of its first argument, whereas **setq** does not evaluate its first argument). Suppose that I tried to use **eval** to define a version of **set**. I could do so as follows:

```
-> (defun my-set (x y) (eval (list 'setq x 'y)))
my-set
-> (setq a 'b)
b
-> (my-set a 'c)
c
-> a
b
-> b
c
->
```

my-set builds up a call to **setq**, and then uses **eval** to evaluate it. As the example indicates, the function seems to work.

However, **my-set** has a terrible bug in it. Can you find it? ... Well, look what happens when I try the following:

```
-> (setq x 'y)
y
-> (my-set x 'z)
z
-> x
y
-> y
Error: Unbound Variable: y
<1>:
```

my-set should have bound **y** to **z**, but instead, **y** remains unbound. What went wrong? Consider what happens when we call **my-set**: The formal parameters **x** and **y** are bound to the values of the actual arguments, in this

101

case, **y** and **z**. Then **list** constructs an expression to evaluate. In this instance, it returns **(setq y y)**. When we **eval** this expression, **y** is indeed bound to **z**. This is what we wanted, *except that* **y** *happens to be a formal parameter of* **my—set**. As soon as we leave **my—set**, **y** is restored to its previous unbound state.

There are a number of solutions to this problem. The simplest is to use strange formal parameter names in these situations, like **%%%x** rather than **x**. This minimizes the chances of variable name conflicts, but does not offer complete protection. Another solution is to allow the user to specify a context within which to evaluate an expression. Franz LISP enables you to do this, but the mechanism is awkward. We will not bother with the details here.

In any case, beware. **eval** is a useful function, but you must be careful to be sure that you are evaluating an expression in the context in which you intend it to be interpreted.

8.5. MAPPING FUNCTIONS

Suppose we want to do the same operation not just to a single set of arguments, but to several sets of arguments. For example, rather than just add *x* to *y*, suppose we also want to add *a* to *b*, *c* to *d*, and so on. LISP provides us with a convenient way to express such computations that involves passing functions as arguments. The technique is called *function mapping*.

The idea behind function mapping is the following. Suppose I had a function of one argument. Normally, we would simply apply this function to its argument. If we want to apply the same function to several different arguments, however, we put these arguments into a list. Then we instruct LISP to apply the function to each element of this list.

Of course, we need some way to instruct LISP to apply a function to each element of a list. We could write a **prog** that does this for a user-supplied function. But LISP provides us with a built-in mechanism that both eliminates the need to write such a function and is usually more efficient to boot.

LISP accomplishes this by supplying the user with functions to do function mapping. The function mapping functions take functions as arguments. They also take as arguments *lists* of the arguments to those functions. Then the mapping function applies its function argument to each element of its argument list.

For example, suppose I want to add 1 to the values 100, 200, and 300.

Rather than write three separate computations **(add1 100)**, **(add1 200)**, and **(add1 300)**, I could use a mapping function to apply the function **add1** to the list of arguments **(100 200 300)**. One such mapping function is named **mapcar**. This can be used to perform the desired computation as follows:

> **−> (mapcar 'add1 '(100 200 300))**
> **(101 201 301)**
> **−>**

Here I supplied **mapcar** with an argument that evaluated to the function **add1**, and an argument that evaluated to a list of arguments to this function. **mapcar** applied the function **add1** to each element of this list of arguments; it returned as its result the list of each resulting value.

Observe that **mapcar** allows us to perform a kind of indefinite repetition. In the example above, it only performed the equivalent of a fixed number of function applications. But suppose I call **mapcar** as follows:

> **−> (mapcar 'add1 x)**

x may be bound to a list of arbitrary length. Since each element of the list is treated as an argument to **add1**, evaluating the above expression may result in an arbitrary number of calls to **add1**.

If the function we wish to use repeatedly requires more than one argument, we can supply more than one argument list to **mapcar**. For example, suppose I want to add 1 to 100, 2 to 200, 3 to 300, and 4 to 400. Here we need two argument lists, the list **(1 2 3 4)** and the list **(100 200 300 400)**. Then we can use **mapcar** to apply **plus** to these lists of arguments:

> **−> (mapcar 'plus '(1 2 3 4) '(100 200 300 400))**
> **(101 202 303 404)**
> **−>**

mapcar evaluates all its arguments. Then it applies the first argument to the **cars** of each latter argument. So **plus** gets applied to **1** and **100**. Then **mapcar cdrs** down the argument lists, and applies **plus** again, this time to **2** and **200**, and so on. **mapcar** collects the results of these computations and returns them all in a list when it is finished.

As another example, suppose we want to know which elements in a list are atoms. We could write a **prog** or a recursive function to do this, but it is easier just to use **mapcar**:

```
-> (mapcar 'atom '(a b c (x y) nil (a b) x y))
(t t t nil t nil t t)
->
```

atom is a function of only one argument, so there is only one list of arguments supplied to **mapcar**. **atom** is applied to each element of this list, and the resulting values are collected into a list and returned as the value of the call to **mapcar**.

8.5.1. The Various Mapping Functions

There are a number of different mapping functions in LISP. Each one goes down its lists of arguments, and applies a user-supplied function to consecutive sets of arguments. Mapping functions differ from one another in exactly how they go down a list and in what value they choose to return, but the basic idea behind all of them is the same.

MAPC

Sometimes the values returned by **mapcar** are less interesting than the side-effects that transpire. For example, suppose I used **mapcar** to define some properties of a bunch of atoms, as follows:

```
-> (mapcar 'putprop
        '(John Fred Bill)
        '(Mary Sue Linda)
        '(mother sister daughter))
(Mary Sue Linda)
-> (get 'John 'mother)
Mary
-> (get 'Fred 'sister)
Sue
-> (get 'Bill 'daughter)
Linda
->
```

putprop is a function of three arguments, so we supply three argument lists to **mapcar**. This worked fine, but note that **mapcar** had to **cons** up the value **(Mary Sue Linda)** in order to return this as its result. This is wasteful, since we have no use for this value in our example, and only throw it away after it is created. As we mentioned above, **cons**ing is expensive. So LISP gives us a mapping function that acts just like **mapcar** except that it does not bother much with a value. This function is called **mapc**. (Do not waste your time trying to puzzle out the motivation for the names of map-ping functions – there is not much of one. However, there is nothing to prevent you from creating your own version of these functions with better names, if you like.) In Franz LISP, **mapc** always returns the value of the first argument list (although in many LISPs, it always returns **nil**).

Let us use **mapc** for the example above:

```
-> (mapc 'putprop
        '(John Fred Bill)
        '(Mary Sue Linda)
        '(mother sister daughter))
(John Fred Bill)
-> (get 'John 'mother)
Mary
-> (get 'Fred 'sister)
Sue
-> (get 'Bill 'daughter)
Linda
->
```

Here we get the same side-effect as with **mapcar**, but save a little overhead by returning a less interesting value.

MAP and MAPLIST

There is also a set of mapping functions that apply a function to the whole list given as an argument to the mapping function, and then to successive **cdr**s of these arguments. This is easier to do than to say. For example, **map** is the **cdr** equivalent of **mapc**, and **maplist** is the **cdr** equivalent of **mapcar**:

```
-> (maplist 'cons '(a b) '(x y))
(((a b) x y) ((b) y))
-> (maplist 'list '(a b) '(x y))
(((a b) (x y)) ((b) (y)))
->
```

In the first example, **maplist** first applies the function **cons** to the entire values of the argument lists, i. e., to **(a b)** and **(x y)** (this is in contrast to **mapcar**, which would have applied the function to the first element of these lists, **a** and **x**, respectively). The resulting value is **((a b) x y)**. Next, **maplist** applies **cons** to the **cdr**s of the two argument lists, namely, to **(b)** and **(y)**, to yield the list **((b) y)**. The **cdr** of each of these two values is

nil, so **maplist** stops and puts the values it has computed so far in a list. This list is returned as the result shown above.

As you might imagine, these mapping functions are not used very frequently. In fact, it is hard to think of a non-contrived example of the use of **map**.

8.5.2. The APPLY-APPEND Trick

It is often the case that we use a function to return a (possibly empty) list of objects that we wish to scrutinize further. If we end up using a mapping function to apply such a function to a list of arguments, we will get a list of lists of objects to further scrutinize. For example, an expression of the form **(mapcar 'find—candidates list—of—arguments)** may return a value like **((a b c) nil (d e) nil (f g h))**, where each element represents the result of each call to **find—candidates**.

A problem with this result is that it contains some list structure that only gets in the way of further computation. The results of each application of **find—candidates** are returned individually wrapped. In our subsequent computation, we would like to examine each item **a**, **b**, **c**, **d**, etc., in turn. But we do not care to know which elements were returned together. Thus we would like to get rid of the list structure that **mapcar** creates, and instead work on the list **(a b c d e f g h)**.

A clever way to do this is to **apply** the function **append** to the value **mapcar** returns. Recall that **append** expects any number of arguments, each of which is a list, and returns a single list containing all the elements of these lists. Since **apply** applies a function to a list of its arguments, **applying append** to the value **mapcar** returns will produce a single list of the form desired. Let us try an example:

```
-> (apply 'append '((a b c) nil (d e) nil (f g h)))
(a b c d e f g h)
->
```

Hence a construct of the form

(apply 'append (mapcar 'find—candidates list—of—arguments))

will return a list of all the candidates that **find—candidates** finds from each application to the arguments in **list—of—arguments**. This is a useful construct to employ whenever we want to use **mapcar** to apply a function that we expect to return a list, and when only the elements of that list are potentially interesting.

There are a few other mapping functions, but understanding them involves some appreciation of LISP internals. For this reason, we will discuss them in Chapter 15.

8.6. SUMMARY

(1) LISP allows the user to supply functions as arguments to other functions. The user may then control function application himself. The function **apply** can be used to apply a function to some arguments.

(2) **apply** takes two arguments, both of which are evaluated. The first should evaluate to a function, and the second, to a list of arguments to that function. **apply** applies the function to the arguments and returns whatever value the function returns.

(3) LISP allows the user to build up s-expressions himself, and evaluate them just as if they were typed into the interpreter. The function **eval** is used to evaluate an s-expression explicitly.

(4) **eval** takes one argument, which is evaluated. Then it evaluates that argument again. Care should be taken when using **eval** to ensure that expressions are evaluated in the correct context.

(5) *Function mapping* is a technique for applying a function repeatedly to a series of arguments. There are a number of function mapping functions. Each takes one argument that should evaluate to a function, and other arguments that should evaluate to lists. There should be as many of these lists as the function argument requires. A mapping function will sequence through the elements of these lists, repeatedly applying the function argument.

(6) The mapping functions differ from one another in how they sequence through the argument lists and in what value they return. **mapc** and **mapcar** apply their function argument to successive **car**s of their arguments; **map** and **maplist** to successive **cdr**s. **mapcar** and **maplist** return the list of the values their function argument returns after each application; **map** and **mapc** just return the first argument list with which they are called.

Exercises

(1)   What are the values of the following expressions:

      (a) (eval (list 'car '(cdr '(b c))))

      (b) (eval (list 'car ''(cdr '(b c))))

      (c) (eval (cons 'cdr '('(a b c))))

      (d) (apply 'cdr '((a b c)))

      (e) (mapcar 'list '(a b) '(c d))

(2)   Write a version of the function **make–assoc–list** using mapping functions. Recall that this function makes a list of the sort **assoc** uses out of two lists of items to be paired with one another. For example, **(make–assoc–list '(a b c d) '(1 2 3 4))** returns **((a 1) (b 2) (c 3) (d 4))**. Compare this version to the iterative version you wrote for the exercise at the end of Chapter 6.

(3)   Write your own version of **mapcar**, or of any of the other mapping functions, using **prog** and **eval** or **apply**. Your version will have to be more limited than the actual LISP function, since we do not yet know how to write functions that accept a variable number of arguments, as does the real **mapcar**. So write your version assuming your function argument will always be a function of exactly one argument.

(4)   Use a mapping function to write a better version of the matrix transpose function described in the exercises in Chapter 6. Recall that we represented a matrix as a list of lists; the transpose of (**(a b) (c d)**) would be (**(a c) (b d)**). (Hint — the most concise version involves **apply**ing a mapping function.)

(5)   Using mapping functions, rewrite the set intersection function described at the end of Chapter 6.

(6)   Suppose a function returns a list of true or false values, e. g., **(nil nil t nil t nil)**. Suppose we want to know if this list contains any non-**nil** value. Use a mapping function in conjunction with a logical operator to make this determination.

(7) One problem with the various mapping functions is that there is no way to stop them before they have run to completion. In many applications, we want to apply a function to arguments repeatedly until a certain condition is true. Therefore, many LISPs include some function applying functions that apply their function only as long as it is necessary to do so. Unfortunately, Franz does not contain such functions. But we now have the tools to create them ourselves.

One useful function that combines flow of control and function mapping is called **some**. This is a function of two arguments, which should evaluate to a function and a list. It applies the function to successive elements of the list *until* the function returns non-**nil**. Then it returns the elements of the *list* from that point on. It returns **nil** otherwise. For example, (some 'numbp '(a b 2 c d)) should return (2 c d).

The function **every** is like **some**, except that it stops as soon as one of the function applications returns **nil**. **every** then returns **nil** as its value. If all the applications return non-**nil**, **every** returns **t**.

Write the functions **some** and **every**.

(8) Define a function **subset** that takes two arguments, which should evaluate to a function and a list. **subset** should apply the function to successive elements of the list. It returns a list of all the elements of this list for which the function application returns non-**nil**. For example, (subset 'numbp '(a b 2 c d 3 e f)) returns (2 3).

(9) We can use **eval** and **apply** to implement a programming technique called "data-driven" programming. In this technique, we store functions along with data, and use the data to suggest which functions to use to manipulate the data.

For example, suppose we had a data base of assorted objects, each of which we want to display according to different rules. People in the data base might be identified by first and last names, books by title and author, cars by make, year, and model, etc.. We could put the code to do this inside a big **cond**, but then we would have to hack this code in order to extend our function to other types of data. A more elegant solution is to first write separate functions for each type of datum:

```
-> (defun car-display (datum)
        (list (get datum 'year)
              (get datum 'make)
              (get datum 'model)))
car-display
-> (defun book-display (datum)
        (list (get datum 'title) 'by (get datum 'author)))
book-display
->
```

and so on. Now we attach one such function to the **display-fn** property of each datum:

```
-> (defprop car13 car-display display-fn)
car-display
-> (defprop book7 book-display display-fn)
book-display
->
```

etc. Of course, we would need to define the other properties of these data as well.

Now we can write a generic display function, **item-display**. This function picks the display function off the property list of the item to be displayed, and applies it to that item. We can extend our displaying capability to new types of data items without modifying this function at all. Instead, we simply write a new display function for the new data type and put it on the property list of each item of that data type.

Write the function **item-display**, and use it to display a small data base of objects.

9

Lambda

9.1. INTRODUCTION

Sometimes it is desirable to define functions that have no name. In this chapter we list some of the reasons for desiring such functions. We show how to implement nameless functions using something called the *lambda notation*. We reveal a fact we have been hiding until now, namely, that the lambda idea underlies all LISP functions. Knowing this fact, we examine some alternative ways of defining functions in LISP. We also present a use of lambda as a way to control variable bindings. Finally, we assess its overall significance.

9.2. FUNCTIONS WITHOUT NAMES

When we use functions as arguments to other functions, as we did in the previous chapter, the need sometimes arises to create a little function that will only be used once. For example, in the last chapter, I used the function **sum−loop** to compute the sum of the cubes of the first **n** integers. To do this, I had to create the function **cubed** that computes the cube of its argument. This simple function will probably never be used again. Even if the need to compute a cube arose elsewhere in my program, it is too easy just to write **(times x x x)** in line than to bother with calling the function **cubed**.

Sometimes a "use-once, throw away" function is created because it fits a very specialized need. For example, suppose we had occasion to determine whether any element of a list were an atom with property **color** and value **red**. We could write an iterative or recursive version of a function that tests a list for this, but it is easier to let **mapcar** do the work. To do this, we first define a function that tests a single atom for this property:

> **(defun red—atom—p (a)**
> **(and (atom a) (equal (get a 'color) 'red)))**

red—atom—p first makes sure that it is looking at an atom; then it gets that atom's **color** property and checks if it is **equal** to **red**.

Now to apply this to a list, we use **mapcar**:

> **—> (defprop b red color)**
> **red**
> **—> (mapcar 'red—atom—p '(a b c))**
> **(nil t nil)**
> **—>**

One problem with this code is that **red—atom—p** is a rather silly function: we are fairly certain never to see it again, and it is a shame to have to waste the storage required to permanently house a new function definition, and waste the time required to think up a name for it.

A solution to this problem is to create a function without a name. To see what this would mean, let us consider more closely what it means to be a function. As we learned in Chapter 3, when we define a function using **defun**, we need to specify a name, a formal parameter list, and some function bodies. **defun** just stores the parameter list and bodies with the name until it needs them during function application. The name serves as a way of associating a formal parameter list with the bodies, and of referring to these some time later on.

Obviously, we need the bodies of code to have a function, because they define what it is the function does. We need a formal parameter list because this specifies which atoms that appear in the code should be treated as formal parameters. But the function name is not really intrinsic to there being a function. If we had some way of associating a formal parameter list with the code directly, we could bypass the need to use atoms to associate these two together.

Putting this another way, the essence of a function is the code that it executes and the way in which it manipulates formal parameters. The function name is not an essential part of this concept, but rather a convenient way of referring to it. In most programming languages, the concept of a function name and the idea of what it means to be a function are closely tied together, so that if you define a function, you must give it a name. And thus far in LISP, this has been the case. However, if we are willing to give up the convenience of being able to refer to every function by name, it should be possible to distill the essence of a function and thereby produce nameless functions.

To produce such a disembodied function, we need some way of associating some formal parameters with a piece of code without using an atom name. This is done in LISP with something called the *lambda notation*. The lambda notation is merely a way of telling LISP that some atoms in a chunk of code are meant to be parameters. To use this notation, the user creates a list that begins with the atom **lambda**. The next element of this list is a list of atoms, and the subsequent elements, some s-expressions. The whole business represents a function, where the list of atoms denotes the formal parameters and the s-expressions, the bodies of code.

For example, suppose I want to make a nameless version of the function **red—atom—p**. I need to tell LISP that **a** is a formal parameter of this function, and that the code is the single expression **(and (atom a) (equal (get a 'color) 'red))**. To do this using the lambda notation, I would write the following expression:

(lambda (a) (and (atom a) (equal (get a 'color) 'red)))

This whole expression denotes a function. The list **(a)** following the occurrence of **lambda** represents the function's formal parameter list; the expression after this denotes the function's single body of code. The entire expression constitutes a function, which, except for the fact that it has no name, is entirely equivalent to the function **red—atom—p** defined above.

Expressions that look like this are called *lambda forms*. Do not type a lambda form into LISP to evaluate it, though, *because lambda forms are not function calls*. It would be meaningless to try to evaluate a list like the one above, because **lambda** is not a function. Rather, the whole form we just typed, **lambda**, formal argument list, and all, is a function. That is, we can stick this form wherever we are used to having atoms designating functions. For example, we are used to putting function names in the beginning of a list, and then following them with arguments. To apply **red—atom—p** to the value **y** we would type **(red—atom—p 'y)**. Since the lambda form given above is entirely equivalent to **red—atom—p**, we can apply it to **y** by putting it in the equivalent position in an s-expression:

-> ((lambda (a) (and (atom a) (equal (get a 'color) 'red))) 'y)
t
->

Take a deep breath and examine this expression. Remember, LISP tries to evaluate lists by assuming that the first element of a list is a function. In this case, the first element of the list is a lambda form. That is okay with LISP, because it thinks lambda forms are functions. Then, as before, LISP evaluates the arguments; in this case, the single argument 'y evaluates to y. Now LISP applies the function to this argument. How? It binds the formal parameter of the function to the value of the actual argument, and then evaluates the function body. It returns the resulting value as the value of the expression, saving and restoring the value of the formal argument in the process.

This is just what happens when we apply named functions that we create using **defun**. The only difference is that, when the function is created via **defun**, we specify the function name and LISP retrieves the previously stored parameter list and function body at function-application time. With the lambda notation, the formal parameter list and body are presented directly to the interpreter. Thus the lambda notation is entirely equivalent to using **defun**, but with one less level of indirection.

This business might strike you as a rather convoluted way of doing a simple thing. After all, could we not just have evaluated the expression **(and (atom 'y) (equal (get 'y 'color) 'red))** and skipped all this hairy stuff? Yes, we could have, in this case. But now let us go back to our **mapcar** example. Here we want to apply a function to a list, and with our lambda form, we can do this as follows:

-> (mapcar
     '(lambda (a) (and (atom a) (equal (get a 'color) 'red)))
     '(a b c))
(nil t nil)
->

Remember, whenever you see a lambda form, try to see a function. The expression above looks exactly like our original call to **mapcar** using **red-atom-p**, except that here, the lambda form appears where **red-atom-p** was previously. The advantage of using the lambda notation is that it eliminates the need to create a permanently stored function named **red-atom-p**. Instead, we create a "function essence" that is useful for expressing what we want to say, without having to dignify it by alloting it the name and permanent storage space granted to a more significant procedure.

114

Since the idea behind lambda is to abstract out the pure essence of what it means to be a function, some people also refer to the lambda notation as *lambda abstraction.*

Let us apply the lambda notation to a more compelling situation. Consider the function **sum—loop** that we defined in the previous chapter. As we mentioned above, **sum—loop** requires a function as an argument. Therefore, it became necessary to define little functions like **squared** and **cubed** just for the purpose of passing them to **sum—loop**. However, with the lambda notation, we can create these functions without going to so much trouble. For example, to define the function **cubed** in the last chapter, we did the following:

>   —> (defun cubed (x) (times x x x))
>   cubed

Then we called **sum—loop**, passing it **cubed** as an argument, i. e.:

>   —> (sum—loop 'cubed 15)
>   14400

To do the same with the lambda notation, let us first express the lambda-form equivalent of the function **cubed**. This would be the following expression:

>   (lambda (x) (times x x x))

Again, this is just the formal parameter list of the function and its function body preceded by the atom **lambda**. Now, let us use this lambda form in the call to **sum—loop**:

>   —> (sum—loop '(lambda (x) (times x x x)) 15)
>   14400

Using the lambda notation, we did not previously have to create a permanent function. Instead, we took the body of code we wanted to execute, **(times x x x)**, and turned it into a function by putting it inside a lambda form.

9.3. def, putd, AND LISP INTERNALS

The lambda form is the basic internal mechanism with which functions are implemented in LISP. For example, when you use **defun** to define a function, **defun** actually builds a lambda form from the arguments you give it and associates the lambda form with an atom. When you put that atom in the beginning of a list to indicate a function call, LISP fetches the lambda form and then uses it just as if it had appeared in the beginning of the list.

Thus if we could peek at the function definition that LISP stored with an atom name, we would see that it is actually kept as a lambda form. In fact, the function **getd** lets us do just this. **getd** takes one argument, which should evaluate to an atom. Then it returns the function previously associated with that atom. For example, after defining **cubed** with **defun**, we can use **getd** to see what LISP has actually attached to the atom:

> **-> (getd 'cubed)**
> **(lambda (x) (times x x x))**
> **->**

So the LISP interpreter is always dealing with lambda forms when it comes to function application; we have been spared this detail until now because the use of **defun** for function definition insulates the user from having to specify lambda forms directly. However, there are LISP functions for defining functions which do require the user to explicitly specify a lambda form. **def** is such a function-defining function. **def** is similar to **defun**, but requires you to specify the lambda form yourself. For example, here is how we can use **def** to define the function **cubed**:

> **-> (def cubed (lambda (x) (times x x x)))**
> **cubed**
> **-> (cubed 3)**
> **27**
> **->**

def takes two arguments, an atom and a lambda form, and associates the form with the atom.

def and **defun** are practically the same; **defun** just saves you the trouble of having to specify **lambda** yourself. Some purists prefer to see the **lambda** in their code, so they use **def**. This is just a matter of taste.

putd is another function for defining functions in which the lambda form is explicit. **putd** is similar to **def**, except that it causes its arguments to be evaluated. For example, to define **cubed** using **putd**, I would type the following:

```
-> (putd 'cubed '(lambda (x) (times x x x)))
(lambda (x) (times x x x))
-> (cubed 3)
27
->
```

Note that **putd** returns the lambda form, rather than the function name, as its value.

putd is actually the most primitive LISP function for defining functions. That is, the LISP functions **def** and **defun** are themselves defined in terms of **putd**. You may occasionally need to use **putd** yourself, for creating your own function-defining function, for example. You may want to do this if you are using some LISP dialect which does not come with both **defun** and **def**. However, it is much more convenient to use **defun** or **def** for the everyday business of defining new functions.

9.4. SOME MORE EXAMPLES

Let us better familiarize ourselves with lambda by considering some more examples. First, here is a function like **cons**, but which accepts its arguments in the opposite order:

> **(lambda (x y) (cons y x))**

Now let us apply it:

```
-> ((lambda (x y) (cons y x)) '(b) 'a)
(a b)
->
```

The formal parameter list of this lambda form contains two elements, **x** and **y**, so the lambda form denotes a function of two arguments. We obligingly supply two arguments, **'(b)** and **'a**.

To emphasize that lambda forms are just functions without names, consider what we would do if we want to create a named function of this function. Suppose we want to call it **xcons**:

```
-> (defun xcons (x y) (cons y x))
xcons
-> (xcons '(b) 'a)
(a b)
->
```

Alternatively, we could have used **def** to define **xcons**:

```
-> (def xcons (lambda (x y) (cons y x)))
```

All three forms are equivalent, except that using **defun** or **def** produces a permanent version of the function that we can use elsewhere in our code; the pure lambda form is used only once, because there is no way to refer again to the function that it defines.

Now here is a lambda of no arguments that always returns the atom **hello**:

(lambda () 'hello)

Since this is a function of no arguments, there will be no other elements in the list when we apply it:

```
-> ((lambda () 'hello) )
hello
->
```

The corresponding named function would be something like

```
-> (defun say-hello () 'hello)
say-hello
-> (say-hello)
hello
->
```

or, using **def**:

```
-> (def say-hello (lambda () 'hello))
say-hello
->
```

9.5. THE FUNCTION function

When you use a function as an argument to some other function, so that the function needs to be quoted, it is considered good practice to use a special version of **quote** that is designed specifically for this purpose. This version of **quote** is called **function**. Here is the **mapcar** example we used above done over with **function**:

```
-> (mapcar
    (function
      (lambda (a) (and (atom a) (equal (get a 'color) 'red))))
    '(a b c))
(nil t nil)
->
```

This will behave exactly as if we used **quote**; unfortunately, there is no standard abbreviation for **function**, as there is for **quote**, so we have to write it out.

You should use **function** to quote named functions as well as lambda forms. For example, if I call the function **sum—loop**, and pass it the function **sqrt** and then the function **(lambda (x) (times x x x))**, I should quote these using **function**:

```
-> (sum—loop (function sqrt) 10)
22.4682781862041
-> (sum—loop (function (lambda (x) (times x x x ))) 15)
14400
->
```

Why use **function** instead of **quote**, if the effect is the same? In some LISP implementations, using **function** will sometimes be more efficient. Also, many programmers think it makes their code clearer. Since it computes the same thing, there is no great harm done if you use **quote**, however.

9.6. USING LAMBDA FOR VARIABLE BINDING

The purpose of lambda is to be able to specify functions. However, we can take advantage of lambda's built-in variable binding mechanism to simplify some common programming constructs. In particular, lambda is useful as a programming device in situations in which we want to change the value of a variable for a short duration.

For example, suppose we wrote a function called **user—utility**. Suppose that **user—utility** normally uses some function internally, but that we want to allow the user the option of specifying some other function for **user—utility** to use in its place in some special cases. We would not want to make this option an argument, because then the user would always have to specify something, and most of the time the user does not want to think about this business at all.

One way to handle this situation is to write **user—utility** so it references a global variable, say **user—utility—function**. **user—utility** will assume that this variable is bound to the function it should use internally. Normally, **user—utility—function** will be set to some default value, but the user can override this default simply by changing the value of **user—utility—function**.

However, if we change this default, we want to be careful to change it back when we are finished. We need to do this because we might call **user—utility** elsewhere in our code, and in those places, we expect **user—utility—function** to be set to its default value. In many programming languages, we might do this in the following style:

```
(setq oldfn user—utility—function)
(setq user—utility—function 'special—function)
(user—utility a b c)
(setq user—utility—function oldfn)
```

In this example, I save the old value of **user—utility—function** so that I can restore it later on. Then I set **user—utility—function** to the value I want in this instance, namely, to a function called **special—function**. Then I call **user—utility**, supplying it with the appropriate arguments. Finally, I restore the binding of **user—utility—function** to its previous state.

We can take advantage of LISP's dynamic scoping to avoid having to explicitly save and restore the old value of **user—utility—function**, however. One way to do this is with **prog**, as in the following example:

```
(prog (user—utility—function)
  (setq user—utility—function 'special—function)
  (user—utility a b c))
```

Here LISP guarantees that **user—utility—function** is restored to its old value upon exiting the **prog**. Since LISP uses dynamic scoping, the last value bound to **user—utility—function** will be the value that **user—utility** finds there. Thus **user—utility—function** will have the right binding, but we need not explicitly worry about restoring its old value when we are finished.

But it is even more elegant to use lambda for this purpose. Now we do not even have to **setq user—utility—function** explicitly:

> ((lambda (user—utility—function) (user—utility a b c))
> 'special—function)

In the **lambda** version, we make the atom **user—utility—function** a formal parameter of a lambda form, and the call to **user—utility** the body of this lambda form. Doing so guarantees that the value of **user—utility—function** will be saved and restored when we finish the call to **user—utility.** Then we apply the lambda form to **special—function** as an argument. This binds the formal argument to this value for the execution of the body, which in this case is merely a call to **user—utility.**

This does the job about as efficiently as possible, although one might complain that, if this is elegance, it is an unsightly elegance at best. However, in Chapter 13 on macros, we will see how to exploit this solution in a more aesthetic manner.

9.7. THE SIGNIFICANCE OF LAMBDA

Some LISP aficionados attach a great deal of significance to the role of lambda in LISP. This may be because the lambda notation is similiar to something called the *lambda calculus,* developed by the logician Alonzo Church. Having the lambda notation seems to give LISP an air of intellectual respectability that is generally lacking in most programming languages.

Lambda is nice because it detaches the idea of a function from the idea of a name. This allows us to have "disembodied" functions, as we have seen above. In addition, it makes LISP rather elegant internally. However, the whole business is probably less of a big deal than many people would like you to believe. Lambda is useful, but most LISP programs would work just as well if lambda did not exist as a separate abstraction.

9.8. SUMMARY

(1)   It is useful to separate the idea of a function from the need to name a function. The *lambda notation* is a way to specify a function without having to specify its name. It is useful to have such functions when they will only appear once in our code, and hence when we do not want to bother to name them and give them permanent storage space.

(2)   We create functions using lambda by building a *lambda form.* A lambda form is a list beginning with the atom **lambda.** Following this should be a list of atoms, and then any number of s-expressions. The list of atoms is interpreted as the list of formal parameters of the

121

function, and the s-expresssions as the bodies of that function.

(3)   Lambda forms can appear wherever LISP expects to find a function. For example, they can appear in the beginning of a list to be evaluated, or as a function argument to **apply** or to a mapping function.

(4)   Internally, LISP function definitions are kept as lambda forms. **defun** allows the user to create function definitions without having to specify the lambda form explicitly. The function **def** also defines functions, but requires the explicit specification of the lambda form. **putd** is just like **def**, except that it causes its arguments to be evaluated. The function **getd** returns the function previously associated with an atom by any of these means.

(5)   While lambda is basically a function definition mechanism, one can also think of it as a way to control the scoping of variables. For example, the construct **((lambda (x) ...code...) arg)** is a good way to temporarily bind **x** to the value of **arg** for the duration of the evaluation of **...code...**.

(6)   The function **function** should be used to quote function arguments, including both lambda forms and named functions. **function** acts just like **quote**. However, the use of **function** informs the LISP system that the next item is a function, and the LISP system can sometimes take advantage of this fact.

Exercises

(1)   Evaluate the following s-expressions:

    (a)   **((lambda (x) (cons x nil)) 'y)**

    (b)   **(apply '(lambda (x y) (list y x)) '(1 2))**

    (c)   **(mapcar '(lambda (x) (quotient 1 (sqrt x))) '(1 2 3 4 5))**

    (d)   **((lambda (x) (setq x 5)) (setq x 4))**

    (e)   **((lambda (x y) (putprop x y 'eats)) 'bird 'worms)**

(2)   A common use of lambda is to create a new function out of an existing function by "fixing" one of the existing function's arguments.
Use lambda to create a function that uses **times** to always multiply its
argument by 3.14.

(3)   The function **sum–loop** in Chapter 6 takes a function and a number,
and returns the sum of that function applied to the integers up to that
number. Suppose we want to use **sum–loop** just to compute the sum
of the first **n** integers. What function do we have to pass to **sum–loop**
to do this computation? Write this function using lambda and call
sum–loop with it.

(4)   You may have noticed that we cannot write recursive functions as
lambda forms. Recursive functions must refer to themselves in their
own definitions, and lambda forms cannot be referred to.

To address this problem, early versions of LISP contained a special
form called the *label form*. The label form allows the programmer to
temporarily attach a name to a lambda form. Label forms begin with
the symbol **label**. This symbol is followed by a literal atom, which is
followed by a lambda form. The whole label form can be applied just
like a lambda form. When you apply a label form, LISP simply applies
the lambda form it contains. The only difference is that, during the
application of the lambda form, the literal atom of the label form will
be bound to the lambda form. The lambda form may reference this
value as a way of self-reference. When LISP has finished applying a
label form, it restores the old value of the literal atom of the label
atom.

For example, consider the following label form:

```
(label fact
    (lambda (n)
        (cond [(zerop n) 1]
              [t (times n (funcall fact (sub1 n)))])))
```

This label form acts just like a lambda form, except the form can be
referred to by the name **fact**. The body of this function can reference
itself by referencing the value of **fact** within the lambda form. In this
manner, we are able to write a recursive (i. e., self-referencing) function, as this example of factorial indicates.

We can apply label forms (awkwardly) just like they were lambda
forms. For example:

```
-> ((label fact
      (lambda (n)
         (cond [(zerop n) 1]
                [t (times n (funcall fact (sub1 n)))]))
   4)
```

would compute 4!.

The label form is used so infrequently that it was not included in Franz LISP. That is, the above expression will cause an error if you typed it into Franz.

About the only interesting application of label forms is in the solution to the following puzzle: What is the shortest self-reproducing non-atomic LISP s-expression? A self-reproducing expression is one that evaluates to itself. **nil** would be an example. But **nil** is atomic, and we seek a non-atomic solution.

You get extra credit if your solution does not cause any side-effects.

Use **label** to formulate a solution to this puzzle.

10

Reading and Writing

10.1. INTRODUCTION

So far, the LISP functions and s-expressions we have created have not done any I/O of their own. They rely on the LISP interpreter to read in their arguments and type out their results. But, as in any programming language, we may want to read and write within a procedure as well.

In this chapter we present the most basic LISP input/output constructs. Then we show some methods for dealing with the input and output of LISP atoms with unusual names. We introduce a new data type called the *string* to facilitate some sorts of I/O. We show how to do I/O with devices other than the terminal, and how to produce neatly formatted function definitions. Finally, we demonstrate how we can use I/O together with the LISP function **eval** to implement the top level of LISP in LISP.

10.2. read AND print

As you might expect, I/O in LISP is done with special I/O functions. Since the basic units of data in LISP are s-expressions, most of these I/O functions deal with entire s-expressions. The most basic functions are called **read** and **print**. **read** is a function of no arguments. When **read** is called, it causes LISP to wait at the terminal for you to type in one s-expression.

When one is entered, this s-expression is returned as the value of **read**.

For example, suppose I evaluate an s-expression that has a call to **read** in it:

    −> (setq x (read))
    (a b c)
    (a b c)
    −> x
    (a b c)
    −>

This interaction with the interpreter requires some explanation. The second argument to **setq** here is a call to the function **read**. This is a function of no arguments, so it appears alone in a list. The function **read** causes the interpreter to go to the terminal and wait for the user to type something in. If you try this example yourself, you will notice that the LISP system pauses, waiting for you to type something; in fact, if you are not on guard, you might think the system crashed, because the interpreter has not yet responded, as it ordinarily would. In this example, I typed in the value (a b c), just as I do when I ask the interpreter to evaluate expressions. However, I did not quote this expression, because LISP was not going to evaluate it. Rather, it merely read in the expression as typed. **read** returned this s-expression as its value, and the computation proceeded. Here **setq** bound **x** to this value. Since **setq** returns the value of its second argument as its value, LISP printed out the value on the terminal. So the first (a b c) was typed by me, the second by the interpreter. Then I queried LISP about the value of **x** just to make sure that everything was done right.

It might be nice to warn the user that the call to **read** was coming, however. We can do so by using the function **print** to display something on the screen. **print** is a function of one argument, which is evaluated. The value of this argument is printed on the terminal and the value **nil** is returned (although other LISPs have **print** return the value of the argument instead). Let us use **print** to display some message to the user, and then use **read** as we did above:

    −> (prog1 (print 'enter) (setq x (read)))
    enter(a b c)
    nil
    −> x
    (a b c)
    −>

I used a **prog1** here, which evaluates its arguments in order and returns the value of the first one. The first expression is a call to **print**. The argument to **print** is evaluated to the value **enter**. This is then given to **print**, which causes the value to appear on the terminal. **print** also returns **nil** as its value. Then LISP starts evaluating the second expression of the **prog1**. This contains a call to **read**, so, as before, LISP pauses and awaits my response. I type in the s-expression **(a b c)**. **x** is bound to this value. A **prog1** returns the value of its first argument, which in this case is **nil**, the value always returned by **print**. LISP prints this value out on the terminal.

These simple examples illustrate some important facts about **read** and **print**:

- **read** does not prompt for input; it merely reads from the terminal. In some LISPs, **read** automatically prompts, but in Franz, the programmer would have to type out some message if he wants to alert the user to input something (probably a good idea most of the time).

- **print** does not print out anything other than the s-expression specified. In particular, it does not output a "newline" character at the end, so the output often looks messy. Some LISPs have **print** automatically output a "newline" character (thereby requiring you use some other function to do the printing when you do not want to start a new line). In most LISPs, including ours, you can start a new line by executing the function (of no arguments) **terpr** (also called **terpri**).

- A value printed by LISP and a value returned by a function are two different things. For example, evaluating the **print** above caused the value **enter** to be printed. However **print** returned **nil** as its value. LISP then printed out this value for us, because LISP always prints out the value of an expression it evaluates on the top level. Remember, though, that internally what counts is the value returned by a function. If I **setq** some atom to the value **print** returns, for example, this atom would get bound to **nil**, regardless of what value was printed. **print** causes the side-effect of something getting scribbled out on the terminal; but once this is done, the only value that will have any subsequent effect on the interpreter is the value that **print** returns.

- **read** and **print** always deal with whole s-expressions, which of course can be either atoms or lists. We cannot directly read or print something like a line of text using **read** or **print**, because a line of text is not a kind of s-expression. Most LISPs contain special functions that do a rough equivalent of this, for example, reading in a line and making it into a list, or some such.

As a further example, suppose I want to write some code that requests a number from the user, computes its square root, and prints out the result. Let us write a loop that does this repeatedly:

```
-> (prog ()
    loop
    (print 'number> )
    (print (sqrt (read)))
    (terpri)
    (go loop))
number> 16
4.0
number> 9
3.0
number> 25
5.0
number> Interrupt:^C
Break nil
<1>: (reset)

[Return to top level]
->
```

In this example, all the **number>** s are printed by **print**; the numbers immediately following them were typed in by me. The results, of course, were output by the second occurrence of **print**. This call to **print** causes its argument to be evaluated, which is a call to **sqrt**. **sqrt** calls **read**, which results in the interpreter going to the terminal and awaiting my input. When I supply it, it is passed to **sqrt**, which returns its square root. This value goes to **print**, which makes it appear on the screen. Then I use **terpri** to start a line and thereby make these interactions more readable. This code constitutes an endless loop, so I had to type the UNIX interrupt character (in my case, CTRL-c) in order to get out of it.

Note, there is nothing special about the atom **number>**. This is just an atom whose name happens to end with a colon. If I want to print out something fancier, for example, an atom ending with a space, I would have to have some way of specifying a space in an atom name. Right now, we do not know how to do this.

I could try to print out a more informative message, however, by enclosing the message in a list:

```
-> (prog ()
   loop
   (print '(Please enter a number>) )
   (print (sqrt (read)))
   (terpri)
   (go loop))
(Please enter a number> )38
6.164414002968976
(Please enter a number> )25
5.0
(Please enter a number> )Interrupt:^C
Break nil
<1>:
```

However, we would prefer this message to be printed without the parentheses around it. We can do this by using **mapc** to apply **print** to a list, but this does not have exactly the effect we seek:

```
-> (prog ()
   loop
   (mapc (function print) '(Please enter a number>) )
   (print (sqrt (read)))
   (terpri)
   (go loop))
Pleaseenteranumber> 64
8.0
Pleaseenteranumber> Interrupt:^C
Break nil
<1>:
```

Since **print** just prints out an s-expression with no frills, all the output runs together. Hence we still need some way to print out characters like space which are not usually part of an atom name.

10.3. READING AND PRINTING ATOMS WITH UNUSUAL NAMES

As the examples in the previous section illustrate, we sometimes wish to have an atom whose name contains an unusual character. This might be a problem if that character normally serves some special function during reading. For example, if we want to have an atom named **ab(cd**, we have no way to type this in. LISP would think the parenthesis marked the beginning of a list, and our intention would get hopelessly garbled.

LISP provides a number of ways to input atom names containing characters

129

normally reserved for other purposes. One method is to precede the reserved character with the special character \ (backslash). LISP does not include the \ in the atom's name, but it does include the following character, regardless of what it is. Thus to input an atom with name **ab(cd**, we can type **ab\(cd**.

\ is sometimes called an *escape character* because it allows the following character to escape from its normal LISP interpretation. However, if a name requires several special characters, preceding each with an escape character is awkward. For example, suppose I want to have an atom named **a b c d e** (i. e., the characters a-e with spaces in between). I could type this in as follows using escape characters: **a\ b\ c\ d\ e**, i. e., by preceding every space by a \. But this is unappealing. To provide a more aesthetic mode of entry, Franz LISP provides an alternative to escaping. If, instead of preceding each problematic character with a \, the whole sequence is surrounded by |'s (vertical bars), LISP interprets the sequence of characters as a single name. Thus the atom named **a b c d e** can be entered by typing **|a b c d e|**. Once again, the vertical bars are not actually part of the atom name, but merely serve to delineate its boundaries. Hence these vertical bars are sometimes called *symbol delimiters*.

print always tries to print out atom names so that they can be read back in by **read**. That is, if we enter an atom by typing **|a b c d e|**, and **print** prints this out as **a b c d e**, LISP would be unable to read this back again as an atom. To guard against this happening, **print** always supplies enough special characters to produce a LISP-readable name. In Franz LISP, this is done by always surrounding problematic atom names with symbol delimiters upon printing (other LISPs use escape characters for this purpose). Since the top level of LISP uses **print** to output the values of the expressions it interprets, we can demonstrate this behavior as follows:

```
-> 'ab\(cd
|ab(cd|
-> '|ab(cd|
|ab(cd|
-> 'a\ b\ c\ d\ e
|a b c d e|
-> '|a b c d e|
|a b c d e|
-> 'ab\cd
abcd
-> '|abcd|
abcd
->
```

Here all the atom names that need special treatment in order to be read in are printed surrounded by symbol delimiters. Note in the last two examples that the backquote and the symbol delimiters are superfluous, as there are no special characters in the atom names. Since this is the case, LISP interprets these names just as if they were typed in without the aid of these devices; they are printed out accordingly.

We are now a step closer to being able to print out an atom name that has a space in it, as we needed for our example in the last section. Let us try using **print** to print out an atom name with a space in it as a prompt for our **sqrt** loop:

```
-> (prog ()
    loop
    (print 'Please enter a number> )
    (print (sqrt (read)))
    (terpri)
    (go loop))
Please enter a number> 27
5.196152422706632
Please enter a number> Interrupt:^C
Break nil
<1>:
```

Here I passed **print** an atom named **Please enter a number>** . The problem is that **print** always outputs such atoms with symbol delimiters, which is not exactly what we wanted. It would not have helped to enter the atom name with escape characters preceding the spaces, because **print** would print this exactly the same way. We would rather print out an atom with an unusual print name in a more pleasing format, without the associated symbol delimiters. Since **print** will not do this for us, we need another function that will.

In Franz, such a function is called **patom**. If given an argument that evaluates to an atom, **patom** will print that atom without any escape characters or symbol delimiters. If the argument evaluates to a non-atomic s-expression, **patom** prints the entire s-expression. **patom** returns the value of its argument.

Consider the following examples:

```
-> (patom 'a b c d e)
a b c d ea b c d e
-> (patom 'ab\(cd)
ab(cdab(cd
```

```
-> (progn (patom 'ab\(cd) (terpri))
ab(cd
nil
->
```

In the first example, **patom** prints the atom name without delimiters. This atom is returned as the value of the call to **patom**, so the top level of LISP prints it out again. Since the top level normally uses **print** to do its output, the second time it is printed the atom name is surrounded by symbol delimiters.

The second example is similar. In the third case, the call to **patom** is inside a **prog** and followed by a **terpri**, which forces a new line. **patom** causes **ab(cd** to be printed; the **terpri** causes us to move to a new line; finally, the top level prints the value of the **progn** (in this case, **nil**).

Let us use **patom** to produce, finally, a correct version of our **sqrt** loop:

```
-> (prog ()
     loop
     (patom 'Please enter a number> | )
     (print (sqrt (read)))
     (terpri)
     (go loop))
Please enter a number> 1024
32.0
Please enter a number> Interrupt:^C
Break nil
<1>:
```

The function **princ** is identical to **patom** except that it always returns **t**. The two different functions exist for the sake of compatibility with various other LISP dialects.

In general, you should use **print** when your emphasis is on producing LISP-readable output, since **print** is guaranteed to output something that, when input by **read**, will produce the same s-expression as was originally passed to **print**. You should use **patom** or **princ** when you are interested in producing human-readable output. Note that the output of these functions may not only not produce the same s-expression when input by **read**, but may not even be acceptable LISP. For example, the expression (**patom 'Please enter a number>)**) will cause the following to be printed: **Please enter a number>** . This would be read in by **read** as four separate LISP atoms. Similarly, the expression (**patom 'ab\(cd)** will cause **ab(cd** to be printed, and this does not constitute a valid s-expression.

10.4. STRINGS

Although we have been quiet about it until now, there are actually a number of data types other than s-expressions supported by most LISP systems. One such data type that is relevant here is the *string*. A string in LISP is denoted by a sequence of characters with a " (doublequote) on either side. Strings, in Franz, evaluate to themselves. For example, all of the following involve strings:

```
-> "foo"
"foo"
-> "hello there"
"hello there"
-> "a b c d e"
"a b c d e"
-> (setq x "ab(cd")
"ab(cd"
-> x
"ab(cd"
->
```

A string looks very much like a funny atom name surrounded by double-quotes rather than symbol delimiters. However, we have already seen one important difference: Strings evaluate to themselves, whereas literal atoms evaluate to their previously bound values. In addition, strings cannot have function definitions or property lists. They are, in fact, nothing more than names.

Strings are useful primarily because they require less storage than literal atoms. This is the case precisely because strings do not require storage to support bindings, property lists, or function definitions. Thus if we are interested in an atom only for its name, as we were in some of the examples above, it is economical to use a string instead.

The function **print** always prints strings with accompanying doublequotes. This is in keeping with **print**'s mission always to print out something that LISP can **read** back in. Similarly, **patom** and **princ** print out strings without quotation marks, in keeping with its intention to produce human-readable output. The best way to implement the prompt for our **sqrt** loop above, then, is to **patom** the appropriate string:

```
-> (prog ()
     loop
     (patom "Please enter a number> ")
     (print (sqrt (read)))
     (terpri)
     (go loop))
Please enter a number> 1024
32.0
Please enter a number> Interrupt:^C
Break nil
<1>:
```

This produces the output that we want, without entailing the overhead of storing an entire atom.

Strings, as well as other miscellaneous LISP data types, will be discussed more fully in a subsequent chapter.

10.5. REDIRECTING I/O

Reading and printing can involve files and devices, not just the terminal. I/O to something other than the standard input or output is done in Franz LISP by supplying an additional argument to an input or output function. This argument should evaluate to a *port,* which is a special LISP data type used just for I/O. The user needs to set up a port using the function **infile** for input or **outfile** for output. Then a call to an input or output function that references this port will do I/O with respect to the file attached to the port, rather than the standard input or output device (usually the terminal). When finished with it, the user should close the port using the function **close**.

For example, suppose I want to write some s-expressions to the file **aleph**. First, I need to set up a port that refers to this file. I use **outfile** for this purpose:

```
-> (setq my-output-port (outfile 'aleph))
%aleph
->
```

outfile returns a port to the file **aleph**; LISP prints ports by preceding the name of the file they refer to by a %. Now we want to write to this file. We do this by passing this port as an additional argument to **print**:

134

```
-> (print '(a b c d e) my-output-port)
nil
-> (print 'razzamatazz my-output-port)
nil
->
```

As you can see, nothing much appeared on the terminal as the result of these calls to **print**, presumably because the output got sent to the file **aleph** instead. Let us close the file and then try to read it back in:

```
-> (close my-output-port)
t
-> (setq my-input-port (infile 'aleph))
%aleph
-> (read my-input-port)
(a b c d e)
-> (read my-input-port)
razzamatazz
-> (read my-input-port)
nil
-> (close my-input-port)
t
->
```

The first **close** returned the value **t**, which indicates that the file was indeed closed as requested. Then we opened the file again for input, and read from it by supplying an additional argument to **read**. When we ran off the end of the file, by trying to **read** one more s-expression than we **print**ed to the file, **read** returned **nil**. If you are worried about distinguishing this from an actual **nil** in the file, you can call **read** with yet another argument. When it reaches an end-of-file, **read** will return the value of this argument. For example, if I read from the file **aleph** with calls of the form (**read** my-input-port 'tzadik), **read** would have returned the same expression as it did above for the first two cases. But when it reached the end-of-file, it would have returned the atom **tzadik** instead of **nil**.

Let us take a final look at the file in UNIX:

```
-> (exit)
% cat aleph
(a b c d e)razzamatazz%
```

Note that the file contains exactly the s-expressions we **print**ed to it, without any additional spaces or "newline" characters. We would have to supply these explicitly if, for some reason, we wanted them in the file.

Most LISP input/output functions conform to this redirection convention. For example, if you supply a port as an additional argument to **patom** or **terpri**, these functions will output to the specified file.

10.6. PRETTY-PRINTING

The function **pp** (for "pretty-print") prints out function definitions in a nice format. Thus to see the function definition of **squared**, we can say

> -> **(pp squared)**

> **(def squared**
>   **(lambda (x)**
>   **(times x x)))**

> **t**
> **->**

pp prints out function definitions as if you had typed them in using **def**. It formats them nicely, so this is a good way to check to see if you have really entered what you thought, or if you dropped a parenthesis somewhere.

Also, **pp** has an option that allows you to redirect output to a file so that you can read it in again later. If an argument to **pp** is of the form **(F filename)**, subsequent arguments will be pretty-printed to that file. For example:

> -> **(pp (F foo) squared)**

> **t**
> -> **(exit)**
> % **cat foo**

> **(def squared**
>   **(lambda (x)**
>   **(times x x)))**
> % **lisp**
> **Franz Lisp, Opus 38.69**
> -> **(load 'foo)**
> **[load foo]**
> **t**

```
-> (squared 5)
25
->
```

10.7. MISCELLANEOUS I/O

LISP has a number of functions for doing character I/O, for determining the number of characters that will be required to print an expression, for checking to see if files exist, etc., and for doing the various internal tasks required by **read**. You can browse through Appendix A to get acquainted with these functions should you find yourself engaged in a task involving considerable I/O programming.

10.8. LISP IN LISP

With the functions **read**, **print**, and **eval** at our disposal, we can make an interesting insight into LISP. The LISP interpreter itself uses these same functions to interpret expressions typed in at the top level. That is, the top level of LISP is really just a chunk of LISP code that is executing the following loop: (1) **read** in an s-expression, (2) **eval** it, and (3) **print** out the result. In fact, with these functions at our disposal, we can write such a loop ourselves in LISP:

```
-> (prog () read-eval-print-loop
      (princ "-< " )
      (print (eval (read)))
      (terpri)
      (go read-eval-print-loop))
-< (setq a 'b)
b
-< a
b
-<
```

A few extra lines of code are needed here to print out the prompt symbol before reading, and the "newline" after printing. However, the bulk of the work in this loop is done by the single line of code **(print (eval (read)))**.

I intentionally used a different prompt symbol from the one LISP normally uses, otherwise it would look like nothing had happened when I evaluate this expression. In fact, we would have little reason to write this exact loop, since evaluating it causes LISP to act pretty much as it did in the first place. What the example does show is that the top level of LISP (i. e., the part of

LISP that we communicate with most of the time) is really not very central to what LISP is. Rather, the heart of LISP is the set of functions provided and the ability to apply and compose them.

10.8.1. Evalquote Top Level

To put this another way, we could have a quite different top level than the one we are now familiar with, and the resulting system would still be recognizable as LISP. Let us create a new top level to illustrate this point. Suppose we mostly enter expressions that cause their arguments to be evaluated, but were tired of enclosing our top level expressions in parentheses, and having to quote our arguments. Instead, I might prefer to enter the function name followed by a list containing all the arguments to that function. For example, to compute **(cons 'a '(b c))**, I would like to be able to type the following instead:

> <−> **cons (a (b c))**
> **(a b c)**
> <−>

(Again, I use a different prompt symbol to indicate an atypical top level.)

To implement this loop, I need to read in two s-expressions, a function name and a list of arguments. Then I need to apply that function to the arguments. We can do this as follows:

> −> **(prog ()**
>   **loop**
>   **(princ "<−> ")**
>   **(print (apply (read) (read)))**
>   **(terpri)**
>   **(go loop))**
> <−> **cons (a (b c))**
> **(a b c)**
> <−> **car ((x y z))**
> **x**
> <−>

This code **read**s in an s-expression, which it assumes will be a function. Then it **read**s in another s-expression, which should be a list of arguments to this function. Then the first input is applied to the second, performing the desired computation. The result of this computation is **print**ed. We loop around to do this operation repeatedly.

Thus we see that it is possible to have rather different top level interpreters for the same underlying LISP language. In fact, the funny top level we just wrote was in widespread use at one time. A LISP interpreter that has this as its normal top level is sometimes called an *evalquote* mode interpreter, because it implicitly quotes arguments before evaluating them. The interpreter whose top level operates as we have become accustomed to is called an *eval* mode interpreter.

Evalquote mode has fallen into disuse, for a number of reasons. In particular, the syntax on the top level is not homogeneous with that for the rest of LISP, and many people find this confusing. Some LISPs provide a means to switch back and forth between the two modes for compatibility's sake (Franz does not, though). But the important point is that either mode can be implemented in the other, making neither idea central to LISP itself.

10.8.2. READ-EVAL-PRINT Loops

Since the essence of the standard top level of LISP involves reading, evaluating, and printing, it is often referred to as a **read-eval-print** loop. As the previous examples illustrate, it is possible to have alternative **read-eval-print** loops for various purposes. One example that we have already encountered is the *break package,* i. e., the mode that LISP goes into when it encounters an error. This is just another **read-eval-print** loop in which some special conveniences are available to aid debugging.

By the way, our user-defined loops behave differently from a real top level of LISP in a few ways. One difference is that, if we encountered an error, and then issued a **reset**, this would throw us back to the original top level of LISP. It is possible to do error handling ourselves, so writing a more authentic top level is a real possibility. This is discussed in Chapter 16 on non-standard flow-of-control.

10.9. SUMMARY

(1)   I/O in LISP is done on the s-expression level. The most basic functions for doing I/O are **read** and **print**.

(2)   **read** is a function of no arguments. It causes the interpreter to read an s-expression from a terminal, and it returns that s-expression as its value.

(3)   **print** is a function of one argument, which is evaluated. The value of that argument is printed on the terminal. **print** returns the value **nil**.

(4)   The function **terpri** (also called **terpr**), outputs a "newline" character.

(5)   We can read atoms with unusual names either by prefacing the unusual characters with *escape* characters (backslashes) or by surrounding the entire name in *symbol delimiters* (vertical bars).

(6)   **print** always prints things out so that they can be read back in by **read**, so it surrounds unusual names by symbol delimiters. The function **patom** prints out atom names without symbol delimiters. **princ** is just like **patom**, except that it returns **t** while **patom** always returns the value of its argument.

(7)   The function **pp** *pretty-prints* the function definitions of its arguments. If an expression of the form **(F filename)** appears in a call to **pp**, **pp** will direct subsequent output to the file **filename**.

(8)   It is possible to **read** to and **print** from arbitrary files. This involves setting up *ports*, using the functions **infile** and **outfile**. If **read** or **print** contains an additional argument that is a port, it will perform I/O with the file specified by that port rather than with the terminal. When we are through with a port, we can close it with the function **close**.

(9)   It is possible to write the top level of LISP in LISP. This is simply a loop that calls the functions **read**, **eval**, and **print**. For this reason, the normal top level of LISP is sometimes called a **read-eval-print** loop.

(10)   There are any number of alternative top levels. The mode that LISP goes into after an error is an example of a useful, alternative top level. Some previous LISP interpreters had a normal top level called *eval-quote* mode, in which the user is expected to enter a function followed by a list of arguments. This is in contrast to the commonly used *eval* mode interpreter, in which the user enters an s-expression to be evaluated.

Exercises

(1)   What do the following s-expressions produce as output? What values do they return?

    (a)   **(cons 'a (print '(b c)))**

    (b)   **(print 'abcd)**

    (c)   **(cons 'a (patom '(b c)))**

    (d)   **(list 'a (princ '(b c)))**

    (e)   **(princ 'ab\ (cd)**

(2)   Write a function that reads in a sequence of s-expressions, terminating with the atom **end**, and returns the list of these s-expressions.

(3)   Write a function to help balance your checkbook. This function will prompt the user for an initial balance. Then it will enter a loop in which it requests a number from the user, subtracts it from the current balance, and prints out the new balance. Deposits can be entered by supplying a negative number. Entering zero should cause the procedure to terminate.

(4)   Write a function that reads s-expressions from a file, designated by an argument, and prints each s-expression on the terminal, separated by blank lines. Your function should print a message indicating when it has reached an end-of-file.

(5)   Write a function **set−rem** that operates like **set**, but which records all calls to it. For example, **set−rem** might use the global variable ***set*** and **cons** all actual arguments with which it is called onto the value of this atom. Then write a function **set−dump** that takes as its argument a file name. **set−dump** writes to this file an appropriate call to **set** for each previous call to **set−rem**. The idea is that when we **load** the file to which we have **set−dump**ed everything, all the bindings created by previous calls to **set−rem** will be reestablished.

(6)   Write your own version of the pretty-print function **pp**. Unlike the built-in version, your version will print all the "interesting" aspects of an atom. This includes its function definition, value, and any user defined properties. For example, the atom might be displayed as follows:

-> **(ourpp foo)**

function: (lambda (x) (list x))

value: (a b c)

color: red

age: 32

nil
->

You might want to use the function **pp** uses to print out these values nicely. This function is called **pp—form**. It prints out any s-expression in a pleasant format.

11

Debugging

11.1. DEBUGGING IN LISP

We have encountered enough of LISP to write some rather serious programs. This capability entails the need for a correspondingly powerful set of debugging tools. In most conventional programming languages, it is difficult to provide very powerful debugging facilities. Usually, the code being executed comes from a compiler, and has a non-obvious relationship to the original source code. The run-time environment of a program probably has little to do with the user's understanding of the language, and the user must rely on debugging aids of varying degrees of quality to tamper with his program.

Fortunately, with LISP, we are somewhat better off. When a LISP interpreter encounters an s-expression it cannot evaluate, it usually has the original source code at its fingertips. Since the code is being interpreted, the environment in which the error occurs is the same environment in which the user created the code. Moreover, the LISP interpreter itself is present, making the full power of LISP available for debugging.

As we have noted, there is no standard LISP language. Methods for debugging are even less standardized. The details of LISP debugging techniques vary from LISP implementation to LISP implementation, from installation to installation, and even from user to user. However, there are some widespread methods of interactively debugging LISP code. In this chapter, we examine the versions of these debugging facilities that are available in Franz LISP. These include the **read-eval-print** loop which LISP enters after an error, various methods for examining the state of affairs at the point of an error, and a method for tracing functions during execution.

These debugging techniques will be useful to you in debugging your Franz LISP programs. Analogous facilities are likely to be available in other LISPs you have occasion to use. But you will have to allow for quite a bit of variation when you get down to the details.

Alternatively, you may have notions of your own on how programs should be debugged. You may decide to replace or enrich the facilities provided for you with ones of your own. This is generally not too difficult to do in LISP. After you have familiarized yourself with the basic debugging techniques, you should feel free to experiment with new ones of your own devising.

11.2.   THE BREAK read-eval-print LOOP

When LISP encounters an error, it enters a special **read-eval-print** loop. This event can be thought of as a kind of pause in the middle of an evaluation. So it is sometimes referred to as a *break*. As we have seen, the prompt symbol used in the break is different from that used at the top level, in order to indicate where we are. However, we are in a genuine **read-eval-print** loop. Since LISP is in the middle of evaluating some s-expression, we can poke around to find some hint of where we are in our code and what might have gone wrong. For example, we can examine the value of variables, including currently bound local variables, simply by asking LISP to evaluate them for us. Here is a contrived example:

```
-> (defun foo (y) (prog (x) (setq x (cons (car 8) y))) )
foo
-> (foo '(a b c))
Error: Bad arg to car 8
<1>: x
nil
<1>: y
(a b c)
<1>:
```

Here LISP encounters an error, prints a message, and enters a **read-eval-print** loop. We interrogate the value of the **prog** variable **x**, and find that it is set to **nil**; the formal parameter **y** can be seen to have the value **(a b c)**. Had this been a bug in a real program, this information might give us some indication of where the error occurred. For example, the value of **x** would suggest that the **prog** variable had been initialized, but not yet **setq**ed.

If we make another error while at this break, LISP simply breaks again. It increments the number within the prompt symbol to indicate the number of current breaks. A call to the function **retbrk**, with no argument, pops up to the previous break (or if there is none, to the top level). For example, below I accidently ask for the value of **z** rather than **x** as I try to investigate an error:

> <1>: z
> **Error: Unbound Variable: z**
> <2>: (retbrk)
>
> <1>: x
> nil
> <1>:

Here my second error causes LISP to enter another break, from which I immediately return by evaluating **(retbrk)**. Then I continue with my intended query.

A call of the form **(retbrk** n**)** moves to the nth break if n is a positive integer, and moves up n breaks if n is negative. Of course, **reset** pops all the way back to the top level.

We can evaluate an arbitrary s-expression during a break, not just ask for the value of a variable. This might be useful if we are confused as to why the error occurred, and want to try to evaluate a piece of the s-expression again. Continuing with our example above, if I do not think **(car 8)** should cause an error, I might test this out by evaluating it again:

> <1>: (car 8)
> **Error: Bad arg to car 8**
> <2>:

11.3. EXAMINING THE STACK

In the case of a real error, however, life is not this easy. In particular, we might not have any idea where the error occurred in our code. **foo** might have been called by **baz**, which in turn might have been called by another function, and so on. An error message stating that there was a bad argument to **car** somewhere would not be of much help in locating the function in which the errant code appears.

Fortunately, LISP has to remember the sequence of function calls it is in the middle of executing. We can take advantage of this fact to help us debug. For example, if LISP is evaluating the s-expression

(cons x (foo l))

it needs to save the fact that it is in the middle of a **cons** while it is evaluating the arguments to **cons**. LISP must remember this fact so it knows how to continue when it finishes evaluating the arguments. Similarly, **foo** is sure to call some other function, and LISP must remember where to continue after this evaluation is completed.

Thus LISP stores on a stack the sequence of s-expressions that it is currently evaluating. Each entry on the stack corresponding to an s-expression is called a *stack frame*. We can use a LISP function to inspect this stack, and help determine where we are in an evaluation.

In Franz, such a function is called **showstack**. In our example above, a call to **showstack** results in the following:

```
-> (foo '(a b c))
Error: Bad arg to car 8
<1>: (showstack)
(showstack)
break-err-handler
(car 8)
(cons <**> y)
(setq x <**>)
(prog (x) <**>)
(foo '(a b c))

nil
<1>:
```

showstack shows the top of the stack first. At the very top, we see the call to **showstack** itself. This was the last thing we did, so naturally it appears on the top of the stack. Directly beneath this is **break-err-handler**, which is LISP's indication that we are in a break caused by an error. Beneath this is **(car 8)**, the s-expression that caused the difficulty. Under this s-expression is the s-expression in which **(car 8)** occurred. Rather than reprint this entire s-expression (in this case, **(cons (car 8) y)**), **showstack** replaces the part it has already printed with the marker <**>. The expression in which this expression was called appears on the line beneath it, and so on, until we get to the s-expression we supplied to the interpreter at the top level, **(foo '(a b c))**.

Using this information, we can trace the sequence of calls from the initial call we made up to the error, thus helping to locate the problem area in our code.

If **showstack** is given an argument of **t**, it will print some forms on the stack that are normally not of interest. Given a numeric argument of n, it will only print the first n items on the stack. A call of the form **(showstack lev n)** will abbreviate expressions of more than **n** levels; a call of the form **(showstack len n)** will abbreviate expressions of more than **n** elements.

11.4. THE DEBUGGER

Sometimes it is not immediately obvious from the sort of output produced by **showstack** why an error occurred or how a program got into its current state. In such a case, some more powerful tools are useful for examining the environment of the error.

For example, suppose **foo** calls **baz**, and that an error occurs during the evaluation of an s-expression in **baz**. Suppose we feel that the value of a formal parameter in **foo**, say **x**, would be useful to know. Unfortunately, **baz** may also have a formal parameter named **x**. Thus typing **x** at the break will not get at the formal parameter in which we are interested.

What we would like to do is temporarily move back to the context of the previous function. In this context, **x** refers to a formal parameter of **foo** rather than to one of **baz**. More generally, we would like to move up and down the stack of active functions, evaluating s-expressions in different contexts.

A *debugger* is a device designed for this purpose. The Franz debugger allows the user to examine more thoroughly the state of the world during an error. With the debugger, the user can

(1) examine the stack in a variety of ways,
(2) evaluate s-expressions in different contexts,
(3) restart the computation at different points.

The Franz debugger is invoked by calling the function **debug** (with no arguments). **debug** enters a special debugging **read-eval-print** loop. The debugging **read-eval-print** loop interprets certain expressions as commands. If the expression is not one of these special expressions, it is subject to normal LISP evaluation. For the sake of an example, let us write a function **baz** that calls **foo**, and which uses the same variable names:

```
-> (defun baz (y)
     (prog (x)
       (setq x 1)
       (foo (cons 'a y))))
baz
->
```

Now let us call **baz** and generate an error. Then we will run the debugger to help out:

```
-> (baz '(b c))
Error: Bad arg to car 8
<1>: (debug)

<------debug------>

:
```

The debugger signals it is ready by issuing the prompt symbol : (colon). Now we can enter commands to help clarify what is going on. For example, the debugger **read-eval-print** loop interprets the symbol **where** as a special command which causes it to print the current stack position:

```
:where

<------debug------>
you are at top of stack.
there are 0 debug's below.

:
```

The function **debug** put the funny form <------**debug**------> on the stack as a kind of reference point. When we ask the debugger where we are, it prints out the item on top of the stack (in this case, <------**debug**------>), and tells us our relative stack position.

We can move up and down the stack using the debugging commands **dn** and **u**:

>   :dn
>
>   (eval (debug))
>   :

dn moves us down the stack one stack frame. We are now at the point of the stack where we made the call to **debug** after entering the break. This is not very interesting from the point of view of debugging our code; in fact, it is a nuisance. So let us move down the stack again:

>   :dn
>
>   (break—err—handler (ER%misc 5 nil |Bad arg to car| 8))
>   :

This intimidating item is the call to the LISP error-handler, which is both obscure and uninteresting. So we move down once more:

>   :dn
>
>   (car 8)
>   :

Finally, we arrive at the piece of code that caused the error. Let us go down the stack one more notch to see where this s-expression came from:

>   :dn
>
>   (cons (car 8) y)
>   :where
>
>   (cons (car 8) y)
>   you are 4 frames from the top.
>   there are 0 cons's below.
>
>   :

Here we can see that the problematic call to **car** occurred within a call to **cons**. This may help us locate the exact point of the call in our original code.

It might also help to get a more complete picture of what is on the stack. We could use **showstack** for this, but the debugger has some more convenient alternatives. For example, the command **bk** prints a listing of the stack, called a *backtrace,* as follows:

149

```
:bk

<-------debug------->
(eval (debug))
(break-err-handler (ER%misc 5 nil |Bad arg to car| 8))
(car 8)
(cons (car 8) y)   <--- you are here
(setq x (cons & y))
(prog (x) (setq x &))
(foo (cons & y))
(prog (x) (setq x 1) (foo &))
(baz '&)
(eval (baz &))
<bottom of stack>

        :
```

bk uses **&** to indicate the part of an expression that appears on the line above it. It also indicates where we are positioned with respect to the stack.

Usually it is too cumbersome to view the whole stack this way. So **bk** allows you to show only the top few elements of the stack:

```
:bk 5

<-------debug------->
(eval (debug))
(break-err-handler (ER%misc 5 nil |Bad arg to car| 8))
(car 8)
(cons (car 8) y)   <--- you are here

        :
```

We can ask for function names instead of entire s-expressions,

```
:bkf

<-------debug------->
eval
break-err-handler
car
cons  <--- you are here
setq
```

```
prog
foo
prog
baz
eval
<bottom of stack>
```

:

and we can include changes to variable bindings as well:

:bkv

```
<——————debug——————>
(eval (debug))
(break—err—handler (ER%misc 5 nil |Bad arg to car| 8))
(car 8)
(cons (car 8) y)   <——— you are here
(setq x (cons & y))
  x = nil
(prog (x) (setq x &))
  y = (a b c)
(foo (cons & y))
  x = 1
(prog (x) (setq x 1) (foo &))
  y = (b c)
(baz '&)
(eval (baz &))
<bottom of stack>
```

:

These options can be combined as you please. For example, a command of the form **bkfv** 7 will be interpreted as a directive to show the top 7 stack frames, printing out only function names, but also including changes to variable bindings:

:bkfv 7

```
<——————debug——————>
eval
break—err—handler
```

```
car
cons  <––– you are here
setq
  x = nil
prog
```

  :

We can also ask for the stack down to the nth occurrence of a function:

:bk 2 prog

```
<–––––––debug–––––––>
(eval (debug))
(break–err–handler (ER%misc 5 nil |Bad arg to car| 8))
(car 8)
(cons (car 8) y)  <––– you are here
(setq x (cons & y))
(prog (x) (setq x &))
(foo (cons & y))
(prog (x) (setq x 1) (foo &))
```

  :

These conventions apply to most debugger commands. For example, **dn 3** will move down the stack three notches, **dn foo** will move down to the next occurrence of **foo**, and **dn n foo** to the **n**-th occurrence of **foo**.

Some other useful commands for viewing the stack are **top** and **bot**, which do pretty much what you would expect. Also, **p** shows the current stack position using the **&** convention; **pp** shows this position without abbreviating s-expressions.

By moving up and down the stack, we can change the context in which an expression is evaluated. For example, at the current stack location, **x** and **y** refer to their values in **foo**:

:x

  x = nil
:y

  y = (a b c)
  :

(Note that the debugger **read-eval-print** loop prints the value of an atom in a special way.) However, I can move further down the stack and evaluate expressions within the context of **baz**. For example, I can move to the point of the stack just before **foo** was called:

> **:dn foo**
>
> **(foo (cons & y))**
> **:x**
>
> > **x = 1**
> **:y**
>
> > **y = (b c)**
> **:**

or to the bottom of the stack, before either variable has a binding:

> **:bot**
>
> **(eval (baz &))**
> **:x**
>
> > **x = ?**
> **:y**
>
> > **y = ?**
> **:**

Being able to continue the computation after a break is another feature of the debugger. One way to do this is to use **setq** within the debugger **read-eval-print** loop to patch up the values of some variables. Then we can try to continue with the computation. The command **redo** will resume evaluation from the current point of the stack. **ok** resumes evaluation at the point of the error. That is, **ok** is equivalent to **top** followed by **redo**. Finally, **return** *e* returns from the current position with the value of the expression *e*.

Let us use **return** to try to get our problem code to continue:

> **:top**
>
> <−−−−−−debug−−−−−−>

```
:dn car

(car 8)
:return 'a
nil
->
```

Our computation continued to completion now, just as if **'a** had appeared in the original code in place of **(car 8)**.

Finally, should you forget the commands the debugger accepts, the command **help** will print a list of them.

Note: For the debugger to work as advertised, LISP needs to maintain some extra information about the forms under evaluation. LISP will maintain this information in accordance with the value of some internal switch. This switch can be set by evaluating the expression (***rset t**). As LISP is normally in this mode, you probably will not have to tamper with ***rset**. However, if the debugger does not seem to be behaving properly, this is a good place to look for the problem.

11.5. TRACING AND BREAKING

Useful as they are, the debugging tools we just described are sometimes inadequate. For example, it is often the case that a piece of code does something that is conceptually incorrect but that is not in itself a LISP error. This mistake may have repercussions that cause the interpreter to choke some time in the future. Unfortunately, examining the state-of-the-world at the time of the actual error will not be particularly revealing about how the problem came about in the first place. Rather, what we would like to do is to run our program again, this time monitoring its behavior so that unexpected events will become apparent.

A *trace package* is an interactive debugging facility that lets the user examine selected function calls as a program is executed. Most trace packages also allow you to suspend execution and examine the current state-of-the-world.

In Franz, the trace package is invoked by a call to the function **trace**. In the simplest case, the arguments to **trace** are the names of functions that you wish to trace. For example, watch what happens when we define and then trace the function **xcons**:

```
-> (defun xcons (x y) (cons y x))
xcons
-> (trace xcons)
[autoload /usr/lib/lisp/trace]
[fasl /usr/lib/lisp/trace.o]
(xcons)
-> (xcons '(b c) 'a)
1 <Enter> xcons ((b c) a)
1 <EXIT>  xcons  (a b c)
(a b c)
->
```

LISP does not normally keep the trace package around. Instead, when the first call to **trace** is made, it is loaded automatically. The output in square brackets above is caused when the trace functions are loaded initially.

Now each time **xcons** is called, LISP will print out the fact that it is being entered, along with the arguments supplied to it; upon exit, the value returned by **xcons** is evidenced.

If a function is called within another traced function, **trace** tries to make this apparent. Suppose **foo** calls **xcons**, as in the following example:

```
-> (defun foo (x y) (xcons x y))
foo
-> (trace foo)
(foo)
-> (foo '(b c) 'a)
1 <Enter> foo ((b c) a)
|1 <Enter> xcons ((b c) a)
|1 <EXIT>  xcons  (a b c)
1 <EXIT>  foo  (a b c)
(a b c)
->
```

From the output of **trace**, we can see that **xcons** was called in the midst of a call to **foo**.

If a function is invoked recursively, **trace** also tries to make this easier to follow. For example, let us define and trace a recursive version of the function **factorial**:

```
-> (defun factorial (n)
        (cond ((zerop n) 1) (t (times n (factorial (sub1 n]
factorial
-> (factorial 4)
24
-> (trace factorial)
(factorial)
-> (factorial 4)
1 <Enter> factorial (4)
2 <Enter> factorial (3)
 3 <Enter> factorial (2)
 4 <Enter> factorial (1)
  5 <Enter> factorial (0)
  5 <EXIT>  factorial 1
 4 <EXIT>  factorial 1
 3 <EXIT>  factorial 2
2 <EXIT>  factorial 6
1 <EXIT>  factorial 24
24
->
```

The numbers at the beginning of each line represent the depth of the recursion; the indentation helps match up each function invocation with its associated termination.

We can turn off tracing by calling the function **untrace**:

```
-> (untrace factorial)
(factorial)
-> (factorial 4)
24
->
```

A call to **untrace** with no arguments will untrace all traced functions.

Sometimes such calls to **trace** result in too much information. LISP therefore gives you a means to exercise selective control over when the trace information should be printed. For example, if, instead of a call of the form

```
(trace foo)
```

we make a call of the form

```
(trace (foo if expression))
```

then the trace information will only be printed if *expression* evaluates to non-**nil**.

The form

> (**trace** (**foo ifnot** *expression*))

works similarly.

Within a call to **trace**, the function **arg** can be used to get at the actual arguments supplied to the function call. For example, the expression

> (**trace** (**foo if** (**eq** (**arg** 1) 4)))

will cause trace information to be printed if and only if the first argument to **foo** happens to be **4**.

In addition to tracing a function call, the trace package lets you suspend execution and explore the current environment. To do this, the trace package is invoked as follows:

> (**trace** (**foo break**))

Now, after **foo** is entered and trace information is printed, a special **read-eval-print** loop is entered. The prompt symbol here is **T>**. As usual, any LISP expression that is entered is evaluated and its value printed. In addition, the expression (**arg** *i*) will cause the *i*-th argument to be printed. When you have finished your exploration, typing the character ˆ**D** (CTRL-d) or the expression (**tracereturn**) will cause execution to continue.

You can combine most of these options. For example, the call

> (**trace** (**foo if** (**eq** (**arg** 1) 4) **break**))

will cause a call to **foo** to break only if the first argument is **eq** to **4**.

There are a number of other variations on the trace theme that allow the user to automatically evaluate expressions upon entry and exit, and so on. Appendix A should be consulted for further details.

11.6. SUMMARY

(1)   Upon encountering an error, LISP normally goes into *break mode*. In this mode, a special **read-eval-print** loop is entered. The current bindings of atoms can now be examined. The stack can be displayed using the function **showstack**. You can return from a break by using the function **retbrk**. The function **reset** will return all the way to the top level.

(2)   The *debugger* can be used to examine the stack more selectively, to evaluate expressions in different contexts, and to restart the computation.

(3)   The debugger is invoked by executing the function **debug**. This enters a **read-eval-print** loop in which a number of expressions are interpreted as commands. Among the more important ones are

dn	move down the stack
u	move up the stack
top	move to the top of the stack
bot	move to the bottom of the stack
bk	show a backtrace of s-expressions
bkf	backtrace with function names
bkv	backtrace with variable bindings
p	show the current stack position
pp	show current position w/o abbreviating s-exps
redo	resume evaluation from current stack position
ok	resume evaluation at the point of the error
return	return from call with specified value
help	list the recognized debugger commands

Many of these commands accept numerical parameters or text strings as arguments.

(4)   A *trace package* can be used to examine flow of control at runtime. This is done by applying the function **trace** to a function argument. Then LISP will print something on the terminal each time that function is entered or exited. The trace package can be used to selectively trace functions upon certain conditions, or to suspend execution when a function is reached.

158

Exercises

(1) Try using the various debugging facilities described in this chapter to help debug some of the functions you have written.

(2) Write a modified version of the debugger that does not display so many irrelevant s-expressions on the terminal. (Note — this involves considerably more knowledge of LISP internals than we have currently presented. You might consider this as a long-term project to do when you become more familiar with the inner workings of Franz LISP.)

12

Other Kinds of Functions

12.1. INTRODUCTION

We have seen that LISP has functions that treat their arguments in different ways. Most of the functions we have seen evaluate all their arguments, while some, like **defprop** and **defun**, do not cause any argument evaluation. A few, like **setq**, only evaluate one argument, and some, like **cond** and **prog**, evaluate their arguments based on certain conditions. In addition, some functions, like **plus**, can tolerate any number of arguments, while others expect a fixed number.

However, all the functions that we have learned to define always cause their arguments to be evaluated. In addition, they tolerate only a specific number of arguments. We have no way of defining a function of our own that does not cause its arguments to be evaluated, or which accepts a variable number of arguments. Sometimes it is useful to define functions that behave this way. Therefore, LISP provides a means to do so.

In this chapter we present alternative LISP function types, and show ways to define them. In particular, we introduce functions that do not evaluate their arguments, and functions that accept an indefinite number of arguments. We examine the forms that underlie these function types, and show various ways of defining them. We also present the notion of a *closure,* which is a way of defining a more specific version of an existing function. Finally, we discuss the role of compiled functions and foreign functions in LISP.

12.2. EXPRS AND FEXPRS

Some terminology is useful here. A function that requires a fixed number of arguments, and which evaluates all of them, is called an *expr* (short for "expression", I guess). This is the most basic form of LISP function. According to this definition, all the functions that we have learned how to define ourselves are exprs. As we have mentioned above, such functions are based on the underlying lambda idea.

LISP supports several other types of functions, however. Another important function type is the *fexpr*. A fexpr is a function that accepts any number of arguments, none of which is evaluated. When we define a fexpr, we only specify one formal parameter. When the fexpr is called, we supply it with as many actual arguments as we like. LISP will take all the arguments that we specify, put them together in a list, and bind this list to the single formal parameter of the function. LISP does *not* automatically evaluate these arguments, as it does in the case of exprs. Rather, it is up to the fexpr to examine the list of arguments with which it is supplied, and decide what to do with them.

We can define a fexpr by using **defun**. This is done by specifying the atom **fexpr** after the name of the function to be defined. This is followed by the formal parameter list, as usual. But the formal parameter list should only have one element in it, as all fexprs have only one formal parameter. Then come the bodies of code, just as if we were defining an expr.

For example, suppose we want to define a version of **get** that does not evaluate its arguments. Remember, **get** takes two arguments, an atom and a property name. It evaluates them, and returns a property value. To write a function that works just like this but does not evaluate its arguments, we could do the following:

```
-> (defun ourget fexpr (l)
       (get (car l) (cadr l)))
ourget
-> (defprop aleph bet gimmel)
bet
-> (ourget aleph gimmel)
bet
->
```

Here I told **defun** that I wanted to create a fexpr by sticking the atom

fexpr after the name of the function I am defining. Then I specified the formal parameter list containing one formal parameter, which I called l. When I call **ourget** later, all the arguments I use will be put in a list, and that list will be bound to l. For example, when I call **ourget** with arguments **aleph** and **gimmel**, LISP puts these into the list **(aleph gimmel)**. Then it binds l to this list. Since what I want **ourget** to do is find the value of the **gimmel** property of **aleph,** I want to apply the function **get** to the values **aleph** and **gimmel**. I can get **aleph** by taking the **car** of l, and **gimmel** by taking the **cadr** of l. So executing the body of this function with l bound to **(aleph gimmel)** is equivalent to typing **(get 'aleph 'gimmel)**.

The function **ourget** is typical of fexprs in a number of ways. First of all, most fexprs end up calling exprs internally to get the job done. For example, **ourget** relies on **get** to do the actual work of examining a property list. In fact, many a fexpr just act as a sort of interface to some expr so that the user does not have to bother quoting arguments.

Second, most of the complexity of fexprs lies in finding the actual arguments in the argument list. In the case of exprs, individual arguments are bound to individual formal parameters, so they are convenient to access. In the case of fexprs, all the arguments are stuffed into a list, so we need to dig them out. Functions like **cadr** and **caddr** tend to appear in fexprs for this reason, each appearance intended to access some actual argument.

Let us look at another example. **load** reads in an s-expression from a file. But it always evaluates the argument given it. This is annoying, because most of the time we know the name of the file and it is painful to have to quote it. Franz supplies us with the function **include** to make life easier. **include** is similar to **load** but does not evaluate its argument. However, we could have written **include** ourselves now that we know how to define fexprs:

```
-> (defun include fexpr (l) (load (car l)))
include
->
```

Remember, when we call a fexpr, all its arguments get put in a list. Thus if I evaluate **(include foo), foo** would be put in the list **(foo)** and this value bound to l. To get at **foo,** then, we have to take a **car** of l. This is precisely what our version of **include** does.

This version of **include** will not work too well if we specified more than one actual argument, however. If we tried to load three files by evaluating the expression **(include lamed vuv nik), include** will simply ignore all but the first argument (this is true as well of the version of **include** that comes with

Franz). But this is a reasonable form to want to enter. So let us write a new version of this function that can handle an indefinite number of arguments. We will call this version **dskin**:

> −> **(defun dskin fexpr (l) (mapc 'load l))**
> **dskin**
> −>

mapc causes **load** to be applied to each element of the value of l. l will be bound to the list of the actual arguments when the function is called. So the expression **(dskin lamed vuv nik)** will do just what we want. That is all there is to it.

12.2.1. NLAMBDA

You might be wondering how fexprs are implemented internally. After all, we said that functions are based on lambda forms. But lambda only defines functions that evaluate their arguments. Therefore, we will need some extension of lambda to accommodate fexprs.

Various LISPs implement fexprs differently. In Franz, fexprs are implemented through something called *nlambdas*. Just as exprs are implemented in terms of lambda forms, fexprs are based on *nlambda forms*. An nlambda form looks just like a lambda form, except that it begins with the atom **nlambda** instead of the atom **lambda**. This is followed by the formal parameter list, which should only contain one element. Then comes the series of function bodies. Nlambda forms can appear wherever functions may appear in LISP. When nlambdas are used as functions, they cause their actual arguments *not* to be evaluated. Instead, the arguments are put in a list and bound to the formal parameter. Then the function bodies are evaluated.

We can create functions explicitly with **nlambda** just as we can with **lambda**. For example, I can specify an nlambda form and use it at the beginning of a list, or as an argument to **mapcar**, just like I can a lambda form. However, in practice, the need to do so rarely arises. Rather, nlambda is used almost exclusively in defining permanent functions. If we use **defun** to define fexprs, however, we never see the underlying nlambda form. But, we can use **def** as well as **defun** to define a fexpr. In this case, we specify the underlying nlambda form explicitly. For example, I can define **dskin** using **def** as follows:

```
-> (def dskin (nlambda (l) (mapc 'load l)))
dskin
->
```

This form is an exact equivalent of the **defun** call to create **dskin** shown above. We can also use the function **putd** to create fexprs; the syntax is the same as that for **def**, except that **putd** evaluates its arguments.

Analogously to the case of exprs, the underlying form of a fexpr is always an nlambda form. This is true regardless of whether the fexpr was created with **defun**, **def**, or whatever. For example, suppose I use **getd** to return the function definition of **dskin** after creating it with **defun**, or **pp** to pretty-print this definition:

```
-> (defun dskin fexpr (l) (mapc 'load l))
dskin
-> (getd 'dskin)
(nlambda (l) (mapc 'load l))
-> (pp dskin)

(def dskin
  (nlambda (l)
    (mapc 'load l)))

t
->
```

These examples show that the definition is stored as an nlambda form. Again, **defun** is just a convenient way of specifying functions without having to deal with all the details of their internal forms. It is lambda and nlambda that are fundamental.

12.2.2. Context Effects in Fexprs

In Chapter 8 on **eval** and **apply**, we noted that these functions can sometimes cause some puzzling effects, having to do with evaluating an expression in a different context than the one the user intended. Since many fexprs end up doing their own evaluation of their arguments, such context effects are particularly prevalent here. The programmer should be vigilant about looking for them.

For example, suppose I want to define my own version of the function **setq**, assuming I had the function **set**. With fexprs at my disposal, I can do this as follows:

(defun mysetq fexpr (l) (set (car l) (eval (cadr l))))

This definition is typical of many fexprs we will have occasion to write. If we call **mysetq** with the arguments **a** and **'b**, say, LISP will put these arguments into the list **(a 'b)** and bind l to this value. **(car l)** will then return **a**, and **(cadr l)**, **'b**. We need to explicitly evaluate this second argument, so we use **eval** to do so. Then we call **set**, passing it the values **a** and **b**.

But this definition has a context bug in it. Can you think of an instance in which it will not work as intended? Suppose I try to use **mysetq** to bind a value to a variable called l on the top level. That is, I would like to type **(mysetq l '(1 2 3))**, and have l bound to **(1 2 3)** thereafter. But look what happens when we try this:

> −> (mysetq l '(1 2 3))
> (1 2 3)
> −> l
> **Error: Unbound Variable: l**
> **<1>:**

When we call **mysetq**, the actual arguments get put in the list **(l '(1 2 3))**, and this gets bound to the formal parameter l of **mysetq**. The first argument to **set**, **(car l)**, evaluates to l, which is what we intended. The only problem here is that l has been declared a formal parameter of **mysetq**. No matter what we change its value to within this function, it will be restored to its original value upon exiting. In other words, this function is just like **setq**, except that it has no effect at all on the particular atom l.

As I mentioned in the section on context problems with **eval**, we can use uncommon local variable names to minimize the occurrence of this problem. Or we can have some way for the user to specify the context in which to evaluate an expression. However, some programmers find this business so distasteful they prefer not to use fexprs at all. Instead, they use a type of function called a *macro*. Macros have many of the advantages of fexprs, but do not usually generate context problems. Macros are a bit more complicated than fexprs, however, so we will save them for the next chapter.

In any case, you should know that context problems may arise when you define fexprs or use **eval**, and take due precautions. In particular, you should consider fexprs as special-purpose items to be used only on special occasions, rather than as part of your day-to-day toolbox of LISP functions.

12.3. FUNCTION DISCIPLINE

We are now ready for a bit more terminology. We refer to the way in which a function treats its arguments as that function's *discipline*. For example, we would say that the discipline of an expr is *lambda,* and that the discipline of a fexpr is *nlambda.*

This terminology is convenient because it applies to different kinds of functions that behave about the same way. For example, a lambda form acts just like an expr, although the term "expr" is usually used to refer only to functions with names. Built-in functions like **car** and **cdr** treat their arguments just like an expr does. Strictly speaking, they are not exprs because their definitions are not written in LISP. However, all three function types can be said to have the discipline lambda.

Similarly, user-defined fexprs, nlambda forms, and built-in functions like **defprop** all treat their arguments the same way. We refer to the discipline of all three types as *nlambda.*

Thus the discipline of a function refers to how a function treats its arguments, without respect to exactly how that function is realized. There are several other types of function disciplines available in most LISPs. We explore these in the remainder of this chapter.

12.4. LEXPRS

We now know how to define functions that take either (a) a fixed number of arguments, all of which are always evaluated (exprs), or (b) any number of arguments, none of which is evaluated (fexprs). But suppose we want to write a function that took a variable number of arguments, all of which are always evaluated. For example, some of our numeric functions like **plus** work this way. True, we could define such a function as a fexpr, and then do the evaluation ourselves. But then we would have to worry about the context effects described above. So LISP gives us another function type just for this purpose.

This type of function is called a *lexpr.* It is not used very frequently, but you should know it is there. Lexprs are called with any number of arguments, all of which are evaluated. In the definition of a lexpr, the user specifies a single formal parameter. When the lexpr is called, this parameter is bound to the *number* of actual arguments supplied in the call. The function body of a lexpr can get at the individual arguments through the use of the special function **arg**. This is a function of one argument, which should evaluate to a number. **arg** will return the value of the argument corresponding to that number.

One way to define a lexpr is with **defun**. To do this, just specify a single non-**nil** literal atom where you normally supply the formal parameter list. For example, here is a rather trivial lexpr that merely prints the number of arguments supplied to it:

```
-> (defun print-no-of-arguments n
        (patom "Number of arguments supplied: ")
        (print n)
        (terpri))
print-no-of-arguments
-> (print-no-of-arguments 'a 'b 'c)
Number of arguments supplied: 3
nil
->
```

As you can see, the formal parameter **n** appears where we would normally put a list if we were defining an expr. Next comes a couple of lambda bodies. The function just prints out the value of **n**, which LISP always binds to the number of actual arguments supplied.

Lepxrs are a good way to write functions that have defaults if a user wants not to have to specify an optional argument. Here is a lexpr, that, if given one argument, squares that argument. If given an optional second argument, however, this function raises the first argument to the power of the second:

```
-> (defun power n
        (expt (arg 1) (cond ((greaterp n 1) (arg 2)) (t 2))))
power
-> (power 3)
9
-> (power 3 4)
81
->
```

power calls Franz LISP's internal exponentiation function, **expt**, always passing it its own first argument. If there is a second argument, **power** passes it as well; if not, it passes **expt** a **2**. Here the lexpr **power** uses the function **arg** to access its actual arguments. It uses the value of its formal parameter to determine how many actual arguments the function is called with.

12.4.1. Defining Lexprs More Conveniently

Because such uses of lexprs are the most frequent, Franz LISP provides the user with a more convenient method of writing them. This method is based on the assumption that, for most lexprs, there will be some arguments that are always supplied, and then some optional ones. The user will want to refer to these arguments by name, as one does in an expr, rather than having to use calls to **arg**.

The function **defun** therefore allows the user to write lexprs in the following way: The user specifies a formal parameter list much like the one he would normally supply to an expr. That is, the formal parameter list can contain any number of formal parameters. These parameters are interpreted as corresponding to the actual arguments that we assume will always be supplied. In addition, toward the end of this formal parameter list, the keyword **&optional** or **&rest** may appear. If the keyword **&optional** appears, then the parameter following it will be bound to the corresponding argument, if one is supplied. Moreover, if, instead of a parameter, the keyword is followed by a list of the form **(name value)**, then **name** is interpreted to be an optional parameter. If an actual argument is not supplied, the parameter **name** will be bound to the default value **value**. If the keyword **&rest** appears, then the parameter following it will be bound to the *list* of all the actual arguments not already associated with specific parameters.

For example, the following definition makes use of this convention to create the lexpr **power** shown above:

```
-> (defun power (x &optional (y 2))
      (expt x y))
power
->
```

In this definition of **power**, the first argument is always expected. Therefore, we designate it by a formal parameter, in this case, **x**. The second argument is optional, so the flag **&optional** appears next. The notation **(y 2)** indicates that we refer to this argument using the parameter **y**, and that we want the value of this parameter to default to **2** if an actual argument is not supplied.

When **defun** sees either the flag **&optional** or **&rest** in the formal parameter list of a function definition, it is alerted to the fact that a lexpr is required. Then it rewrites the function internally as a real lexpr, using calls to **arg**, etc. Since **defun** has to create so much code of its own to translate what you have written into a real lexpr, the resulting code may not be very recognizable if you pretty-printed it out. Nevertheless, what you have to write is considerably more lucid than the form you would otherwise have to supply. In the next chapter, we will see how to write functions of our own that behave this way.

defun accepts one other flag. If the symbol **&aux** appears in the formal parameter list, **defun** treats the next symbol as a variable local to the function definition. If the next argument is a list of the form (*name expr*), **defun** treats *name* as a local variable and sets its initial value to the value of *expr*. Otherwise the local variable is initialized to **nil**.

12.4.2. Lexpr Forms

Lexprs are implemented differently in different LISPs. In Franz, lexprs are implemented using a special *lexpr form*. This is analogous to the lambda form. It enables you to define lexprs explicitly using **def** rather than **defun**. For example, here is a version of the trivial lexpr **print−no−of−arguments** in which the lexpr form is explicit:

```
-> (def print-no-of-arguments
      (lexpr (n)
         (patom "Number of arguments supplied: ")
         (print n)
         (terpri)) )
print-no-of-arguments
-> (print-no-of-arguments 'a 'b 'c)
Number of arguments supplied: 3
nil
->
```

Note that, in the lexpr form, the formal parameter must be enclosed in parentheses, whereas in the standard call to **defun** it must not be. This inconsistency arises because these two function defining functions arose from different LISP schools of thought. Franz incorporates both of them for compatibility. It is probably a good idea to pick one convention or the other and stick with it.

In any case, we refer to the discipline of lexprs also as *lexpr*. Of course, lexpr is the discipline of lexpr forms, and of built-in functions that behave the same way.

12.4.3. Other Lexpr Functions: LISTIFY and SETARG

Franz LISP provides two other functions that are useful in conjunction with lexprs. The function **listify** returns a list of the first n arguments to the current lexpr, where n is the value of the argument to **listify**. If n is negative, **listify** will return a list containing the last −n arguments to the lexpr.

The function **setarg** takes two arguments. The first should evaluate to a number between 1 and the number of actual arguments supplied to the lexpr. **setarg** will set the corresponding argument of the lexpr to the value of its second argument. Thus, after evaluating **(setarg n 'val)**, evaluating **(arg n)** will return **val**.

12.5. CLOSURES

Suppose we want to write a function that saves some value it can examine the next time it runs. For example, functions that generate random numbers often use the previous random number generated to help generate the next. To do so, we need some place to squirrel away a value so that a function can get at it next time.

We can use a global variable or a property list to store such a value. But this solution is not without risk. We might get careless, and write another function that happens to use the same global variable or property. Then the two functions may interact adversely. It is even more problematic if we want to have several incarnations of the same function around, each remembering what it computed previously, but not interfering with one another. Using a single, global object does not accommodate this.

For example, suppose I want a function that will give me the next even number each time it is called. We could write this as a function that uses the global variable **evenseed** to remember the last value it computed:

```
-> (defun even-generator () (setq evenseed (plus evenseed 2)))
even-generator
-> (setq evenseed 0)
0
-> (even-generator)
2
-> (even-generator)
4
```

    -> (even-generator)
6
    ->

This works fine, but some other function could come along and clobber **evenseed** in between calls. And I could not use **even-generator** to generate two streams of even numbers simultaneously, each independent of the other.

A solution to this problem is to make a version of a function that has variables only it can access. This is done by taking a function that references some free variables, and producing a new function in which all those free variables are "frozen" at their current values (recall that *free variables* are atoms whose values are referenced within a function, but which are not formal parameters of that function). When this new function is run, it unthaws these "frozen" variables. When it finishes running, it puts these variables back in the freezer. Thus, if the values of some of these variables are changed, their new values will be remembered for the next time the function is run. However, changes to these formerly free variables will not have any effect outside of this function; moreover, the values of these variables cannot be accessed or altered outside of this function.

In the case of our example above, we would like to produce a version of **even-generator** that has its own private copy of the free variable **evenseed**. When we create this version of **even-generator**, we would like its version of **evenseed** to be frozen at whatever value **evenseed** currently has. No matter what happens subsequently to the original version, this will not affect the new version. When we run this new version, it would update its private copy of **evenseed**. This would not affect the version of **evenseed** known to the original function. But the new, updated copy of **evenseed** would be available to the new function the next time it is run.

In other words, we take a sort of snapshot of a function with respect to the current values of its free variables. We now manipulate this picture rather than the function itself. The picture has about the same logical structure as the original, but if I change something in the picture, the original does not change. In fact, I should be able to take any number of such snapshots, and manipulate each one a bit differently. The alterations to each snapshot would serve to record its current state of affairs. But each snapshot could be looked at and altered quite independently of the others.

When we take such a snapshot of a function, it is called a *closure* of that function. The name is motivated by the idea that free variables of that function, normally "open" to the world outside that function are now closed to the outside world.

In Franz LISP, closures of functions are called *fclosures,* and are created by the function **fclosure**. This function requires two arguments (both evaluated): a list of variables that should be closed, and a function in which to close them. It returns a snapshot of the function argument with the specified variables closed off to the outside world.

For example, I can use **fclosure** to produce a snapshot of the function **even−generator** that includes the free variable **evenseed** in the picture:

```
−> (setq even−gen−1 (fclosure '(evenseed) 'even−generator))
fclosure[8]
−> (funcall even−gen−1)
8
−> evenseed
6
−> (funcall even−gen−1)
10
−> evenseed
6
−> (even−generator)
8
−> evenseed
8
−>
```

Here we create an fclosure of the function **even−generator** in which the variable **evenseed** is closed off to the outside world. We save this fclosure by binding **even−gen−1** to it. Next, we use **funcall** to invoke this function. (Remember, **funcall** is like **apply**, but expects the arguments right after the function name. In this case, there are none, as both **even−generator** and therefore, the various fclosures based on it, are functions of no arguments.) LISP prints out an fclosure as **fclosure[n]**, where the **n** has to do with the amount of storage the fclosure occupies.

We run this fclosure a couple of times, and each time it produces a new value. Then we check on the value of **evenseed**, and see that it is unchanged, as promised. The fclosure has its own version of **evenseed** to twiddle with, and manipulating one does not affect the other. Finally, we run the original function again. It behaves just as if the fclosure had never been created or run. After all, one would hardly expect an object to change just because we altered a photograph of it.

We can create as many independent fclosures of the same function as we like. For example, suppose I make another fclosure of **even−generator** right now. Note that I ran **even−generator** once since I made the first fclosure of it. The free variable **evenseed** has therefore been updated since that time. The fclosure I now make will reflect this new state of affairs:

```
-> (setq even-gen-2 (fclosure '(evenseed) 'even-generator))
fclosure[8]
-> (funcall even-gen-2)
10
-> (funcall even-gen-2)
12
-> (funcall even-gen-1)
12
-> (funcall even-gen-1)
14
-> (funcall even-gen-1)
16
-> (funcall even-gen-2)
14
-> evenseed
8
->
```

This fclosure starts off with its version of **evenseed** at the value **even-generator** left it. However, the two fclosures and the original function now constitute three independent functions. Each references a different and independent version of **evenseed**.

In an actual program, I would most likely create an fclosure of **even-generator** and use it if I need some even numbers. I would probably never run the original function. Instead, I would keep it around for grain seed. Then if I needed an additional stream of even numbers, I would clone the original function again.

You can make an fclosure of any type of function. This includes atoms with function definitions, lambda forms, or even other fclosures. The last case applies when you close off only some of the free variables of a function. Then the fclosure created still has some free variables in it. More of these variables can be closed off to make an fclosure of an fclosure.

12.5.1. Closing a Set of Functions

When we close off the free variables of a function, a new problem presents itself. The closed variables are inaccessible outside of the fclosure. So it would be difficult to write a set of functions that shared the same closed variable.

For example, suppose we want to write a pair of functions. One returns the next even number, and the other the next odd number. However, we want them to work in tandem, so that a call to one advances the other. For example, if we call the even number generator three times in a row, it should return **2**, **4**, and **6**. Then a call to the odd number generator should return **7**. If we call it again, it should return **9**. The next time we call the even number generator, it should return **10**.

It is easy to write a single pair of such functions. For example, we could do the following:

```
-> (defun even-gen ()
      (setq seed (cond ((evenp seed) (plus seed 2))
                        (t (add1 seed]
even-gen
-> (defun odd-gen ()
      (setq seed (cond ((oddp seed) (plus seed 2))
                        (t (add1 seed]
odd-gen
-> (setq seed 0)
0
-> (even-gen)
2
-> (even-gen)
4
-> (even-gen)
6
-> (odd-gen)
7
-> (odd-gen)
9
-> (even-gen)
10
->
```

However, if I want to make fclosures of these functions, I am in trouble. If I use **fclosure** to produce an fclosure of each function, each fclosure would get its own version of **seed**. The fclosure of **even-gen** could not influence the fclosure of **odd-gen**, and conversely. But this is not what we want.

The solution is to have a function that creates fclosures of a bunch of functions together. The functions closed together would share their variables with one another, but not with anyone else. This can be done using the function **fclosure-list**. The call to **fclosure-list** is a sequence of pairs of arguments. Each pair is a list of variables to be closed, and a function to close them in. The result is a list of fclosures which all share whatever variables were closed at the same time. For example, to close **even–gen** and **odd–gen** together, I would do the following:

```
-> (setq fns (fclosure–list '(seed) 'even–gen '(seed) 'odd–gen))
(fclosure[8] fclosure[8])
-> (funcall (car fns))
12
-> (funcall (car fns))
14
-> (funcall (cadr fns))
15
-> (funcall (cadr fns))
17
-> (funcall (car fns))
18
-> (even–gen)
12
->
```

The call to **fclosure–list** produces a pair of fclosures, an fclosure of **even–gen**, and one of **odd–gen**. This pair shares access to an otherwise private copy of the variable **seed**. We could define as many of these pairs as we like, each pair sharing a variable all its own.

12.6. COMPILED AND FOREIGN FUNCTIONS

If you try to look at the function definitions of most LISP built-in functions, you will find that they look rather mysterious. For example, suppose I use either **getd** or **pp** to examine a built-in function, like **car**:

```
-> (getd 'car)
#c3e2–lambda
-> (pp car)

pp: function car is machine coded (bcd)

t
->
```

The reason we do not get a nice s-expression here is that the function **car** is not coded in LISP. This is not too surprising. **car** is a rather basic function, and so it is written in machine language. When the interpreter tries to **print** out a function that is written in machine language, it usually ends up printing out the machine address where the function lives, and either a **lambda** or **nlambda** to indicate the function's discipline. (There is no special form for machine-coded lexprs; these also appear with a **lambda** after the uninformative number.) When **pp** is asked to display a function written in machine language, it prints out the message you see above, indicating that the function is composed of *binary coded data.*

In addition to the most basic LISP functions, which must be written in machine language, more complex functions are often written in machine language as well. This is done for efficiency's sake. To facilitate this process, there exists a LISP *compiler,* that takes as input functions written in LISP, and produces as output machine language versions of those functions. The resulting functions can then be used in place of the original LISP functions, and will generally run much faster. Of course, you give up some readability and ease of debugging to get this increase in performance.

So it is possible to take all the functions you have written yourself and, when you are finished debugging them, compile them into machine language to speed up your program. The process of doing this is a bit involved, and we will deal with it in Chapter 20. However, in the meantime, if you peek at a function whose definition is opaque to you, you will know where it came from.

Another possibility is that the function definition was written in another language altogether, and then interfaced with LISP. In Franz, it is possible to load routines that were written in many other languages, and run them as LISP functions. Of course, these so called "foreign functions" had better obey various conventions of the LISP nationality, or they will wreak havoc. These functions will be **print**ed out just like compiled functions, except that the output will include a keyword like **subroutine** or **c−function** rather than **lambda** or **nlambda**, after the cryptic number. These refer to special disciplines that foreign functions may have. Clearly, this is not the stuff for beginning LISP programmers to be concerned with.

Virtually all LISP functions fall into one of the categories we have now seen (the only exception is the *macro,* to which we devote the entire next chapter). For example, **car**, **cdr**, and **cons** are binary coded versions of exprs; **setq**, **def**, and **defprop** are binary coded version of fexprs; and **plus** and **times** are binary coded versions of lexprs. LISP programmers loosely refer to these functions as being of the type from which they were derived. For example, LISP programmers will call **car** an expr, and **setq** a fexpr, even though, strictly speaking, these are binary coded functions.

12.7. EXTENDED LAMBDA FORMS

In the original version of LISP, functions were only allowed to have a single function body. If you wanted to write a function that did two things one right after the other, you would have to use some explicit construction to do so. LISP was later extended to allow any number of bodies in a function. Sometimes LISP programmers refer to this style of LISP as having *extended lambda forms,* meaning that the various function definition mechanisms, including the basic lambda building blocks, support multiple function bodies.

12.8. SUMMARY

(1) LISP supports several different schemes for function argument handling. We refer to the way in which a function treats its arguments as its *discipline.* Functions which require a fixed number of arguments, all of which are always evaluated, are said to have the disciple *lambda*; functions with a variable number of arguments, none of which is automatically evaluated, have the discipline *nlambda*; functions of a variable number of arguments, all of which are always evaluated, have the discipline *lexpr*.

(2) User-defined functions whose discipline is lambda, nlambda, or lexpr are called *exprs, fexprs,* or *lexprs,* respectively. These are implemented internally by *lambda, nlambda,* and *lexpr forms,* respectively. Each of these forms has the same structure. It begins with a keyword, either **lambda**, **nlambda**, or **lexpr**. It is followed by a formal parameter list; in the case of nlambda and lexpr forms, this list should contain only one element. Then comes any number of bodies of code. All three forms may appear anywhere that a function is expected in LISP. The definitions of user-defined function are stored as either lambda, nlambda, or lexpr forms, regardless of how they are entered initially.

(3) When an expr is called, LISP evaluates each argument, and binds each formal parameter to the corresponding value. When a fexpr is called, LISP puts all its actual arguments in a list, and binds the single formal argument of the fexpr to this list. When a lexpr is called, LISP evaluates each argument, and binds the single formal parameter of the lexpr to the number of actual arguments. In all cases, the previous values of these formal parameters are saved and then restored when the function call is completed.

(4) Lexprs have a number of associated functions that are useful for accessing arguments. The function **arg** takes one argument, which should evaluate to a number between 1 and the actual number of

arguments supplied in the call. **arg** returns the corresponding actual argument. **listify** returns a list of the first n arguments to the current lexpr, where n is the value of the argument to **listify**; if n is negative, **listify** will return a list containing the last −n arguments to the lexpr. **setarg** can be used to change the value of an argument to a lexpr.

(5)   All of these function types can be defined by **def** or **putd**, both of which expect a function name followed by a lambda, nlambda, or lexpr form; **putd** evaluates its arguments, whereas **def** does not.

(6)   All three function types can also be defined by **defun**. To designate a fexpr, the keyword **fexpr** should appear after the formal parameter list; to designate a lexpr, the formal parameter list should be replaced by an atom denoting the single formal parameter. In addition, **defun** will recognize the keywords **&optional** and **&rest** in a formal parameter list as denoting a lexpr. If no special notation is used, the function defined by **defun** will be an expr.

(7)   An *fclosure* is a version of a function with its own private copy of some free variables. A call to an fclosure may access or change its own copy of a variable. But it cannot access or influence those of other functions, including other fclosures of the same function. Nor may other functions access or change its private copies.

(8)   An fclosure can be produced by the function **fclosure**. This function takes as arguments a list of variables to close, and a function object to close them in. An fclosure can be made out of any kind of function object. The function **fclosure–list** can produce several fclosures which share the same private copy of a variable.

(9)   Functions can be machine coded for efficiency. We can translate LISP functions into machine-coded functions using a LISP compiler. In addition, we can interface "foreign" functions into LISP. All functions in a LISP system that are not written in LISP are **print**ed as an address in memory accompanied by a keyword that indicates how the arguments to the function should be treated.

Exercises

(1)   Define fexpr versions of the functions **cons** and **set**. The latter is particularly useful for initially defining data, in just the way **defprop** is.

(2)   Write a function **msgs**, a sort of generic message-printing function. **msgs** accepts any number of arguments, and works as follows: If an argument is an ordinary s-expression, **msgs** will output it, unevaluated, using **patom**. If the argument is the atom **t**, **msgs** does a **terpri**; if it is a number, it outputs that many spaces. Finally, if the argument is an expression of the form (**e** *s-expr*), **msgs** evaluates the expression *s-expr*.

(3)   I mentioned above that the function defining functions **defun** and **def** are implemented in terms of **putd**. As an exercise, write your own version of **def** in terms of **putd**.

(4)   We can also define our own functions for defining functions. For example, some programmers define a function called **df** especially for defining fexprs, and a function **de** just for defining exprs. These functions have the same syntax as the basic call to **defun**, but define only fexprs and exprs, respectively. For example, with **df**, I could define **dskin** as follows:

        -> (df dskin (l) (mapc 'load l))
        dskin
        ->

Write the functions **de** and **df** that work as advertised.

(5)   The built-in functions **and** and **or** are implemented as nlambdas. Write your own definition of each of these functions.

(6)   Write a function that takes any number of arguments, evaluates them all, and computes the square root of the sum of their squares.

(7)   Write a version of **cons** called **mcons** that takes any number of arguments, all of which are evaluated. The value of the next-to-last argument should be **cons**ed onto the last; the value before that should be **cons**ed onto the resulting value, and so on. For example, (**mcons 'a 'b 'c '(d e)**) should return (**a b c d e**).

(8)   Write a function **close—enough** which determines if two numerical values are within a certain tolerance of one another, where the tolerance is given by some free variable. Now produce functions that determine if two numerical values are within a certain tolerance of each other, for various different specific tolerances.

13

Macros

13.1. INTRODUCTION

We have now encountered all the major LISP function types save one, the
macro. Macros are sufficiently different from other types of LISP functions
to merit special attention. Learning to use macros is a bit harder than learning to use more prosaic LISP functions. However, once they are mastered,
they provide the user with enormous flexibility at a low cost.

In this chapter we motivate the use of macros, and then present some ways
of defining them. We also discuss some techniques to make macro writing
easier. Some particular macros are presented, some of which are useful
enough to add to one's standard repertoire of LISP programming techniques. Some of these sample macros suggest a certain programming style
which many programmers find aesthetically pleasing. This style is presented
for your consideration.

13.2. USING MACROS TO WRITE MORE READABLE CODE

One reason that symbolic LISP functions seem a little strange at first is that
they have no "real world" semantics. By this I mean that they do not really
have much meaning outside of LISP. This is not the case for more banal
programming language functions, such as numerical operations. For

example, the operation **plus** is meaningful outside of LISP (or FORTRAN or PASCAL, for that matter). But **car** and **cdr** only seem to make sense within the LISP world.

Of course, the idea is to use **car** and **cdr** to implement other functions that have some a priori meaning to us. For example, suppose I represent locations by lists of the form **(city state zip)**. Then taking the **cadr** of a datum of this form would be conceptually equivalent to stating "give me the 'state' part of a location".

There is a problem with a program that accesses data fields this way, however. The inherent meaninglessness of symbolic operators makes the code rather opaque. For example, if we look at a piece of code that contains the expression

> **(cadr loc1)**

it is difficult to determine that this is a reference to the "state" part of a data structure.

One way to write more transparent code would be to define a function called **get−state−field**. The body of this function definition would simply be a call to **cadr**. But now our code looks more meaningful:

> **(get−state−field loc1)**

Not only is the code more meaningful, but we have obeyed an important general rule of programming. We have insulated the rest of our program from low-level implementation decisions. Now if I decide to change my location representation, I need only change **get−state−field** and a few other access functions. I do not have to run through my code in search of all references to "location" data.

But I have paid a price for this convenience. Applying **cadr** is an extremely simple LISP operation. But applying **get−state−field** entails the additional overhead of a new function call − fetching the function body, saving old lambda variable values, binding new ones, etc. This is probably several times as costly as the original call to **cadr**. If such data accesses represent a significant portion of the time spent by my program, I may have greatly decreased its efficiency.

What I would really like to do is provide a convenient way of expressing what I want to say, but avoid any additional overhead this might entail.

Macros are a kind of LISP function that can be used to fulfill this goal.

Macros provide an extremely flexible mode of expression. In addition, in most systems, macros can be made to result in efficient code, combining the best of two worlds.

How do macros achieve such wonders? The basic idea is the following. Whereas other functions in LISP produce a result that is passed on as their value, LISP macros first *produce a result that is itself another piece of code.* This fabricated piece of code is then evaluated to produce the value that the code returns. In other words, the LISP interpreter evaluates a call to a macro twice. The first evaluation should return an executable s-expression. This s-expression is evaluated again. The result of this second evaluation is returned as the value of the call to the macro.

For example, suppose I define **get–state–field** as a macro. I would do so in such a way so that calling **(get–state–field loc1)** would first produce the piece of code **(cadr loc1)**. LISP would then evaluate this piece of code, which accesses the "state" part of **loc1**. This is just as if the actual code turned into **(cadr loc1)** before execution.

In general, macros may turn into arbitrarily complicated pieces of code. Thus, macros are a convenient way to express something whose appearance would otherwise be more cumbersome or less meaningful.

But macros sound like they would require more work than other LISP function calls, not less. After all, macros have to produce code as well as evaluate it. So how can macros be efficient? The trick is that most LISPs have some way of saving the code produced by the first phase of macro execution. Remember, macros first produce code that they subsequently evaluate. The code that the macro produces will be the same each time the macro is called. That is, each time we evaluate the expression **(get–state–field loc1)**, LISP will produce the code **(cadr loc1)** for subsequent evaluation. (Of course, each time this code is evaluated, it may return a different value, depending on the value of **loc1**.) So our interpreter remembers the value of the code produced by the call to the macro the first time it is evaluated. The second time the interpreter comes around to execute the line of code, it finds the code produced from evaluating the macro call last time. Then it merely executes this code. For example, the second time the interpreter encounters the code that was originally **(get–state–field loc1)**, it finds the code **(cadr loc1)**, and only has to execute a **cadr**.

Thus, with the exception of the initial expense of executing the macro for the first time, code written using a macro will run as fast as if we had written the code produced by the macro. But the code we actually wrote containing the macro will be much nicer to look at.

13.3. DEFINING MACROS

We can define a macro in Franz using either **defun** or **def**. Using **defun**, macros are defined by inserting the keyword **macro** after the function name. This is similar to defining a fexpr. Thus macros can be defined by calls to **defun** that have the following general form:

> (**defun** *function-name* **macro** *(symbol) body-of-code*)

(Actually, macros can have any number of function bodies, just like any other LISP function. However, the initial phase of macro application can only produce one piece of code for subsequent evaluation. Therefore, it does not make much sense to write a macro with more than one body.)

We can also define macros using **def**. Here we are required to define a macro using an underlying *macro form*. This is exactly analogous to a lambda or nlambda form. Like nlambda forms, macro forms almost never occur in line. Rather, they appear only in function definitions. In the case of **def**, we can define a macro by putting a macro form after the function name. The general format is as follows:

> (**def** *function-name* (**macro** *(symbol) body-of-code*))

Macros look something like fexprs in that their formal parameter list always contains exactly one parameter. However, macros are evaluated differently. When a call to a macro occurs, LISP takes the *entire s-expression* involved in the call and binds it to the formal parameter of the macro. Then the body of the macro is evaluated. This evaluation presumably results in a new body of code, which LISP then evaluates again.

For example, if **foo** were defined as a macro, a call of **(foo a b c)** would result in the entire expression **(foo a b c)** being bound to the formal parameter of the macro. Like a fexpr, none of the actual arguments is evaluated. But if **foo** were a fexpr, only **(a b c)**, rather than the entire calling expression, would be bound to the formal parameter.

Let us write a version of **get–state–field** as a macro as an example. Remember, we want a call of the form **(get–state–field loc1)** to turn into **(cadr loc1)**. To do this, we can define **get–state–field** as follows:

> —> (**defun get–state–field macro (l)**
>   **(cons 'cadr (cdr l)))**

When we evaluate an expression like **(get–state–field loc1)**, the formal parameter l will be bound to the entire calling expression, e. g., (get—state—field loc1). Thus the body of our macro needs to take a **cdr** of the value of l to get at the argument. Then it can **cons** the literal atom **cadr** onto the beginning of this value to yield the desired expression, e. g., **(cadr loc1)**. Let us try this macro and see how it works:

> —> (get—state—field '(Berkeley California 94720))
> **California**
> —>

In evaluating this function call, the interpreter took the following steps: First, it took the entire s-expression that constitutes the call, and bound the formal parameter of the macro to this value. In this case, the formal parameter l got bound to the value **(get—state—field '(Berkeley California 94720))**. Then the body of the macro got evaluated. This **cons**ed the atom **cadr** onto the value of the **cdr** of l. This produced the value **(cadr '(Berkeley California 94720))**. Then LISP evaluated this expression. This returned the value **California**, which was returned as the value of this macro call.

13.4. MACRO EXPANSION

If you define the **get—state—field** macro, and then test it as we did above, you will notice a small difficulty. LISP evaluates the code produced by a macro immediately after producing it. Therefore, when you use a macro, you get to see only the result of the entire evaluation of the macro. But you do not get to see the code produced by the macro along the way. Since it is sometimes useful in debugging to view this intermediate code, LISP provides us with a way of doing so. The Franz LISP function **macroexpand** is an expr that takes as input an s-expression that may contain a call to a macro. It produces as output an s-expression obtained by replacing calls to macros with the code they produce. (Most LISPs have some function like **macroexpand**, although the name may vary from LISP to LISP.) Let us run **macroexpand** on a call to **get—state—field** and see what happens:

> —> (macroexpand '(get—state—field loc1))
> **(cadr loc1)**
> —>

Here the code produced by the call to the macro **get—state—field** is returned by **macroexpand**. This code is not evaluated, but just returned for our perusal. We can now examine this code to decide if it is what we want.

The code produced by macros is generally longer than the call to the macro itself (although this is not the case for our example above). Hence the phase of interpreting the macro to produce code is called *macro expansion*. For example, we would say that the expression **(cadr loc1)** is the macro expansion of the expression **(get—state—field loc1)**.

13.5. SOME SAMPLE MACROS

FLAMBDA

Let us take a look at a few convenient macros. We noted previously that when we quoted functions, such as lambda forms, it is proper to use the special quoting function **function** rather than **quote**. We have no convenient abbreviation for **function**, however. Since lambda forms almost always need to be quoted, we can define a macro that makes writing quoted lambda forms a bit simpler. We do so by defining a macro **flambda** that expands into **(function (lambda ...))**:

```
—> (defun flambda macro (l)
       (list 'function (cons 'lambda (cdr l))))
flambda
—> (macroexpand '(flambda (x y) (cons y x)))
(function (lambda (x y) (cons y x)))
—>
```

flambda works by just sticking the atom **lambda** on the front of its actual argument list. The resulting lambda form is put in a list that begins with the atom **function**. Thus the sample "flambda form" given above as an argument to **macroexpand** can be seen to be a shorthand for writing the full **(function (lambda ...))** business.

POP

A more interesting function is the macro **pop**. **pop** takes as its argument an atom bound to a list. It reduces this list to its **cdr**, and returns the first element of the list as its value. In effect, **pop** treats the list like a stack, and pops off its top element.

We can implement **pop** by code of the following form:

(prog1 (car stack) (setq stack (cdr stack)))

Recall that **prog1** evaluates all its arguments in sequence, returning the value of the first one. Thus, for any particular list, we can execute a line of code like the one shown above, which carries out the desired function. What we would like to do is to define a macro that expands into code of this form. Thus we want (**pop stack**) to expand into the **prog1** shown above. So we have the following definition:

```
-> (defun pop macro (l)
        (list 'prog1
                (cons 'car (cdr l))
                (list 'setq (cadr l) (cons 'cdr (cdr l)))))
pop
-> (macroexpand '(pop stack))
(prog1 (car stack) (setq stack (cdr stack)))
->
```

Now let us try this macro to see how it works:

```
-> (setq stack '(a b c))
(a b c)
-> (pop stack)
a
-> stack
(b c)
->
```

pop returned the first element of **stack** as its value. In addition, it reduced **stack** to its **cdr**.

Note that it would be difficult to write this function as an expr, since it needs to get at the actual stack name to change its value. We could have written it as a fexpr, though. But then the function would have had to do an explicit **eval** in order to get at the value of the stack. As we mentioned above, explicit **eval**s inside fexprs sometimes lead to context problems. However, we have no such difficulty with macros. Since a macro expands into code which is then evaluated, the resulting code gets evaluated within the context of the calling program. Thus there are none of the usual context problems of fexprs associated with macros, because no macro context exists at the time the code produced by the macro is evaluated.

For this reason, many LISP programmers prefer not to use fexprs at all. They use macros instead whenever the need arises. The only drawbacks of macros are: (1) Not every LISP system supports macros. This is not too serious a problem, because of the wide availability today of LISP systems that do support them. (2) Macros produce code that looks very different than the code you wrote. Once we expand a macro, it may be hard to recognize it as the code you wrote. (3) Your LISP system needs to be set up in such a way that macros are not expanded each time they are encountered.

If you cannot do so, the cost of using macros may be prohibitive.

13.6. MACRO WRITING TECHNIQUES

As we can see from the example above, even simple macros are difficult to write. A macro is code that produces code, and this code manipulates data which are of the same form as code. Sometimes all these levels get confusing. You can avoid some of this confusion by following the following procedure whenever you write a macro:

(1) First, write down an example of the call to the macro you would like to be able to make. In the case of **pop**, for example, this might be the call **(pop stack)**.

(2) Then write down the code that you would like the macro to produce. In our example, this would be **(prog1 (car stack) (setq stack (cdr stack)))**.

(3) Now write a macro that transforms the likes of the first into the second.

Let us apply this procedure to define a macro called **push**. This macro will expect two arguments, and will produce code that pushes the first onto the stack named by the second. The code will return the entire new stack as its value.

(1) A typical call to **push** might be this:

   (push a stack)

   Remember, the formal parameter of the macro will get bound to this entire call.

(2) Now let us write the corresponding target code:

   (setq stack (cons a stack))

(3) Now let us write a function that builds this code from the call. To build the subexpression **(cons a stack)**, we can first get the expression **(a stack)** by taking the **cdr** of the formal parameter. Then we could stick the atom **cons** onto this list. Thus part of the macro definition will be the code **(cons 'cons (cdr l))**, where l is the formal parameter. Now we need to put this value in a list prefaced by the atoms **setq** and **stack**. The **stack** we can get by taking the **caddr** of the parameter's

187

binding. The **setq** is a constant. So we have the following definition:

      −> **(defun push macro (l)**
                (list 'setq (caddr l) (cons 'cons (cdr l))))
    push
    −>

Let us test it to check that it is correct:

      −> **(macroexpand '(push a stack))**
    (setq stack (cons a stack))
    −> **stack**
    (b c)
    −> **(push 'a stack)**
    (a b c)
    −> **stack**
    (a b c)
    −>

13.6.1. DEFMACRO

Even following the macro-writing procedure of the previous section, writing macros is often awkward. Not the least of the problems is the strange macro calling convention, which passes the entire calling expression rather than just the arguments. Since the bodies of almost all macros make use of only the arguments, this calling convention makes getting at the arguments unnecessarily complicated.

Fortunately, Franz provides a special function for defining macros that makes accessing the arguments more convenient. This function is called **defmacro**. When you define a macro using **defmacro**, you get to specify a formal parameter list just like you do for an expr. Each argument in your formal parameter list will get bound to each (unevaluated) argument in a call to the macro. The body of the macro can be written to reference individual arguments by name.

For example, here is a definition of **push** written using **defmacro**:

      −> **(defmacro push (e stack)**
                (list 'setq stack (list 'cons e stack)))
    push
    −>

In this definition, the formal parameter **e** will be bound to the first argument in the actual call to the macro, and **stack** to the second. This code is a bit clearer than the code we wrote above, because here we do not have to use any **caddr**s, etc., to access the actual macro arguments.

It is instructive to see how **defmacro** works. Let us use **pp** to see the function definition created for **push** by **defmacro**:

> **-> (pp push)**

```
(def push
  (macro (defmacroarg)
    ((lambda (e stack)
        (list 'setq stack (list 'cons e stack)))

      (cadr defmacroarg)
      (caddr defmacroarg)))))


  t
->
```

pp shows the definition as a macro form. We can see from this form that **defmacro** created a macro definition with the formal parameter **defmacroarg**. The body of this macro form is a call to a function which is defined as a lambda form. This lambda form was created out of the code we specified in the call to **defmacro**. The lambda form is applied to forms that will access the actual arguments by **cdr**ing down the value of **defmacroarg**. In effect, this code is an instance of the technique we discussed in the chapter on lambda in which lambda is used as a quick and clean way to temporarily bind values to some variables.

So **defmacro** produces some code on its own, in addition to the code with which we actually supply it. We have seen some other functions that do likewise. For example, we noted that **defun** will build lambda, nlambda, and lexpr forms from a rather different surface syntax. How do these functions perform such transformations? Anytime you see a function that produces some code of its own, you should suspect that a macro is at work. And indeed, such is the case here. **defmacro** and **defun** are themselves macros. A call to **defmacro** expands into a call to **def** of the form shown above, and a call to **defun** also expands into the appropriate call to **def**.

There is nothing special about the definitions of the macros **defun** or **defmacro**. They are macros that happen to have the effect of defining other functions. We could write them ourselves with what we now know. We will not go into the details of these function definitions here, however. But you should go through the above examples and be sure you understand all the different levels involved.

13.7. THE let MACRO

As we mentioned, the code produced by **defmacro** uses lambda as a way of
scoping variables. When we introduced this idea in the section on lambda,
we mentioned that, while this code is efficient, it has a certain visually
displeasing aspect to it. We also promised to show a more aesthetic version
that uses macros. To refresh your memory, we gave the following example.
In this example we used lambda to change the value of the global variable
user−utility−function for the duration of a call to **user−utility**:

> **((lambda (user−utility−function) (user−utility a b c))**
>   **'special−function)**

Here **user−utility−function** is bound to the value **special−function** for the
duration of the call to **user−utility**. This function presumably references
the free variable **user−utility−function** during its execution. The value of
this variable is automatically restored to its previous value when the application of the lambda form is completed.

To make this prettier, we introduce the **let** macro. This macro has the following syntax:

> **(let ((***par1 val1***) (***par2 val2***) ... (***parn valn***))**
>   *exp1 exp2 ... expm*)

A call to **let** causes the following to happen: Each of the parameters *par1,
par2,* etc., is bound to the value of the corresponding *val1, val2,* etc. Then
the expressions *exp1* through *expm* are evaluated. Finally, the parameters
are restored to their old values.

let works by turning the call to **let** into a **lambda**. Thus the general call to
let shown above turns into the following:

> **((lambda (***par1 par2 ... parn***)** *exp1 exp2 ... expm*)
>   *val1 val2 ... valn*)

For example, the lambda form we used for **user−utility** could have been
written with **let** as follows:

> **(let ((user−utility−function 'special−function))**
>   **(user−utility a b c))**

Most programmers find this more pleasing than allowing a lambda form to appear explicitly.

The macro definition for **let** is somewhat more complicated than those of other macros we have seen. **let** has to do a bit of work in order to build a lambda form from its input. This is mostly because the variables and values in the call to **let** appear in a very different arrangement than they do in the lambda form. But in principle, this definition is no different than simpler ones. Fortunately, **let** is defined for us in Franz, so we need not bother with the complexities of its definition here.

13.8. setf

There are several LISP functions we have seen that change things. For example, **setq** changes values, and **putprop** changes property values. There are some other functions for changing other kinds of values we will encounter later on. However, rather than have a diverse set of functions to alter various kinds of values, some programmers prefer to have only one function for changing things. Depending upon how we call this function, it might perform any of the operations mentioned above.

Franz LISP provides this facility with the built-in macro **setf**. Depending upon how you call **setf**, it will change into the appropriate alteration function. For example, if I call **setf** specifying an atom on the left-hand side, **setf** turns into a **setq**, e. g.:

> $->$ **(macroexpand '(setf a 'b))**
> **(setq a 'b)**
> $->$

However, if the left-hand side of the call to **setf** is a call to the function **get**, the **setf** turns into a **putprop**:

> $->$ **(macroexpand '(setf (get x 'color) 'red))**
> **(putprop x 'red 'color)**
> $->$

In general, a call to **setf** is interpreted as a command to change the value that would be accessed by the first argument to the value of the second argument.

Using a macro like **setf** is mostly a matter of taste. If you have a version of **setf** that you can modify, you may find it easier to extend **setf** rather than write a new setting function for a new type of change operation.

13.9. AESTHETIC USE OF MACROS

The use of macros is limited only by your own creativity. For example, if you are appalled by the lack of mnemonic value for the names of LISP's mapping functions, you can define a macro to remedy this. Let us call this macro **for**. Depending on how it is called, **for** will turn into a call to the appropriate mapping function. The basic call to **for** could have the following form:

>   (for (x in l) (do (foo x)))

Here the literals **in** and **do** are keywords that denote which form of mapping is desired. The clause containing the keyword **in** means that we want the function to apply to successive **cars** of a list. The list is specified next. In other words, **in** means that we want to produce either a **mapc** or a **mapcar**. The clause beginning with **do** allows us to specify the body of the function to be applied to the formal argument; in particular **do** means that this body should simply be executed, and the results thrown away. Thus, **do** would be used if we want to specify either a **map** or a **mapc**. The combination of **in** and **do** is therefore equivalent to **mapc**. Hence the following would be the macro expansion of the call to **for** given above:

>   (mapc 'foo l)

Similarly, using the keyword **on** instead of **in** might denote a mapping function which applies to successive **cdrs** of a list. And in addition to **do**, we might have a number of options. For example, the keyword **save** would mean to collect the result of each function application in a list, and return this as the value. Thus we would have the following calls and associated expansions:

>   (for (x on l) (do (foo x))) =>
>   (map 'foo l)
>
>   (for (x in l) (save (foo x))) =>
>   (mapcar 'foo l)

We can add additional flourishes. For example, we can have an optional **when** clause that allows the specification of a condition which must be met before the action clause is executed, e. g.:

>   (for (x in l) (when (test x)) (do (foo x))) =>
>   (mapc '(lambda (x) (cond ((test x) (foo x)))) l)

for is a relatively smart macro. It performs a complicated translation operation. For example, sometimes it will actually produce a lambda form with a formal parameter in it. Sometimes it will throw away the user-specified formal parameter because it can use a map function directly. We will not show a definition for **for** here, but a definition for a nearly identical macro is given in Charniak et al. (1979).

13.10 MACRO ODDS AND ENDS

Macros are the most general LISP function type. You can do anything with a macro that you can do with a fexpr, lexpr, or expr (although doing so may not be as efficient). Alternatively, you can simulate most of the power of macros using fexprs. This can be done by defining a fexpr that creates the desired piece of code and then explicitly **eval**s it. One problem here is that there is no good way to replace the call to such a fexpr with the intermediate code the macro produces, so this technique is inherently more inefficient than using real macros. Also, fexprs are only passed the argument list, and not the entire s-expression appearing in a call. Thus you cannot use a fexpr to simulate a macro that depends on receiving the entire calling s-expression (although such macros are extremely rare).

Some programmers object to the liberal use of macros of the sort suggested above. Their complaint is directed mostly at macros like **for** and **let**, which have their own internal syntax. The problem here is that each of these macros has its own complicated internal structure. Hence one needs to learn what is essentially a new language in order to manipulate programs containing such macros. The macro definitions collectively constitute the compiler for this language. Thus, one is no longer programming in LISP, but in some other language in which some of the elegance and simplicity of LISP are lost.

I find this argument to be valid, but not too damaging. One does indeed often use LISP as a way to implement the language one really wishes one had in the first place. But this is probably an important reason why researchers in artificial intelligence like LISP. Problems in AI are generally less well understood than those in other areas, so the basic primitives that one would want in a language are less clear. Instead, AI needs a language where it is easy to define what you want as you go along.

So it is true that many AI programs are in effect written in their own language. But it is probably the case that the need to develop these languages is intrinsic to the problem. It is a strength of LISP that one can develop such languages so easily. And of course, all the aspects of LISP still are operative in these languages. So the full power of LISP is available in each case.

13.11. MACRO REPLACEMENT

Most LISPs give you a choice of whether you want macros in your code to be replaced by the code they produce the first time they are run. In Franz, if you set the global variable **displace—macros** to non-**nil**, the interpreter will replace macros with their expansions. If you leave this variable set to **nil**, LISP will re-expand your macros each time it encounters them.

For example, suppose a call to the macro **let** appears in a function definition:

```
-> (defun test-function (x) (let ((y x)) (list y)))
test-function
->
```

test—function is just an expr that binds **y** to the value of **x**. Then it returns the list of this value.

Initially, the value of **displace—macros** is **nil**, so executing this function definition will not change anything:

```
-> displace-macros
nil
-> (test-function '(a b c))
((a b c))
-> (pp test-function)

(def test-function
  (lambda (x)
    (let ((y x)) (list y))))

t
```

But now let us change the value of **displace—macros** and try this again:

```
-> (setq displace-macros t)
t
-> (test-function '(a b c))
((a b c))
```

```
-> (pp test-function)

(def test-function
  (lambda (x)
    ((lambda (y)
       (list y))
     x)))

t
->
```

The actual code we wrote has been changed. The function definition now contains the code produced by the call to the macro **let** instead of the call to the macro itself. The next time we evaluate this function, it will not have to expand the macro again. Therefore, it will execute faster than it did the first time. The price we pay for this is that the code no longer looks just like the code we wrote.

13.12. SUMMARY

(1) A *macro* is a LISP function that is evaluated in two phases. The first phase produces a piece of code, called the *macro expansion*. In the second phase, the macro expansion produced in the first phase is evaluated.

(2) A macro is a good way to write aesthetically pleasing but efficient code. Macros are efficient if the LISP implementation allows for calls to macros to be replaced by their macro expansions after they are initially evaluated.

(3) A macro can be defined by either **defun**, **def**, or the special macro defining function **defmacro**. The underlying *macro form* tolerates only a single formal parameter. However, the function **defmacro** lets the user specify any number of formal parameters.

(4) When a call to a macro occurs, the formal parameter of the macro is bound to the entire calling expression. None of the actual arguments supplied to the macro is evaluated. Then the body of the macro is evaluated to produce an executable s-expression. This s-expression is then evaluated and its value returned as the value of the macro call.

(5) The expr **macroexpand** is useful to debug macro definitions. **macroexpand** expands the macro calls in its argument, and returns the resulting code as its value.

(6). A good way to write macros is to first write down a sample macro call and the code it should produce. Then write a macro definition that translates one into the other.

(7) Some useful general macros are **pop, push, let**, and **setf**. In addition, some familiar built-in LISP functions like **defun** turn out to be written as macros.

(8) In Franz, calls to macros will be replaced by their macro expansions if the atom **displace—macros** is bound to a non-**nil** value.

Exercises

(1) Write macros **head** and **tail** which expand into calls to **car** and **cdr**, respectively.

(2) Write a macro **IF** that translates calls of the form **(IF a THEN b)** into **cond**s of the form **(cond (a b))**, and `calls of the form **(IF a THEN b ELSE c)** into **cond**s of the form **(cond (a b) (t c))**.

(3) Write a version of the **for** macro described above that provides a uniform way of expressing calls to mapping functions.

(4) Some LISP programmers prefer not to use **go**s explicitly in their code. Instead, they write macros that expand into **prog**s.

Define a macro **while** that can be called with expressions of the form **(while test exp1 exp2 ...)**. As long as the expression **test** evaluates to true, **while** repeatedly evaluates the expressions **exp1, exp2**, etc.

while should translate into a call to **prog** which contains an explicit call to **go**. It is possible to write a more complete (and more complicated) version iteration macro. See Charniak et al. (1979) for an example of such a macro.

(5) Write the functions **de** and **df** as macros. Recall that **de** and **df** are used to define exprs and fexprs, respectively. Write a macro **dm** that can be used similarly to define macros.

14

Read Macros

14.1. INTRODUCTION

So far in this book, we have been largely concerned with how s-expressions are evaluated by the LISP interpreter once they have been read in. This is not remarkable, since the process of evaluation is central to LISP. However, we have also made an effort to consider LISP as a real programming language and not an abstract formalism. As such, issues such as the user interface, implementation details, error handling, debugging, compiling, and interacting with the operating system become equally important. The rest of this book is primarily concerned with such issues.

In this chapter we examine a technique that gives the LISP programmer the ability to modify the way expressions are read in by the interpreter. This involves the use of a device called a *read macro*. Through the use of read macros, the user can designate special characters which act in unusual ways. This gives the user the ability to establish some useful shorthands that simplify some programming tasks. We discuss how to define read macros, and suggest some uses for them. One particularly useful read macro, called the *backquote* macro, is discussed in some detail.

197

14.2. EXECUTING FUNCTIONS DURING read

Suppose Franz LISP had no special symbol for **quote**. With the machinery we have seen so far, we would have no way to extend Franz to accept the special notation we have been using. Of course, this is not a real problem. Virtually all LISPs come equipped with a built-in special symbol for **quote**. But we may need to define other special symbols that behave similarly to **quote**. And right now, we have no way to do so.

To provide such a facility, some LISP interpreters allow the programmer to attach arbitrary functions to individual characters. When LISP reads in a character that has a function attached to it, LISP fetches the function associated with that character, and evaluates it. LISP throws away the original character, and instead, returns the value computed by the attached function.

For example, if we wanted to set up a special character for **quote**, assuming that none existed, we could do so by attaching the following function to the **quote** character ':

> **(lambda () (list (quote quote) (read)))**

First, note that this is a function of no arguments. Hence we can always evaluate its body without worrying about there being actual arguments to apply it to. When we do evaluate this body, LISP will produce a list whose first element is the atom **quote**, and the second the s-expression read in by the explicit call to **read**. If we attach this function to the character ', and type **'a**, this would turn into the list **(quote a)**.

Thus the special character for **quote** works by expanding into a normal LISP s-expression. For this reason, characters that have functions so attached to them are called *read macros*. Like ordinary macros, the body of a read macro produces as its value a piece of LISP code. However, unlike ordinary macros, which are expanded during evaluation, read macros are expanded during the **read** phase of LISP's **read-eval-print** loop.

The example above illustrates an important point about read macros. Note that for our read macro for **quote** to work, it had to read in the next s-expression explicitly. That is, **read** does not anticipate what a read macro will do or try to help out in any special way. If the read macro wants to get at something in the input stream, it must call **read** again recursively. (This is recursive because we must already be inside a call to **read** in order to be evaluating a read macro to begin with. Most of the time, this call to **read** will be implicit within LISP's top level **read-eval-print** loop.) This recursive call to **read** will swallow up a bit of input. When control is returned to the outer level, the outer **read** just continues by reading in the characters

198

following those swallowed up by the recursive call. So if our **quote** character occurs in the middle of an expression, as in **(a 'b c)**, the read macro will cause **b** to be read in explicitly, and will return **(quote b)**. The **read** in which all this is going on will see **c** as the next atom to be read, and will therefore return the list **(a (quote b) c)**. This is just the result we want.

Let us look at another simple example. Suppose we want a shorthand for saying **(pp foo)** (recall that **pp** pretty-prints function definitions). One way to do this is to attach a function to a character, say >, so that >**foo** will turn into **(pp foo)**. To do so, we need only attach the following read macro definition to the colon character:

> **(lambda () (list 'pp (read)))**

This definition is almost identical to that for **quote**. If we attach this function to >, then >**foo** will expand to the list **(pp foo)**. LISP will then evaluate this expression, resulting in the function definition of **foo** being pretty-printed.

14.3. DEFINING READ MACROS

We have not yet seen how to attach a read macro definition to a character. Unfortunately, the syntax for doing so in Franz LISP is a bit baroque. To implement the previous read macro, for example, I would have to type the following:

> — > (setsyntax '> 'vmacro '(lambda () (list 'pp (read))))
> **t**
> — >

setsyntax is a general Franz LISP function for altering the way LISP reads individual characters. Here we are using **setsyntax** to set the syntax of > to **vmacro**, which is Franz's way of designating a read macro. Finally, we specify the function for this particular read macro.

setsyntax has many other uses which do not concern us here (see Appendix A if you are interested). However, it would be simpler if we had a function just for defining read macros. That is, we could have a fexpr or macro **drm** (for "define read macro ") that is called as follows:

> — > (drm > (lambda () (list 'pp (read))))
> **t**
> — >

drm would work by calling **setsyntax**, but is a bit simpler to use. Writing **drm** is a fairly simple task. I leave it as an exercise to the reader.

Using either **setsyntax** or **drm** to define a read macro for >, I could then do the following:

>   —> **(defun foo (x y) (cons y x))**
> **foo**
> —> **>foo**
>
> **(def foo**
>   **(lambda (x y)**
>   **(cons y x)))**
>
>
> **t**
> —>

Note that if you define a character as a read macro, it becomes just about unusable anywhere else. For example, if I want to have a variable named **a>b**, I would have to say **a\ >b**, where the \ instructs LISP to take the next character literally. The first example would be interpreted as two separate s-expressions, namely, **a** and **(pp b)**, as the read macro is treated as a separator and causes **read** to think it has finished reading an atom.

There is a way in Franz to circumvent this problem, and to define read macros that are only effective if they do not appear in the middle of what would otherwise be an atom. We will not worry about this flourish here.

14.4. SPLICING MACROS

Suppose we want to use a read macro to define a comment character. A reasonable way to do this would be to have the read macro read individual characters, discarding them until it came to the end of the line. For example, we could do the following:

> —> **(drm \! (lambda ()**
>   **(prog () loop (cond ((not (equal (readc) Newline))**
>   **(go loop))))))**
> **t**
> —>

Note that in this example, I backquoted **!**. This is not really necessary in this case, as **!** is an ordinary LISP character. But in general, characters used for read macros will tend to be unusual ones, so it is safest to backquote them. Also, **readc** is a function that reads in a single character and returns it as an atom; I assume that **Newline** is bound to the UNIX "newline" character. This is not true in Franz to begin with, so we would need to have bound it explicitly for this to really work.

Even if we did so, this definition of ! would not work very well. Read macros always return a value to the call to **read** in which they occur. ! returns **nil**. Thus if a comment using ! appeared within an s-expression that ran on for a few lines, we would end up with an extra **nil** in the expression. For example,

> **(and (foo x) !here is a comment**
> **(baz x))**

would turn into

> **(and (foo x) nil (baz x))**

where the **nil** came from the comment read macro. And this can hardly be what we want!

To solve this problem, we need to introduce a new kind of read macro. This is called a *splicing macro*. A splicing macro is just like a read macro, except that rather than returning its result to **read**, the result of a splicing macro is spliced into the list that **read** is currently putting together.

To illustrate this idea of splicing, suppose we had an ordinary read macro % that simply returned **(a b c)**, e. g., **(x % y)** would be read as **(x (a b c) y)**. But if % were a splicing macro, the same input would be read as **(x a b c y)**. The list returned by the macro was spliced into the list **read** was building, rather than stuck into the list as a single element.

Getting back to our comment character example, suppose we define ! as a splicing macro, but with exactly the same definition as given above. ! will still ignore all characters to the end of a line, and return **nil**. But this result will now get spliced into the list currently being read in, rather than inserted into this list. However, since the value computed by ! is the empty list, splicing this value into another list does not change that other list at all. Of course, this is just the effect we were trying to achieve.

To define a splicing macro, we make a call to **setsyntax**, but supply an argument of **vsplicing—macro** rather than **vmacro**. For example, to define !, we type the following:

```
-> (setsyntax '\! 'vsplicing-macro
        '(lambda ()
              (prog () loop (cond ((not (eq (readc) Newline))
                                  (go loop))))))
t
->
```

Of course, we could define a function **dsm** ("define splicing macro") to make writing these macros easier.

The nature of splicing macros imposes some constraints on them. Since there must always be some list for a splicing macro to splice into, splicing macros must always appear inside some other s-expression. Similarly, since the value computed by the splicing macro is to be spliced into a list, splicing macros must always return a list. In practice, splicing macros are used very rarely, and almost always return **nil**.

14.5. THE BACKQUOTE MACRO

Franz LISP contains some useful built-in read macros. One of these is called the *backquote* macro. It is particularly useful when writing macro function definitions.

The idea of the backquote macro is the following. Usually, in LISP, we evaluate expressions, and prevent evaluation by preceding an expression by **quote**. However, an expression that is backquoted works just the opposite way: All its elements are not evaluated *unless* they are preceded by something that explicitly indicates evaluation.

In Franz, the character ` (backquote) indicates the backquote read macro; the character , (comma) within a backquoted expression indicates evaluation.

For example, if we backquote an entire expression, all the elements in it are not evaluated. This is just as if we used **quote**:

```
-> `(a b c)
(a b c)
->
```

However, if any of these elements are preceded by a comma, then its *value* will be used instead. For example:

```
-> (setq b '(x y z))
(x y z)
-> '(a ,b c)
(a (x y z) c)
->
```

The interpretation of backquote, then, is "do not evaluate any of elements in a backquoted s-expression, unless the s-expression is preceded by a comma".

In addition, if an expression within a backquoted s-expression is preceded by the characters ,@ (comma followed by at-sign), the value of the expression is spliced into the backquoted list, rather than inserted into it. So we have the following:

```
-> '(a ,@b c)
(a x y z c)
->
```

We sometimes refer to the comma as "unquote" and the comma-at-sign as "splice-unquote".

Note that the unquote and splice-unquote designators can appear anyway within a backquote s-expression. For example, the following is perfectly legal:

```
-> '(a (b (c (d ,b e) f) g) h)
(a (b (c (d (x y z) e) f) g) h)
->
```

Let us consider for a moment how the backquote macro works. When a backquote appears, the backquote read macro is thereby executed. It explicitly calls **read** to read in the next s-expression. The next s-expression is likely to contain occurrences of the unquote and splice-unquote read macros. Each of these macros explicitly reads in the next s-expression. Each simply returns a list of the argument prefaced by a special symbol. For example, **,a** might expand into something like (***unquote* a**), and **,@a** into (***splice—unquote* a**). Thus the s-expression backquote reads in will arrive with all occurrences of unquote and splice-unquote macros expanded to contain forms like the above. For example, if we type in **'(a ,b c)**, the backquote macro will get to see the s-expression (**a (*unquote* b) c**).

So the backquote macro will call **read** on an input like (**a ,b c**), and **read** will return an s-expression like (**a (*unquote* b) c**). The backquote read macro looks for the appearance of special forms beginning with ***unquote*** or

∗**splice—unquote**∗ in the list it reads in. If it sees them, it composes whatever sequence of function calls is necessary to build up the appropriate list. In our example above, it would need to build an s-expression that **cons**s the value of **b** onto the list (**c**), and then **cons**s the value of **a** onto the result. That is, backquote would have to return an expression like (**cons 'a (cons b '(c))**). Remember, backquote is just a read macro. The s-expression it returns will normally be evaluated by LISP's **read-eval-print** loop. So backquote must return a LISP s-expression that evaluates to the desired list.

We can see the form that backquote actually creates before it is evaluated simply by quoting the expression that is read in. For example,

```
-> ''(a ,b c)
(cons 'a (cons b '(c)))
->
```

Remember, read macros get expanded at **read** time, not during evaluation. Therefore, they are expanded as soon as they are read in, even if they appear in an expression that is not evaluated. This would not be true of ordinary macros. If I quoted an expression that began with an ordinary macro, it would not be evaluated and the macro would not be expanded. But an expression that begins with a read macro, like '(a ,b c), will always get expanded, in this case, to (**cons 'a (cons b '(c)))** .

Be warned that the backquote macro may do a considerable amount of transparent **cons**ing. In order to produce expressions like the one above, backquote must generate whatever calls to **cons** are necessary to do the job. For example, suppose we backquote a relatively long expression:

```
-> ''(a (b (c (d ,b e) f) g) h)
(cons 'a
       (cons (cons 'b
               (cons (cons 'c
                       (cons (cons 'd
                               (cons b '(e)))
                             '(f))
                      '(g)))
              '(h)) )
->
```

As we can see, the expression whose value we wanted occurs deeply within this list. So we must do quite a bit of list building to compute the desired list.

You should think of the backquote macro as a shorthand for writing code that builds up s-expressions. This is quite a contrast to **quote**, for example, which just prevents evaluation of an existing expression.

14.5.1. Using Backquote in Macro Definitions

The·primary purpose of backquote is to help write macro definitions. Remember, macros always return code that is then evaluated. The body of a macro spends all its energy building up an s-expression which is mostly the same from occurrence to occurrence. The only thing that changes is the part of the code that comes from the actual arguments. Backquote is a great help here. It allows us to specify our macro function definition as a kind of template of the code we would like to have it produce.

For example, consider the definition of the macro **push** in the last chapter. Recall that a call to **push** of the form **(push e stack)** should turn into code of the form **(setq stack (cons e stack))**.

Even using **defmacro**, our definition of this macro looked rather opaque:

```
-> (defmacro push (e stack)
        (list 'setq stack (list 'cons e stack)))
push
->
```

However, using backquote, we can write this as follows. We can backquote a template of the code we would like to produce. Within this template, the parts of the code that come from the arguments will be prefaced by unquote read macros. Thus we would have the following alternative definition:

```
-> (defmacro push (e stack)
        `(setq ,stack (cons ,e ,stack)))
push
->
```

This definition is almost identical to the code we want it to produce.

Remember, one should think of backquote as a shorthand for writing code that builds up an s-expression. Backquote just saves us the trouble of writing out a lot of **cons**es, etc., by hand. The body of the functions so produced will still contain all these **cons**es in it. For example, here is the actual definition produce by the call to **defmacro** above:

```
-> (pp push)

(def push
  (macro (defmacroarg)
    ((lambda (e stack)
           (list 'setq stack (list 'cons e stack)))

      (cadr defmacroarg)
      (caddr defmacroarg)))))


t
->
```

14.6. SUMMARY

(1)   A *read macro* is a function that is attached to an individual character and executed when that character is seen by **read**. The result of a read macro is inserted into the s-expression currently under construction by **read**. The character to which the read macro is attached is discarded.

(2)   A *splicing macro* is a kind of read macro. Unlike ordinary read macros, which insert the value they compute into the list under construction, splicing macros splice the value they compute into the list under construction. A splicing macro should always return a list as its value.

(3)   Both ordinary read macros and splicing macros are defined using the expr **setsyntax**. This takes three arguments: the character to which the read macro should be attached, the symbol **vmacro** or **vsplicing—macro**, and a function of no arguments to attach to the character.

(4)   A particularly useful read macro is called *backquote*. It is designated by the character ' (backquote). The elements in a backquoted s-expression are not evaluated, unless they are preceded by the character , (comma) or @, (comma followed by at-sign). In the former case, the value of the element is inserted into the backquoted expression; in the latter, it is spliced into it. Backquote is particularly useful for writing macro function definitions.

Exercises

(1)   Implement the read macro > that pretty-prints out the next symbol. However, use your own definition of pretty-print that you wrote as an exercise in the chapter on I/O.

(2)   Write the macros **drm** and **dsm** that define read macros and splicing macros, respectively.

(3)   Rewrite the macro definitions of the previous chapter using the backquote macro. For example, write a macro definition of **pop**, and of the macros **while**, **de**, and **df** given in the exercises.

(4)   Create a new comment character called %. Unlike the standard LISP comment character, the new character will ignore everything up to and including the next occurrence of %.

(5)   Many artificial intelligence programs use a technique called *pattern matching*. (We will discuss pattern matching in detail in Chapter 21.) A basic application of pattern matching is to have a data base of facts of the form **(human John)**, **(human Bill)**, **(dog Fido)**. Then, to find out which elements are known to be human, the program can query the data base with a *pattern* like **(human ?x)**. The item **?x** is meant to denote a sort of variable that matches actual items. The result of the query should be a list of all elements in the data base that match the entire pattern.

However, we need to let our pattern matcher know that items like **?x** are meant to be treated specially. One way to do this is to make **?** a read macro so that **?x** turns into a form like **(*var* x)**. Then the pattern matcher can be on the lookout for forms of this kind.

Define **?** as a read macro having the behavior just described.

15

Dotted Pairs and Other Internals

15.1. INTRODUCTION

All the s-expressions we have seen have been either lists or atoms. S-expressions are actually somewhat more general than this, due largely to the way LISP is implemented. I have avoided discussing general s-expressions thus far because it is better to have an understanding of LISP in terms of lists first. But there are some aspects of the language for which an understanding of the implementation is necessary.

In this chapter we present the data structures that underlie lists, which are called *dotted pairs*. We show how lists are implemented in terms of dotted pairs, and how to enter and manipulate dotted pairs directly. We look at some of the consequences of this implementation. In particular, we examine the problems that arise from having multiple pointers to the same data object. We discuss some LISP operations that make sense in terms of this implementation, namely, the modification of existing lists. The possible horrors that may result from such manipulation are graphically depicted. Finally, we discuss when such implementation details should be considered to gain advantages in efficiency.

15.2. INTERNAL REPRESENTATION OF LISTS

Lists are represented in LISP using binary trees. As we all know, binary trees have nodes with exactly two pointers in them, one pointing to the left subtree and one pointing to the right subtree. In addition, binary trees can also have terminal nodes; in the case of LISP, terminal nodes are always atoms. LISP uses binary trees to represent lists as follows: The left subtree of a node points to the first element of a list, and the right subtree points to the rest of the list. For example, the list **(a b c)** is represented as the following binary tree:

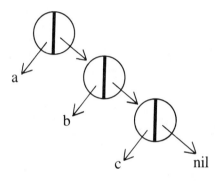

Note that the last node of the tree contains a right pointer to the atom **nil**. This is a convention indicating that there are no more elements in the list.

A list may have an element that is itself a list. Such a list will have a some- what more complicated appearence, but will still conform to the structure described above. For example, here is the LISP representation of the list **(a (b c) d)**:

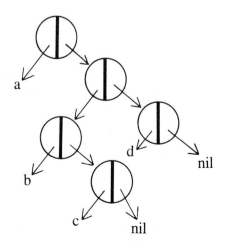

Here the left pointer of the second node of the top level list points to an object which itself represents a list.

Since lists are implemented in terms of binary trees, the various list manipulation functions we have seen carry out their function in terms of binary tree manipulation. For example, when we bind an atom to some value, LISP implements this by associating with that atom a pointer to the desired value. If the value is a list, the pointer points to the root node of the tree representing that list. Thus if **x** were bound to the list **(a b c)**, the value pointer of **x** would point to the root of the tree representing **(a b c)**.

When we perform a **car** or a **cdr**, we are actually passing around LISP pointers. For example, when we ask LISP to evaluate **(cdr '(a b c))**, LISP starts at the root node of the tree representing **(a b c)**. It merely returns the right pointer of this node. This pointer points to a tree that represents the list **(b c)**, which is what we want. Similarly, **car** just returns the left pointer, which by convention points to the first element of the list. **cons** works by fetching an unused node from memory, and making its left pointer point to the first argument and its right pointer to the second. Then **cons** returns a pointer to this new node. You should make sure you understand why this implements **cons**.

15.3. DOTTED PAIR NOTATION

A node of a LISP binary tree is often called a **cons** cell. Each cell can be specified explicitly by the LISP user. This is done much in the same way in which LISP allows you to specify lists. To specify a single binary tree node, the user enters the values for the left and right parts of the cell, separated by the character **.** (period), and encloses the whole business in parentheses. For example, if I want to designate a node with left pointer pointing to **a** and with right pointer pointing to **nil**, I would type **(a . nil)**.

This notation for a node of a binary tree is called a *dotted pair*. The function **read** recognizes dotted pair notation. However, LISP is usually used to manipulate lists. Thus wherever possible, the function **print** tries to print out binary trees using the sort of list notation with which we have become familiar. The top level of LISP, which uses **read** and **print**, will therefore accept dotted pair notation. But it will usually print things out using list notation. For example, look what happens when I type the following dotted pair into LISP:

```
-> '(a . nil)
(a)
->
```

read recognizes the input as a representation for the list **(a)**. Had we actually typed in **(a)**, **read** would have built exactly the same internal representation. In either case, the structure can be interpreted as a list. Therefore, **print** outputs the structure using list notation (i. e., without dots) as opposed to the dotted pair notation we used to enter the object.

Since every list is represented by a binary tree, we can enter any list using dotted pair notation. For example, consider the list **(a b c)**. As we can see from its binary tree representation given above, this list consists of three dotted pairs, one corresponding to each internal node of the binary tree in the diagram. The first node is equivalent to **a** dotted with the list **(b c)**. This list, in turn, consists of **b** dotted with the list **(c)**, which in turn consists of **c** dotted with **nil**. Or using dotted pair notation, we could express the whole list as **(a . (b . (c . nil)))**.

To make sure we got this right, let us type it into LISP:

```
-> '(a . (b . (c . nil)))
(a b c)
->
```

We typed in a complicated dotted pair. LISP cleverly recognized this representation as denoting a list, and, upon output, printed it out using list notation.

List notation is just a user convenience. It is easier to type and read **(a b c)** than **(a . (b . (c . nil)))**, so LISP was designed to accept the former notation on input and use it on output whenever it can. Internally, remember, both notations turn into exactly the same binary tree structure. This structure is more transparently reflected by the dotted pair notation, but the list notation tends to be more convenient for the user.

You can freely mix these notations if you like. For example, I could also have entered the list **(a b c)** as follows:

```
-> '(a . (b c))
(a b c)
->
```

Well, it seems as if the dotted pair notation is just a cumbersome way of typing in lists. It is true that this notation is inferior to the list notation for typing in lists. But the notation is necessary because *there are dotted pairs that are not lists.* Note that in all the examples we have seen, the last node of the tree representing the list always had a right pointer of **nil**. As we stated, this is a convention used to indicate the end of the list. But given the dotted pair notation, what is to prevent us from entering a dotted pair that ends in something other than **nil**? Nothing:

```
-> '(a . b)
(a . b)
->
```

Here is a dotted pair whose right pointer points to the atom **b**. As this does not correspond to any list, **print** is forced to print it out using the more cumbersome dotted pair notation.

As we mentioned above, the functions that we learned for symbolic manipulation on lists really operate on dotted pairs. Thus even though dotted pairs are a more general data type than lists, we need not learn a new set of functions to operate on them. For example, we can apply **car** and **cdr** to dotted pairs that are not lists:

```
-> (car '(a . b))
a
-> (cdr '(a . b))
b
->
```

and we can use **cons** to create a new dotted pair that is not a list:

```
-> (cons 'a 'b)
(a . b)
-> (cons 'a nil)
(a)
->
```

As we can see, the case where the underlying objects happen to be lists is really a special case. In general, if you want to determine if it is reasonable to take a **car** or **cdr** of some LISP object, the correct thing to do is to ask if that object is a dotted pair. LISP supplies a predicate just for this purpose, called **dtpr**. Thus we have the following:

```
-> (dtpr '(a b c))
t
```

```
-> (dtpr 1)
nil
-> (dtpr 'a)
nil
-> (dtpr nil)
nil
->
```

15.4. MULTIPLE POINTERS TO THE SAME OBJECT

The underlying representation used by LISP gives us some important insights into the way the basic LISP functions operate. For example, as mentioned above, the function **cdr** works by following the right pointer of a binary tree node. This means that, if the value returned by **cdr** is remembered by one's program, we may end up with more than one pointer to the same data object. For example, suppose we did the following:

```
-> (setq x '(a b c))
(a b c)
-> (setq y (cdr x))
(b c)
->
```

cdr returns a pointer to the second node of the tree representing **(a b c)**. **setq** just associates this pointer with **y**. Hence **y** and the right pointer of the root node of **(a b c)** point to exactly the same internal LISP structure. We can diagram this situation as follows:

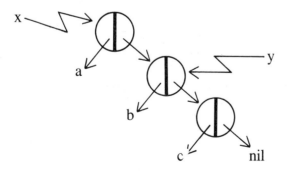

Note that if I assigned a value to **y** by typing **(setq y '(b c))**, LISP would allocate new storage to represent **(b c)**. Then the values of **x** and **y** would not share anything in common. This situation would have the following

213

internal representation:

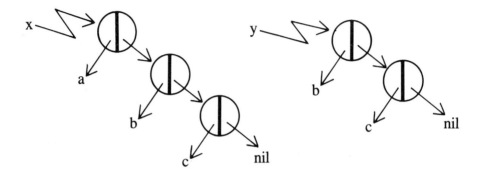

But we now have a somewhat tricky situation on our hands. Quite different LISP internal configurations can look exactly alike as far as their LISP value is concerned. For example, in the two cases just cited, the value of **x** is **(a b c)** and the value of **y** is **(b c)**. However, in the first case, **x** and **y** share the representation for **(b c)**. In the second case they do not. The values are the same, but the internal representations are different.

15.4.1. EQ

As yet we have no reason to care about this, because all the functions we have seen operate solely on values. They do not care whether a structure is really the same as another or just has the same value as another structure. But sometimes it is important to make this distinction. LISP provides us with a simple means to do so. This is via the function **eq** (pronounced "eek"). **eq** is an expr of two arguments. It returns true if the arguments evaluate to the same internal LISP pointer. It returns false otherwise.

Note that **eq** is fussier than **equal**. The latter function returns true whenever its two arguments evaluate to equivalent LISP values. In the case of **eq**, they must also point to the same exact internal representation. Thus in the two cases above, the value of **y** will always be **equal** to the value of **(car x)**, because they are both **(b c)**. But only in the first case are these **eq**, because only then do they point to the same internal representation.

Let us do an example to see that this works:

$\rightarrow$ **(setq x '(a b c))**
(a b c)

```
-> (setq y (cdr x))
(b c)
-> (equal (cdr x) y)
t
-> (eq (cdr x) y)
t
-> (setq z '(b c))
(b c)
-> (equal y z)
t
-> (eq y z)
nil
->
```

Here we first bind **x** to a value, and then bind **y** to the **cdr** of this value. In this case, both **y** and the **cdr** of **x** point to the same internal representation. Thus these values are both **equal** and **eq** to each other. Next, we bind **z** to a new list of the same form as that bound to **y**. Since it is of the same form, this new list is **equal** to the value of the **y**. But they are different lists, and hence are not **eq** to one another.

Since atoms are unique, all atoms will always be **eq** to themselves. That is, (**eq 'a 'a**) is always true. We can use this fact to define **equal** in terms of **eq**. Two s-expressions have the same value if either they are the same atom or if they are dotted pairs and their **cars** are the same and their **cdrs** are the same. Thus we have the following recursive definition:

```
-> (defun equal (x y)
       (cond [(or (atom x) (atom y)) (eq x y)]
             [(equal (car x) (car y)) (equal (cdr x) (cdr y))]))
equal
->
```

In fact, the actual definition of **equal** that LISP uses looks very much like this one.

As we can see in this definition, **eq** is not only more primitive than **equal**, but much more efficient. **equal** must run a recursive test to determine if two things are the same value. But **eq** need only check if two things are the same pointer. In most implementations, this requires only a single machine instruction. Thus most LISP programmers try to use **eq** in preference to **equal** whenever they can get away with it. For example, **eq** is used if the values one is to compare are known to be atoms, since these are guaranteed to be unique. But **equal** must be used if we want to test for equivalence of value among arbitrary lists.

Since **eq** is more efficient than **equal**, LISP generally supplies an **eq** version of every function that does some testing for equality. For example, we mentioned that **member** tests if its first argument is a member of its second. Since it uses **equal** to make this test, **member** will be needlessly slow if the list contains only atoms. So LISP provides an **eq** version of **member** called **memq**. **memq** works just like **member**, except that it uses **eq** rather than **equal** as it goes down the list.

15.5. THE EVIL OF rplaca AND rplacd

Most of the functions we have seen so far do not change existing objects. For example, although we said informally that **car** and **cdr** tear apart lists, we noted several times that they are actually non-destructive. These functions work by merely passing around pointers to parts of an s-expression. Similarly, **cons** creates a new dotted pair that points to old ones. But it leaves the old ones unchanged.

It is possible in LISP to alter an existing LISP object. But before I tell you how to do this, let me warn you. *There is nothing more dangerous or irksome in LISP than modifying an existing object.* Here is why. As we mentioned above, after doing some **cars** and **cdrs** on an existing LISP value, we often end up with several pointers to the same internal structure. Normally, if we only compare this structure with others or make new structures point at it, this would not cause any problems. However, suppose I *altered* the list I found at the end of one of these pointers. Since other LISP objects may point to this same list, I may have unknowingly altered the value of any number of other objects. When your program crashes because of this, it will no doubt crash when you are manipulating one of these unintentionally changed objects. You will not know where to look for the problem, because it really occurred when your program was doing some conceptually unrelated task.

Even worse, the program is likely to work just fine the first time through, but leave behind a data structure that resembles a plate of spaghetti. The second time through, everything will not look as it should, and the program will flounder.

It is even hard to look at some of the structures that can be created this way. For example, it is possible to construct circular lists that point to themselves. When LISP tries to print these out, it blindly follows pointers and so prints something like

216

> **circular-list**
> **(a b c a b c a b c ....**

until you stop it.

So. Whenever you find yourself writing a piece of code that involves actually changing a list, stop. Ask yourself why you are doing it and if it is really necessary. Are you sure? Are you sure it will work? Better have answers to these questions then, or you may never know what hit you.

And do not say that you were not warned that the following material is for mature audiences only.

The basic LISP functions for altering lists are called **rplaca** and **rplacd**, for "replace car" and "replace cdr", respectively. Each is an expr of two arguments. **rplaca** replaces the left pointer (i. e., the **car** side) of its first argument with its second. The altered **cons** cell is returned as its value. **rplacd** does the equivalent to the right (i. e., **cdr**) pointer of the first argument.

For example, suppose **x** were bound to **(a b c)**. If I **rplaca** the value of **x** with **d**, say, the value bound to **x** would now be **(d b c)**. To wit:

> **(setq x '(a b c))**
> **(a b c)**
> **(rplaca x 'd)**
> **(d b c)**
> **x**
> **(d b c)**
>

Note that this is quite different from taking the **cdr** of **(a b c)**, **cons**ing **d** on the front of it, and **setq**ing **x** to this value. Both processes result in lists of the same value, but in very different internal structures. Most significantly, in the case where **rplaca** is used, if another LISP object contains a pointer to the list we are changing, that value will change as well. In the **setq** case, such unnerving side-effects will never occur. Consider the following example:

> **(setq x '(a b c))**
> **(a b c)**
> **(setq y x)**
> **(a b c)**
> **(eq x y)**
> **t**

```
-> (rplaca x 'd)
(d b c)
-> x
(d b c)
-> y
(d b c)
-> (eq x y)
t
->
```

Here we see how using **rplaca** changes the value bound to **y**, a variable that does not occur in the call to **rplaca**. Using **setq**, on the other hand, would not cause changes in an unmentioned value:

```
-> (setq y (cons 'e (cdr x)))
(e b c)
-> y
(e b c)
-> x
(d b c)
```

In spite of the danger involved, these list-altering functions are useful in a number of circumstances. The most compelling reason for their use is efficiency. For example, suppose I had two lists I wanted to connect together into a one big list. I could use **append**, as follows:

```
-> (setq x '(a b c))
(a b c)
-> (setq y '(d e f))
(d e f)
-> (setq z (append x y))
(a b c d e f)
-> x
(a b c)
-> y
(d e f)
-> z
(a b c d e f)
->
```

This did what we want, but was rather costly. **append** had to build a new list, for which some additional **cons** cells were required. (Actually, **append** did not have to build an entirely new list. It just had to build a copy of its first argument. Then it could point the right pointer of the last **cons** cell of this new list at the second argument. It needs to copy the first argument, of course, because if it diddled with a **cons** cell of the actual argument, it would destructively change the value of that argument. In general, if we call **append** with several arguments, it would have to make copies of all but the last one.)

consing is expensive. So if we are not too concerned about preserving the integrity of the arguments to **append**, we might be tempted to alter the last **cons** cell of the first actual argument to point to the second. This would avoid the cost of **cons**ing up a fresh copy of the first argument. To do this, we would have to follow the first argument to its last cell. Then we could do a **rplacd** to make this cell point to the second argument.

Fortunately, LISP supplies us with a built-in function that does most of this work for us. It is called **nconc**. **nconc** takes any number of arguments, all of which are evaluated. It follows each argument to its end, and destructively changes its last right pointer to point to the next argument.

Let us use **nconc** on the lists appended together in the previous example:

```
-> (setq x '(a b c))
(a b c)
-> (setq y '(d e f))
(d e f)
-> (nconc x y)
(a b c d e f)
-> x
(a b c d e f)
-> y
(d e f)
->
```

nconc changed a pointer in the final cell of the value of **x** to point at the beginning of **(d e f)**. While the value produced is the same as that produced by **append**, **nconc** altered the value of **x**. In contrast, a call to **append** would never change the value of one of its arguments.

nconc is often useful in conjunction with function mapping. In the chapter on mapping functions, we described a situation in which a function returns a list of items that fit some description. We might like to apply this function to each element in a list of arguments, and then do something with all the resulting items. The problem is that if we use **mapcar** to apply this function we will get back a list that looks something like this:

((a b c) nil (d e) nil (f g h))

That is, each application of our function returns a (possibly empty) list. But we would rather get back one big list with all the interesting elements in it, and without any additional structure:

(a b c d e f g h)

We previously mentioned one way to get the list we seek from the result of a **mapcar**. This is to apply **append** to the result of the **mapcar**. For example, if our function is called **foo**, and the list of objects we wish to apply it to is **l**, then we can do the following:

−> (apply 'append (mapcar 'foo l))
(a b c d e f g h)
−>

As we mentioned above, **append** is rather costly. However, if we are sure it is safe to alter the lists **foo** returns, we can apply **nconc** to this structure instead. This will also produce the desired result, but much more efficiently. Again, we better be sure that **foo** creates its lists from scratch. Otherwise the use of **nconc** is likely to be catastrophic.

LISP provides us with a mapping function that does all this for us. It is called **mapcan**. **mapcan** is just like **mapcar**, except that it **nconcs** together all the values that result from each function application. For example, if I had used **mapcan** in the example above, I would have gotten exactly the result I wanted:

−> (mapcan 'foo l)
(a b c d e f g h)
−>

There is also a **cdr** version of **mapcan**, called **mapcon**. In both cases, the function being applied must always return a list. And since both **mapcan** and **mapcon** use **nconc**, the lists that the function returns should not be referred to by any other structure.

Incidentally, LISP must use destructive functions for certain internal purposes. This is generally harmless, because the behavior is well understood in these cases. For example, the function **putprop** sets a given property on a property list. To do so, it must actually change the property list associated with an atom, because it would be much too expensive to build a new list every time. Since LISP users do not normally maintain their own pointers to property lists, this does not cause a problem. But should you decide to do so, be forewarned that the value at the end of your pointer may magically change after you update the property list of some atom.

15.6. SUMMARY

(1)   Lists are represented internally as binary trees. The left-hand pointer of a binary tree node points to the next element of a list; the right-hand pointer points to the rest of a list. The terminal nodes of these trees are always atoms. To represent the end of a list, a pointer to the atom **nil** is used.

(2)   We can refer to the individual nodes of a binary tree using *dotted pair* notation. The notation consists of two s-expressions separated by a dot, and surrounded by parentheses. The LISP function **print** always tries to avoid using the dotted pair notation whenever it can. It uses the list notation instead.

(3)   There are dotted pairs that are not lists. These are the dotted pairs whose right-hand pointer points to an atom other than **nil**.

(4)   Internally, LISP functions are implemented in terms of dotted pair manipulation. List processing is just a special case of dotted pair processing.

(5)   It is possible to have many pointers to the same internal LISP object. To differentiate between two pointers to the same object and two pointers to identically configured but different objects, the function **eq** can be used. **eq** returns true only if its two arguments evaluate to the identical LISP object.

(6)   Existing LISP objects can be altered using the functions **rplaca**, **rplacd**, and **nconc**. Altering an object is extremely risky and should not be attempted casually.

(7)   The functions **mapcan** and **mapcon** are equivalent to **(apply 'nconc (mapcar ...))** and **(apply 'nconc (maplist ...))**, respectively.

Exercises

(1)   Write a function that prints out an s-expression in dotted pair notation. (Hint − This is extremely simply if you write a recursive function.)

(2)   Represent the following s-expressions in terms of **cons** cells and pointers (i. e., as binary trees):

    (a)   **((a))**

    (b)   **(x (y) z)**

    (c)   **(x y . z)**

    (d)   **(((nil . c) . b) . a)**

(3)   Suppose we evaluate the following s-expressions:

    −> (setq x '(c d))
    (c d)
    −> (setq y (append '(a b) x))
    (a b c d)
    −> (eq (cddr y) x)
    ???

What value does the last s-expression evaluate to? Why?

(4)   Write the following representations as LISP would print them out:

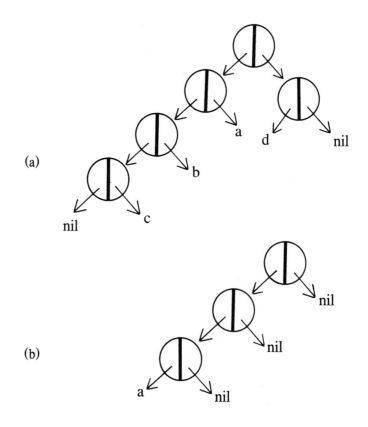

    (a)

    (b)

(c)

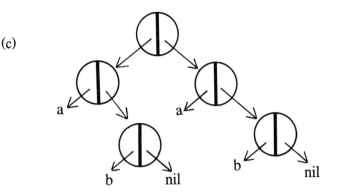

(5) Suppose we evaluated the following s-expressions:

> **-> (setq x '(a b c))**
> **(a b c)**
> **-> (setq y x)**
> **(a b c)**
> **-> (rplaca (rplacd y nil) 'd)**
> **(d)**
> **-> x**
> **????**

What is the value of **x**? What happened to the list **(a b c)**?

(6) What is the value of the following expression:

> **-> (mapcan '(lambda (x) (list x (add1 x))) '(1 2 3 4 5))**

(7) It is easy to add something to the beginning of a list in LISP. But it is harder to add something to the end. One way to ameliorate this situation is to carry around a pointer to the end of a list. Then it is easy to find the end of the list and update it.

A *tconc structure* is a special list whose **car** is a list, and whose **cdr** points to the end of the list pointed to by the **car**. The function **tconc** takes two arguments, the first of which should be a tconc structure. It updates the tconc structure to include the second argument as its last element.

For example, I can start out with an empty tconc structure, and add an element to it:

> —> (setq foo (tconc nil ’x))
> ((x) x)
> —>

The tconc structure prints out in this unusual manner because its **cdr** always points to the last part of its **car**. Now let us stick some elements onto the end of the list within this structure:

> —> (tconc foo ’y)
> ((x y) y)
> —> (tconc foo ’z)
> ((x y z) z)
> —> foo
> ((x y z) z)
> —>

Use **tconc** to implement *queues*. Recall that a queue is a data structure in which we add elements to one end, and take them off the other. Write functions **in—queue** and **de—queue**, which add objects to and remove objects from existing queues, respectively.

16

Error Handling and
Nonstandard Flow of Control

16.1. PROGRAM CONTROL OVER ERRORS

As we mentioned in a previous chapter, upon encountering an error, LISP normally forces a break and enters a special **read-eval-print** loop. Once in this loop, user intervention is required to continue. However, some sorts of errors can be anticipated, and the corresponding actions codified. In these cases, it may be possible to eliminate the need for user interaction. Instead, it may be possible to include error handling routines as part of the user program, thus automating some aspects of error processing.

An example of the utility of automatic error processing is determining whether an expression can be evaluated. For example, suppose I want to examine the value of a variable, and if it has a value, use this value in some subsequent computation. However, I cannot inspect the value of the global variable easily. This is because, if the variable were undefined, just examining it would cause an error. What I would like my program to do is examine the variable, and, if it has a value, use it. But if examination causes an error, I would like to ignore the error and go on.

To implement such processes, LISP provides a facility to exert control over error handling from within a user program. This facility allows the user to monitor the evaluation of a particular expression for the occurrence of an error. If an error occurs during this evaluation, control is transferred to a predetermined location. The code to which control is transferred may then try to analyze the error, and specify how to continue.

In this chapter we describe LISP's facility for allowing program control over error handling. Since this involves some nonstandard flow of control, the more general facility to implement alternative control schemes is presented as well.

16.2. errset

Control over errors is exerted in LISP through use of the function **errset**. **errset** takes an s-expression as an argument, and tries to evaluate it. If no error occurs during the evaluation of this s-expression, **errset** returns as its value the *list* of the value of the argument. However, if an error does occur anywhere in the evaluation of this s-expression, control is returned to the **errset**, which exits immediately with the value **nil**.

errset also takes an optional second argument. If this is **nil** then the error message LISP would normally print on the terminal is suppressed. If the argument is missing or non-**nil**, then the normal error message is printed before control is returned to the call to **errset**.

As an example, consider the case mentioned above. We would like to examine the value of a variable that may not have a binding. We can do so by evaluating the variable inside a call to **errset**: If the variable has the value **val**, say, **errset** will return **(val)**, i. e., the list of this value; if the variable is unbound, **errset** will return **nil**. Thus we might write a function that contains the following segment of code:

```
(setq result
      (car (cond ((errset x nil))
                 (t '(default–value)))))
```

Here the **errset** evaluates the s-expression **x**. If **x** has a value, **errset** returns the list of this value. This is guaranteed to be non-**nil**, so the **cond** returns it as its value. Passing on the **car** of this value binds **result** to the value of **x**. On the other hand, if **x** has no value, trying to evaluate it causes an error. Evaluation terminates immediately, and control is passed back to **errset**, which returns **nil**. The second **cond** clause will then be used. This returns the literal **(default–value)**, the **car** of which is eventually used to set **result**. We use a second argument of **nil** in the call to **errset** so that no message is printed in the case where **x** is unbound.

Actually, Franz LISP has a special function, **boundp**, just for determining if an atom is bound to a value. So **errset** is not really needed in this particular example. However, a LISP without an analogous function would have to rely on **errset**. Moreover, the **errset** technique is rather general. It will work when evaluating any s-expression, not just when examining the value of a literal atom.

16.3. SIMULATING ERRORS WITH err

The user may interface his program with the LISP error handling machinery, including **errset**, through use of the function **err**. **err** takes one argument, which is evaluated. **err** then forces a leap to the last previous call to **errset**. When **err** forces such a leap back, it passes the value of its argument to the call to **errset** to which it returns. That call to **errset** will return the value **err** passes it as its value. If there is no **errset** to catch this value, a break occurs and LISP enters the error **read-eval-print** loop.

With **err**, a user can write a LISP function that generates a real error if it encounters a circumstance it cannot handle. For example, the internal Franz LISP function **chdir** is used to change to a new directory. If the directory requested by the user does not exist, **chdir** cannot satisfy the user's request. This is considered an error, and requires user intervention. However, **chdir** is itself written in LISP. It tests to see if the directory requested exists, and if it does not, it calls **err** to throw control to the LISP error handling apparatus. In this manner, the function **chdir** cleanly interfaces with the normal LISP error handling machinery, just as if it were built into LISP. The user can write code that uses **err** to interface with LISP's error handling facility in exactly the same way.

16.4. catch AND throw

errset violates the normal LISP flow-of-control pattern: An error anywhere within the expression given as the argument to **errset** will cause an immediate transfer of control to the call to **errset**, without a transition through intermediate levels. For example, suppose our call to **errset** had the following form:

(errset (fn1 x y z) nil)

Unlike our previous examples, here the expression being evaluated contains a function call. Suppose further that **fn1** calls **fn2**, which calls **fn3**, and so on. Now assume that somewhere in the midst of all these calls, an error occurs. Control would immediately be passed to the **errset** *without going*

227

through the imtermediate steps of **fn3** *returning to* **fn2** *returning to* **fn1**, *etc.* In most other circumstances we have encountered, when we enter a function, we must exit it in order to go on. Thus we can think of **errset** as a way of enabling a return from a deeply nested function call to a higher level function call without having to go through the bother of returning through all the intermediate levels.

This ability to leap to a higher level is useful even if we do not have a real error. For example, suppose **fn1** is called from a function **fn**, and that **fn1** calls **fn2**, which calls **fn3**, etc. Suppose also that each function is searching for a certain value, which, if it is found, it will want to pass back to the calling function **fn**. If **fn3** finds this value, for example, it will have to return it to **fn2**; **fn2** will have to be set up to recognize this value as one it should return to its calling function; **fn1** will have to be set up the same way. This makes our code rather awkward and redundant, since each intermediate function must recognize and plan for the cases recognized by the functions that it calls.

However, if we could use the **errset** facility to return from a deeply nested function upon demand, we could avoid these unfortunate complications. If we could allow some deeply nested function to return directly to some higher level function, the intermediate functions would not have to know anything about the values that the lower level functions return. All we would need to accomplish this action are (1) some way to explicitly invoke the transfer of control and (2) some way of transmitting a value from a lower level to a higher one. So far these happen only if there is a real or simulated error.

To allow explicit access to the nonstandard flow-of-control required for **errset**, we introduce two functions, **catch** and **throw**. **catch** is somewhat like an **errset**, in that it provides a point to which control can be transferred later on. **throw** is similar to **err** − it causes control to leap to a previous **catch**.

catch takes as an argument an s-expression, which it evaluates. If it evaluates normally, **catch** simply returns this value as its value. However, if a call to **throw** occurs during this evaluation, flow of control will be abruptly returned to the **catch**. The value returned by the **catch** will then be the value of the argument to the **throw**. In effect, the **throw** throws the value of its argument through any number of levels of intermediate function calls directly to the most recent **catch**.

For example, using **catch** and **throw**, the code to implement the functions **fn**, **fn1**, **fn2**, etc., alluded to above might look something like the following:

```
(defun fn (...)
  (catch (fn1 ...) ))

(defun fn1 (...)
  (cond ((user—test1 ...) answer1)
        ((and (user—test2 ...) (fn2 ...)) answer2)
        ( ... )))

(defun fn2 (...)
  (cond ((user—test3 ...) (throw answer3))
        ((user—test4 ...) 'useful—value—but—not—an—answer)
        ((user—test5 ...) (fn3 ...))
        (t (fn4 ...) (fn5 ...)))))
```

Here **fn** simply establishes a **catch** to handle subsequent **throw**s. The functions **fn1**, **fn2**,... do all the work. **fn1** makes a test, and if it pans out, returns the answer. It uses the ordinary LISP flow-of-control mechanism since there are no intermediate functions between it and **fn**. If the test fails, **fn1** tries another test that includes a call to **fn2**. **fn2** may simply return a value that helps **fn1** continue its computation. However, in the course of computing this value, it may itself come upon the answer. In this case, it **throw**s the answer directly back to the **catch**, ignoring what **fn1** was trying to do.

As this example illustrates, **catch** and **throw** are needed mostly when some code is trying to serve two functions. If the functions **fn1**, **fn2**,... were only to search for a value, we could just have used the ordinary LISP flow-of-control regime. However, in this instance it was desirable to have a function such as **fn2** which has two functions: It might return a value to be used by some other function, but it might also find the big answer along the way. We use **catch** and **throw** here to write the code so that, from the point of view of **fn1**, **fn2** appears just as a utility. However, should **fn2** decide it found something more important, it can return to **fn** without **fn1** having to worry about what **fn2** was doing.

16.4.1. More Selective CATCHing and THROWing

Used as just described, one **catch** will catch anything that is thrown by any **throw** that is executed during the evaluation of its argument. This would make it difficult to have several different **catch-throw** scenarios operating simultaneously. This problem can be overcome by making **catch** and **throw** more selective. To do so, **catch** and **throw** both take an optional second argument. The optional second argument to **catch** should always be a literal atom, or a list of literal atoms; the second argument to **throw** must be a literal atom. When a **catch** has an explicit second argument, it will only catch those **throws** having a corresponding second argument (in the case where the second argument to **catch** is a list, this will catch any **throw** whose second argument is a member of this list).

A **catch** without a second argument will catch any **throw**, regardless of whether or not it has a second argument. However, a **throw** without a second argument can only be caught by a **catch** with no second argument. A **throw** that is not caught by anyone is an error.

In sum, we have the following kinds of **catch-throw** behavior:

```
-> (catch (...(throw 'x)...) )
x
-> (catch (...(throw 'x tag1)...) )
x
-> (catch (...(throw 'x tag1)...) tag1)
x
-> (catch (...(catch (...(throw 'x tag1)...) tag2) tag1)
x
-> (catch (...(throw 'x)...) tag1)
Error: No catch for this tag  nil
<1>:
```

In the first example, a general **catch** catches a general **throw**. In the second case, the **throw** is more specific, but the **catch** is general. In the third example, a specific **catch** catches a specific **throw**. In the next case, the **throw** throws through the first **catch** to the one bearing the same tag as it. Finally, an undifferentiated **throw** is not caught by the specific **catch**, thus causing an error.

16.5. errset AND err VERSUS catch AND throw

Since **err** can initiate a nonstandard flow-of-control leap, and since it can return a specific value to **errset**, the programmer can use **err** in conjunction with **errset** to implement a kind of **catch** and **throw** discipline. In fact, internally in Franz, an error is treated as just a special kind of **throw**.

However, it is best not to use **err** and **errset** to implement such a flow-of-control regime. Although they use virtually the same internal apparatus as **catch** and **throw**, the latter have been designed just for this purpose. Using them will make for much more transparent code. Use **err** only when you want to interface with LISP's error handling mechanisms, including **errset**. Use **catch** and **throw** if you are interested in a nonstandard flow-of-control regime.

16.6. AUTOLOADING

The Franz LISP error handler has a built-in feature that takes the place of some sorts of user intervention. When LISP encounters an undefined function name, it first checks to see if that name has the property **autoload** defined. If the value of this property is non-**nil**, then Franz interprets it as a path name. It reads in the designated file in hope of finding the function's definition. This feature allows the user to have functions whose definition is read in only on demand.

Franz also checks the property **macro—autoload**. This property is really designed for autoloading macro definitions for use by the LISP compiler, which is discussed in a later chapter.

16.7. SUMMARY

(1)   The function **errset** allows the user to process errors within his programs. Within a call to **errset**, the occurrence of an error during the evaluation of the argument to **errset** will transfer control back to the call. **errset** will return **nil** if an error occurs within it, and the list of the value of its argument otherwise.

(2)   The function **err** can force a return to the previously established **errset**. The value of the argument to **err** will be returned as the value of the **errset**. If there is no previous **errset**, control is transferred to the LISP error processing machinery.

(3)   Nonstandard transfer of control can be accomplished through the use of the functions **catch** and **throw**. **catch** sets up a reference point to which a subsequent **throw** can transfer control and transmit a value. **catch** and **throw** use labels to allow selective catching and throwing.

(4)   The LISP error handler looks for the property **autoload** on symbols with undefined function definitions. It interprets its value as a file name and loads it in an effort to define the function.

Exercises

(1)   Use **errset** to write your own **read-eval-print** loop that will not be exited by a user error.

(2)   Use **catch** and **throw** to implement a perfect number generator. Recall that perfect numbers are equal to the sum of their proper divisors. Write this code by writing a low level function that searches for the next perfect number each time it is called. When it finds one, it **throw**s it to the calling routine. This calling routine should consist of a loop that **catch**es that value thrown by the low level routine, prints it out, and iterates this procedure.

17

The LISP Symbol Table

17.1. read RECONSIDERED

In a previous chapter, we discussed the fact that LISP represents s-expressions internally in the form of binary trees. However, input to LISP consists of strings of characters, that is, of text typed in by the user. LISP must convert these strings of characters into binary trees in order to perform LISP operations on them.

The burden of this translation is borne by the function **read**. **read** acts as LISP's general purpose interface between the world of character strings and the world of LISP's internal representations. In our discussion of input/output, we showed how the LISP programmer can use **read** to input s-expressions to his own program; we also mentioned that LISP's **read-eval-print** loop uses this same function to input the s-expressions typed in by the user for LISP to evaluate. In both cases, **read** must recognize the s-expression being described by the string input, and build the corresponding internal representation. Once **read** has done this job, all other LISP functions can operate on the internal representation **read** produces. These other functions can then be completely oblivious to the details of the textual denotation of s-expressions.

read has a considerable job to do. For example, **read** must recognize the boundaries of atoms, detect the occurrence of imbedded s-expressions, as well as be sensitive to read macros and other syntactic quirks. In sum, **read** must embody a full-fledged scanner and parser to detect LISP tokens and syntactic structures.

Thus **read** does much of the work that is done by a compiler in more conventional programming languages. All programming languages allow one to specify programs as strings of characters. Some translation system then converts these strings to an internal form. In the case of a compiler, the internal form is usually a parse tree that serves as the basis for code generation. In the case of LISP, the internal representation is a binary tree, which serves as the basis for evaluation.

Hence the LISP **read** function does a great deal more than the input procedures of most languages. These generally do nothing more sophisticated than converting a string of digits into a number. In contrast, **read** performs the entire scanning and parsing phases of language translation. Fortunately, LISP's syntax is very simple and closely parallels its internal representation, so these tasks can be done rather efficiently.

LISP is somewhat unusual in that it performs scanning and parsing functions intermittently. That is, because it is interpreted, some scanning and parsing are performed each time an s-expression is typed in for evaluation. Also, LISP's data structures are identical to its programming language constructs and are denoted by the same textual conventions. Thus, scanning and parsing must also occur when data are input by a program. This identity of data structures and program constructs allows for the same mechanisms to be used in either case. Namely, these are the mechanisms employed by the single LISP function **read**.

This chapter is concerned with one aspect of the LISP input phase, namely, the role of the LISP symbol table. The routine use of this object by **read** is discussed. Then direct user manipulation of the LISP symbol table is examined. This includes ways for users to create new atoms and remove existing ones. The possible dangers of such manipulation are discussed, along with some useful applications.

17.2. TRACKING ATOM NAMES

One aspect of the processing performed by **read** involves the treatment of literal atoms. Most programming language translation systems keep track of the appearance of names of variables and functions during scanning and parsing. This is done to be sure that names are used consistently. A symbol table is used for this purpose. The LISP function **read** must also maintain a sort of symbol table for LISP atoms, since LISP guarantees that all atoms having the same name are the same atom. For example, if we bind a value to an atom named **foo**, and then ask LISP to evaluate an atom named **foo**, LISP must make sure that both names reference the same atom so that the latter operation will produce the previously stored value.

Since we have become accustomed to LISP operating in this manner, enforcing this constraint might seem like a trivial consideration. But LISP must do some work in order to maintain the uniqueness of atom names. In particular, LISP must distinguish between new atoms and previously encountered ones. In the case where a name refers to a previously encountered atom, LISP must find the representation of the old atom and use it in building the representation of the new s-expression being read in. If the atom is a new one, then a new representation for it must be created.

17.3. THE REPRESENTATION OF ATOMS

To make this process a bit clearer, consider first how literal atoms may be represented in LISP. We have the following information about each individual atom that LISP has to store: An atom may have a value bound to it; it may also have a property list and it may have a function definition; and of course, it has a name. In Franz LISP, an atom is represented by a chunk of memory, each of whose cells points to one of these aspects. Thus the first memory location of an atom is a pointer to its value, the second to its property list, the third to its function definition, and the fourth to its print name. There is also a fifth memory location used for internal purposes. (Other LISPs use a similar scheme, although some use property lists to represent some of the aspects of an atom that merit a special memory location in Franz.)

When LISP refers to an atom internally, it does so by pointing to the first location of the memory chunk that represents that atom. For example, in the internal LISP representation of the list **(a b c)**, the **car** half of the first **cons** cell designating the list points to the first memory location of the chunk of memory representing the atom named **a**. All other references to this LISP atom also point to this same memory location.

Thus when **read** scans the character string **(a b c)**, and recognizes a reference to the atom named **a**, it must check to see if a representation for **a** has already been built. If so, then **read** must build a representation for this list that includes a pointer to the existing representation of **a**. It is to maintain this unique association of atom names with their internal representations that a symbol table is useful.

17.4. THE OBLIST

In LISP, the symbol table is called the *oblist,* for "object list". Virtually every atom known to the current LISP process will appear on the oblist. This includes standard LISP atoms like **car** and **cdr**, as well as literal atoms introduced by the user. Atoms that appear on the oblist are said to be *interned.*

Every time the function **read** encounters a literal atom name, **read** looks for an atom with that name on the oblist. If an atom with the name just read in is already on the oblist, **read** will use the existing representation for that atom; otherwise it will create a new atom representation, and enter the new atom on the oblist.

The oblist is stored as a kind of hash table indexed by atom name. This facilitates efficient look-up by name to find the internal representation. However, this indexing structure is fairly well hidden. The oblist will appear just like an ordinary list to LISP functions that examine it.

You can access the oblist in Franz through use of the function (of no arguments) **oblist**. However, it is not recommended that you use this function on the top level. The oblist is usually quite long and some of its members are apt to contain non-printing characters. Instead, this function is useful when you want to do something to every atom that LISP has encountered. For example, the function **length** returns the number of elements in a list; applying this to the value returned by **(oblist)** will tell us the number of atoms this LISP process has encountered so far (including the ones it knew about from the beginning):

```
% lisp
Franz Lisp, Opus 38.59
-> (length (oblist))
1283
-> 'baruch
baruch
-> (length (oblist))
1284
->
```

In this example, I started out with a fresh LISP process. Then I measured the length of the oblist. Afterwards I merely typed in an atom name I am sure LISP has never seen before. When I measure the oblist again, its length has been increased by one. This happened because a new representation for the previous unencountered atom had to be created, and added onto the oblist. If I mention this atom again, it will already be on the oblist, and

read will not have to make a new entry for it:

> -> 'baruch
> baruch
> -> (length (oblist))
> 1284
> ->

This example illustrates some of the processing that is always going on behind the scenes in LISP. Typing in a quoted atom for evaluation does not seem like asking LISP to do much. However, doing so forces LISP to run through the oblist. It may also have to allocate storage and build a new represention, just in response to your mentioning an atom name.

17.5. OBLIST MANIPULATION FUNCTIONS

Woody Allen, in a treatise on mythical beasts, describes a creature called the Great Roe. The Great Roe has the head of a lion, and the body of a lion,... but not the same lion.

A similar situation can result if you manipulate the oblist yourself. For example, using oblist manipulation functions, it is possible to arrive at a situation in which there are several distinct atoms, all having the same name. Such atoms are as confusing as the Great Roe, as it is almost impossible to tell them apart. Programs in which this is the case are rarely correct, and are extremely difficult to understand and debug.

17.5.1. Making New Atoms

We can create a brand new atom using the function **maknam**. The argument to **maknam** should evaluate to a list of literal atoms or numbers. **maknam** returns as its value a new atom whose name is the result of concatenating together the first characters of each of the elements in this list. For example, to create an atom with the name **abc**, we can do the following:

> -> (maknam '(a b c))
> abc
> ->

maknam *does not put the atom it creates on the oblist.* Thus if there already exists an atom named **abc**, or if we make one later on, this will be a different atom than the one created by **maknam**. To demonstrate this point, let us save the atom created by **maknam**, and compare it to an atom

237

of the same name created by **read**:

```
-> (setq x (maknam '(a b c)))
abc
-> (eq x 'abc)
nil
-> x
abc
->
```

Even though two atoms here have identical names, they are otherwise unrelated, as evidenced by applying **eq** to them.

We can intern an atom on the oblist using the function **intern**. For example, if I intern the result of **maknam**, subsequent references to that name will behave more conventionally:

```
-> (setq x (intern (maknam '(u v w))))
uvw
-> (eq x 'uvw)
t
->
```

intern will not put an atom on the oblist if there is already one there by the same name. Instead, **intern** will return as its value the atom already on the oblist.

The function **implode** is just like **maknam**, except that it automatically interns its result. Similarly, the function **concat** takes any number of arguments, evaluates them, and produces an interned symbol whose name is the concatenation of the resulting values (like **maknam**, **implode** only uses the first character of a name); **uconcat** creates an atom in a like fashion, but does not intern it.

17.5.2. Automatic Name Generation

Sometimes the need arises to automatically create new atom names. The function **gensym** serves this purpose. **gensym** takes one argument, which should evaluate to an atom. It returns a new uninterned atom whose name begins with the first character of this value; the rest of the name is of the form **0nnnnn**, where **nnnnn** is the number of times **gensym** has been called. For example:

```
-> (gensym 's)
s00004
-> (gensym 's)
s00005
-> (gensym 'x)
x00006
-> (gensym)
g00007
```

As you can see, **gensym** defaults to the lead character **g** if no argument is given.

Each call to **gensym** is guaranteed to produce a new atom. There are many applications for this. For example, some programmers like to give names to each datum of a certain type their program encounters. If the program is going to store facts about an indefinite number of people, say, it could generate one atom for each new person. Facts about this person can be represented by attaching properties to the corresponding atom, or by similar techniques.

There is a set of functions with a similar purpose that some programmers prefer. These allow for a number of symbols with independent counters. (Note that in Franz LISP, **gensym** does not keep different counters for symbols with different lead characters.) To have several independent symbol series, the function **newsym** can be used. **newsym** is similar to **gensym** except that it allows you to have independent symbols series beginning with arbitrary symbols. **newsym** also interns its result. For example, the following example has two series, one beginning with the symbol **john** and the other with the symbol **mary**:

```
-> (newsym 'john)
john0
-> (newsym 'john)
john1
-> (newsym 'mary)
mary0
-> (newsym 'mary)
mary1
->
```

To get the last symbol in a series generated by **newsym**, the function **oldsym** can be used:

```
-> (oldsym 'john)
john1
->
```

The function **allsym** returns all the symbols generated so far in a series:

```
-> (allsym 'john)
(john0 john1)
->
```

And the function **initsym** allows you to start counting at an arbitrary point:

```
-> (initsym '(bill 5) 'alice '(fred 2))
(bill5 alice0 fred2)
-> (newsym 'bill)
bill6
-> (newsym 'alice)
alice1
-> (newsym 'fred)
fred3
->
```

The function **remsym** removes fabricated symbols from the oblist. For example,

```
-> (remsym 'john '(mary 1))
(john1 mary1)
->
```

removes from the oblist all **newsym**ed symbols whose names begin with **john** and those **newsym**ed symbols whose names begin with **mary** from **mary1** on. **remsym** returns the current symbols in each series.

Finally, **symstat** returns each requested symbol with its current counter:

```
-> (symstat 'joe 'bill)
((joe nil) (bill 6))
->
```

17.5.3. Removing an Atom from the Oblist

We can remove an atom already on the oblist using the function **remob**. However, if we do so, and type in an atom of the same name, a new atom will be created. We may have s-expressions pointing to the representation

of the old atom, so we could end up with several atoms with the same name
this way. Here is an example:

        -> (setq x 'foo)
        foo
        -> (remob 'foo)
        foo
        -> (eq x 'foo)
        nil
        -> x
        foo
        ->

In this example, I first remove **foo** from the oblist. When **foo** appears in the
next s-expression, **read** no longer finds **foo** on the oblist. Thus it creates a
representation for a new atom named **foo**. The atom **x** is still bound to the
old **foo**, however. **eq** demonstrates these to be distinct atoms, even though
they bear the same name.

We can use these oblist manipulation functions to have several atoms of the
same name around, and switch back and forth between the one **read** will
identify. In the following example, I distinguish two different **foo**s using the
property named **whoami:**

        -> (defprop foo foo1 whoami)
        foo1
        -> (setq x foo)
        foo
        -> (remob 'foo)
        foo
        -> (defprop foo foo2 whoami)
        foo2
        -> (setq y 'foo)
        foo
        -> (get 'foo 'whoami)
        foo2
        -> (remob 'foo)
        foo
        -> (intern x)
        foo
        -> (get 'foo 'whoami)
        foo1
        -> (remob 'foo)
        foo

```
-> (intern y)
foo
-> (get 'foo 'whoami)
foo2
->
```

After I remove **foo** from the oblist the first time, the appearance of **foo** in the next **defprop** causes a new atom named **foo** to be created. The old **foo** is pointed to by **x** and the new one by **y**. I can switch back and forth between these two **foo**s by alternately **remob**ing one and **intern**ing the other.

17.6. AN APPLICATION—VARIABLES LOCAL TO A MODULE

We can use the ability to move things on and off the oblist to implement the LISP equivalent of a variable local to a module. That is, suppose we want a function or set of functions to share an atom. But we do not want this atom to be accessible from other functions. **prog** or **lambda** will not do, because they only localize the *value* of the atom. Changes to properties of **prog** or **lambda** variables are global.

We can implement a truly local variable by removing that variable from the oblist before reading in a chunk of code. After the code has been read in, any new atom by the same name is removed, and the old atom is re-interned. Subsequent references to that name will refer to the original atom, not to the one used by the protected segment of code.

Here is one implementation of this idea. **beginlocal** is used to start a code segment in which several variables are to be local, and **endlocal** to end one:

```
-> (def beginlocal
      (nlambda (l)
       (mapc '(lambda (x)
               (remob x)
               (intern (copysymbol x nil))
               (putprop (intern x) x 'savedatom))
           l)))

t
```

```
-> (def endlocal
      (nlambda (l)
        (mapc '(lambda (x)
                 (remob x)
                 (intern (get x 'savedatom)))
             l)))

t
-> (beginlocal a b c)
(a b c)
-> (def ...)
   .
   .
   .
-> (def ...)
   .
   .
   .
-> (endlocal a b c)
(a b c)
->
```

This definition of **beginlocal** makes use of the Franz function **copysymbol**. This produces a new uninterned symbol whose name is the same as that of its first argument. Thus **beginlocal** produces a new copy of an old atom. It replaces the old with the new, remembering the old symbol on the property list of the new one.

Therefore, in the block of code between the call to **beginlocal** and the call to **endlocal**, any references to **a**, **b**, or **c** will be local to the block. Then **endlocal** removes the new copy and replaces it with the old. Subsequent references to these symbols will then refer to the original versions.

It is hard to heartily recommend this idea, which is due to Chris Riesbeck*. Fooling around with the oblist is a dangerous game in general. For example, should a break occur during a call to a function defined within a **beginlocal-endlocal** block, you will not be able to examine the value of a protected variable by name. This tends to be hopelessly confusing, since you will no doubt have forgotten that the variable in question is protected. This fact will not be at all reflected when you examine the function definition.

---

*Personal communication

In general, it is good programming practice to write code that manipulates the oblist only as a last resort.

17.7. SUMMARY

(1) The function **read** acts as the general purpose interface between the world of character strings and the world of LISP's internal representations. Therefore, **read** performs the equivalent of scanning and parsing each time it is called.

(2) In particular, **read** is concerned with "uniquifying" atoms — making references to the same names refer to the same atoms. **read** accomplishes this through the use of a kind of symbol table called the *oblist*. Every atom known to **read** appears exactly once on the oblist. Such atoms are said to be *interned* on the oblist.

(3) The function **oblist** returns the oblist as its value. The expr **intern** ensures that its argument is on the oblist, inserting it there if it is not there already. The expr **remob** removes its argument from the oblist.

(4) The functions **implode, maknam, concat,** and **uconcat** create new atom names from their arguments. **implode** and **concat** automatically intern their results, while **maknam** and **uconcat** do not.

(5) The functions **gensym** and **newsym** create new atom names. These provide a useful way to create new atoms on the fly.

(6) One application of oblist manipulation is to produce atoms that are truly local to a piece of code.

(7) In general, functions that manipulate the oblist should be used with great caution. They can result in multiple atoms with the same name. This can make debugging the code in which they appear exceedingly difficult.

Exercises

(1) In the chapter on property lists, we showed how we can represent a data base on a library of books. However, to create a representation of a book in this example, the user had to supply a name like **book3**. Write a version of the function **add-book** defined in that chapter which generates its own names for books.

(2)   In an exercise in the chapter on property lists, we discussed the technique of *marking*. In that exercise, we supposed we had two lists of atoms, and wanted to compute the intersection of these lists as sets (that is, the list that contains exactly one instance of all the elements on both lists). For example, the intersection of (**a b c c d e**) and (**x c b d d**) is (**b c d**). A straightforward way of doing this is to take each element of one list and determine if it is a member of the other. This requires comparing each element of one list against each element of the other, for a total of 2*n comparisons, if we assume each list is of length n.

However, it is much faster to go through one list and put a property on each atom. For example, we can set the value of the **marker** property to **t**. Then we can go through the second list, and hold onto each element that has this property value. The resulting list will be the intersection we require. This version requires only around 2*n operations, as it only involves a single sequencing through each list.

However, there is an annoying problem with this function. If we use it several times, some of the atoms we encounter are likely to have marks on them from previous calls to this function, and we will get a spurious result.

One way around this problem is to clean up after each use. But this requires doing more work. A better solution is to use a unique marker each time. For example, we can have our intersection function first create a **gensym**ed atom and use this to mark the atoms in one of the lists. That is, rather than mark the atoms with a property named **marker**, we can mark them with a property name created by **gensym** (alternatively, we can use the property name **marker**, but use a property value created by **gensym** instead of the property value **t**). Then we can check for this particular mark on the atoms of the other list. Since each call to our intersection function would create a brand new marker atom, we would not have to worry at all about the effects of previous calls.

Write a version of such an intersection function that uses **gensym**ed atom names to avoid having to clean up after itself.

18

Other Data Types

18.1. INTRODUCTION

We have noted that LISP programs are represented as s-expressions, and that the data they manipulate consist primarily of s-expressions. The homogeneous nature of LISP programs and data has some interesting benefits. It is often possible and desirable in LISP to execute data, for example, through the use of functions like **eval** and **apply**; we both read in our programs and read in our data through the same mechanism, the function **read**.

However, there is nothing about LISP that restricts it to the manipulation of s-expressions. For example, in the beginning of this tutorial, we first applied LISP to numeric quantities. We used the machinery of LISP to write programs that do mathematical computation. The resulting programs are not substantially different from those that might be written in FORTRAN or PASCAL, except that they conform to LISP's syntax.

LISP might not be the best programming language to write such algorithms (it is probably not the worst, either). But sometimes it is useful in LISP to use data types and data structures other than atoms and dotted pairs. For this reason, almost all LISPs augment these main data types with other types. For example, most LISPs also support arrays and strings; some LISPs, such as Franz, have special data types like ports, which are useful for I/O.

246

In this chapter, we examine some of the less frequently used LISP data types. In doing so, we present a more thorough picture of what is available in Franz LISP. We present methods for creating and accessing these various data types. We also make suggestions about their respective uses. However, we do not show much in the way of specific applications of them. This is because the set of available data structures encompasses just about all the well known types. Also, most of these are not especially specific to LISP. Thus this chapter tends to highlight the LISP peculiarities involving these structures, rather than describe their general features.

Support of non-s-expression data types varies considerably from one LISP implementation to the next. The user should be aware that some of the data types described in this section are apt not even to exist in other LISPs. Where they do exist, the details of their structure and function may differ in important ways from those of Franz LISP.

18.2. THE DATA TYPES AVAILABLE IN FRANZ

As Franz supports more than a few data types, it is sometimes useful for a programmer to be able to query a piece of data to determine its type. The expr **type** evaluates its argument and then returns its type. The possible values **type** will return are those which Franz LISP recognizes as distinct data types. These are given below. The function in parentheses next to the name of the data type is the Franz predicate that will return true if and only if its argument evaluates to the corresponding data type:

list (**dtpr**)
> This type is a slight misnomer. All dotted pairs are considered to be of type **list** by Franz LISP, including those dotted pairs that are not properly lists (e. g., **(a . b)**). There is no distinct data type in Franz that distinguishes true lists from arbitrary dotted pairs.
>
> **nil** is not considered to be a dotted pair, i. e., **(dptr nil)** returns **nil**. However, the function **listp** returns **t** if and only if its argument evaluates either to a dotted pair or to **nil**.

symbol (**symbolp**)
> This refers to literal atoms.

(As we mentioned previously, the predicate **atom** returns **t** if and only if its argument evaluates to either a symbol or a number. The predicate **numbp** (also called **numberp**) determines whether its argument evaluates to a number. However, "number" is not a fundamental data type in Franz. Franz LISP, like most LISPs, distinguishes several different types of numbers. The three types of LISP numbers are described next.)

fixnum (**fixp**)

Fixnums are integers between -2^{31} and $2^{31}-1$.

flonum (**floatp**)

This is the type of double precision real numbers. **read** creates a flonum whenever it sees a decimal point or scientific notation (e. g. **12.3E6**, meaning 12400000.0).

bignum (**bigp**)

Bignums are integers of magnitude greater that fixnums. Franz tends to convert the results of arithmetic computations into bignums as required, and into fixnums if possible.

binary (**bcdp**)

This value is returned for machine coded functions, that is, those functions written in machine language rather than in LISP. For example, most functions that come with LISP have **binary** as the type of their function definitions:

>   **−> (type (getd 'car))**
>   **binary**
>   **−>**

We can create our own functions of this type using a LISP compiler, which is described in another chapter.

string (**stringp**)

Strings of characters are a data type in many LISPs, including Franz. For example, the names of atoms are stored as strings. Users can enter strings directly, as we saw in the chapter on input/output.

array (**arrayp**)

Arrays are blocks of contiguous storage. They are created and manipulated by functions especially designed for these purposes.

hunk (**hunkp**)

A hunk is a vector of from 1 to 128 LISP values. Hunks exist to provide a form of storage that is more efficient than arrays, if somewhat less flexible.

vector (**vectorp**)

Vectors are currently an experimental data type in Franz. Vectors are similar to hunks, but can be of arbitrary size and have a sort of property list. They are used internally to implement closures, and are useful for communicating with functions written in other languages.

vectori (vectorip)

These are *immediate-vectors,* which are similar to vectors. Immediate-vectors allow the storage of binary data directly within the vector. As such, they are useful for efficiently storing string data and the results of functions written in other languages.

value (valuep)

A value is a pointer to another LISP value. These arise mainly in conjunction with arrays.

port (portp)

Ports are used to do I/O in LISP. They were discussed in the chapter on reading and writing.

other

It is possible to obtain a value that was not allocated by the LISP system. This may happen when you use a foreign function within LISP which uses LISP to allocate its storage, for example. Such values are classified as type **other**.

We now look at each of these data types that have not received adequate treatment thus far.

18.3. STRINGS

Strings are sequences of characters. As we saw in the chapter on input/output, strings are denoted in Franz by surrounding a sequence of characters with double quotes. For example, **"abc"**, **"string"**, and **"string with spaces"** are all strings. In Franz, strings always evaluate to themselves.

Strings look very much like atom names; in fact, the names of literal atoms in Franz are stored as string data. The advantage of using strings explicitly is that they do not incur the overhead of storing an entire atom. For example, if you want to print out the words **Welcome to program FOO**, you could do this by creating an atom with the name **Welcome to program FOO**, and then **princ**ing it out. But this is somewhat inefficient, because the atom will require storage for a property list, a value, and a function definition. These will never be used in this case. In addition, the atom takes up space on the oblist, which also slows down **read** ever so slightly.

A more efficient solution is to store "**Welcome to program FOO**" as a string. The string is not interned, nor does it incur the overhead of storage that an atom does. We would need a LISP function to print out this string, but, fortunately, most functions that work on symbolic atoms also work on strings. We can apply **princ** to this string and it will be printed out without the surrounding double-quotes.

Because most LISP functions that apply to literal atoms also apply to strings, most LISP functions that are used for string manipulation are not specific to strings per se. For example, **concat**, which concatenates the values of its arguments into a new atom name, will accept arguments that are either atoms or strings. Thus it is possible to evaluate the following:

> ```
> -> (concat 'abc "xyz")
> abcxyz
> ->
> ```

The result is an atom whose name derives from the atom **abc** and the string "**xyz**".

Other examples of functions that are useful for string manipulation are **maknam** and **implode**. These were discussed in the section on **read**. In addition, the function **getchar** (also called **nthchar** and **getcharn** in Franz) is often applied to strings. **getchar** returns the nth character of a string or literal atom name:

> ```
> -> (getchar "abcde" 3)
> c
> ->
> ```

Note that **getchar** always returns an atom.

The function **explode** returns the list of characters (as atoms) that **print** would use to print the argument:

> ```
> -> (explode 'foo)
> (f o o)
> -> (explode "foo")
> ("| f o o |")
> ->
> ```

Similarly, **explodec** returns the list of characters that **princ** would use.

250

These functions will apply to any s-expression, although they are occasionally useful for character string manipulation. An efficiency-minded user might want to use the functions **aexplode** and **aexplodec**, which are internal versions of these functions that work only on symbols and strings.

As atoms are more commonly desired than strings, these functions all return atoms rather than strings as their result. However, Franz LISP stores atom names as strings, so it is always possible to get at the atom name in string form. We can access the name of an atom using the function **get_pname** (get print name):

>   −> **(get_pname 'foo)**
> **"foo"**
> −>

The function **substring** is somewhat more specific to strings. **(substring string nth)** returns the substring of **string** starting at the **nth** character:

>   −> **(substring "abcedfghij" 5)**
> **"dfghij"**
> −>

If you apply **substring** to an atom, LISP will apply it to the atom's name:

>   −> **(substring 'abcedfghij 3)**
> **"cedfghij"**
> −>

Similarly, the function **alphalessp** returns true if its first argument is alphabetically prior to its second; if the arguments are literal atoms, LISP uses their names for the comparison.

Finally, the function **stringp** returns **t** if and only if its argument is a string.

18.4. ARRAYS

Arrays allow the LISP user to create and access a contiguous block of data. These serve pretty much the same function as arrays do in other programming languages.

In most LISPs, including Franz, we define an array using a special array definition function. We access the array by using the array name where we would normally expect a function to appear. The arguments to the function are treated as subscripts of the array access.

The simplest kind of array in Franz is defined using the function **array**. This takes a number of arguments. First comes the name of the array; next a flag indicating the type of the data to be stored in the array (**t** −> arbitrary LISP s-expressions, **fixnum** −> fixnums, etc.); the rest of the arguments are interpreted as the dimensions of the array. For example, to create an array named **foo** of dimensions 4 by 7, containing arbitrary s-expressions, we can type the following:

>   −> (array foo t 4 7)
>   array[28]
>   −>

array[28] is how LISP prints out the array object itself.

The subscripts of these arrays are zero-based, so the first element of this array is referenced by the expression **(foo 0 0)**. The next element is **(foo 0 1)**, and so on. These look just like function calls, but LISP knows that **foo** is an array and interprets these expressions as array references. For example,

>   −> (setq x (foo 3 6))

would reference the last element of **foo**, and set **x** to the value it contains.

array initializes the arrays it creates in accordance with their type. Arrays of arbitrary s-expressions are initialized to **nil**; arrays of fixnums are initialized to **0**, etc.

To change the value of an array element, the function **store** is used. **store** takes as its first argument an array reference, and as its second an expression whose value is to be stored in the array element referenced by the first argument. For example, to store the value **baz** in the last element of the array **foo**, we would type

>   −> (store (foo 3 6) 'baz)
>   baz
>   −>

18.4.1. Fancier Array Accessing Schemes

The type of array just described is modeled after MacLISP style arrays. It is functionally identical to the sort of arrays commonly available in other programming languages. However, in Franz, arrays are implemented in terms of more primitive functions. These underlying array implementation functions are capable of supporting more general array manipulation schemes.

In its most general form, an array in Franz is a data structure with a number of components, including an access function, a block of contiguous data, and other pertinent information. When LISP encounters a reference to an array, it simply calls the access function included in the array, passing it the arguments the user supplied. This access function is responsible for figuring out exactly what element of the array to access and what to do with it.

For example, the **array** function described above merely sets up arrays with access functions that determine the location of an element from subscripts in the standard way. Similarly, the function **store** is a macro: **(store (foo a b) c)** just turns into **(foo c a b)**. Evaluating this expression results in calling the same access function as is invoked when we evaluate **(foo a b)**; it is up to this access function to count the number of arguments supplied and decide whether to change the value of an element of the array, or just return one.

The Franz programmer can build his own arrays using whatever kind of access scheme he wants. We will not go into the details here. The finer aspects of array structure are described in Appendix A. However, this generality entails some additional costs. To implement simple, small vectors of objects, hunks may be an economical alternative.

18.5. HUNKS

Hunks are contiguous chunks of storage that are accessed much like vectors. The primary advantage of a hunk is efficient access. Accessing an element of a hunk, while slower than accessing a **cons** cell, is faster than accessing an array. Hunks can range from 1 to 128 elements in size. (Actually, storage for hunks is allocated only in sizes which are powers of 2; most LISP functions that manipulate hunks just act as if the allocated but unasked-for portion of the hunk were not there.) Once a hunk is created, its size cannot be changed.

Hunks are printed out in Franz surrounded by curly brackets. For example, a hunk of length three containing the elements **a**, **b**, and **c** is printed as {**a b c**}. However, this notation is not recognized by **read**. In fact, there is no built-in way to enter an entire hunk using **read**.

Instead, hunks are created by the functions **hunk** and **makhunk**. **hunk** takes any number of arguments, and allocates a hunk whose length is equal to the number of arguments given. It returns this hunk as its value. **hunk** initializes each element of the hunk to the value of the corresponding argument. For example, **(hunk 'a 'b 'c 'd)** returns the hunk {a b c d}.

The function **makhunk** takes only one argument. If it evaluates to a fixnum, then a hunk of that length is created. Its elements are all initialized to **nil**. If the argument evaluates to a list, then a hunk of size equal to the length of the list is created. It is initialized to the elements of this list. So **(makhunk '(a b c d))** is equivalent to **(hunk 'a 'b 'c 'd)**; **(makhunk 4)** returns the hunk {**nil nil nil nil**}.

Hunk elements are accessed using the function **cxr**. This function is named so as to indicate that hunks may be thought of as generalizations of dotted pairs. **cxr** takes two arguments. The first should evaluate to a fixnum, and represents an index (starting at 0). The second should evaluate to a hunk. Thus **(cxr 0 foo)** will return the first element of the hunk to which **foo** is bound. The functions **cdr** and **car** can also be used to access the first two elements of a hunk. But note that **cdr** will reference the first element of a hunk, and **car** the second.

The value of any element of a hunk can be changed using the function **rplacx**. This is a function of three arguments, which should evaluate to an index, a hunk, and a target value. The functions **rplacd** and **rplaca** can also be used to modify the first and second elements of a hunk, respectively.

Finally, the function **hunksize** returns the number of arguments in a hunk.

It is generally desirable to use hunks rather than arrays when possible. This is because hunks require very little overhead. Of course, should you want to use a more complicated access scheme, you will have to pay the additional overhead incurred by arrays.

18.6. VECTORS AND IMMEDIATE-VECTORS

Vectors are an experimental data type. The following description is therefore tentative and subject to change.

Vectors were designed primarily to provide a simple, contiguous data type not subject to the size limitation of hunks. In addition, vectors have a kind of tag associated with them. The idea is that the user can mark vectors with this tag, and thus distinguish different subtypes of vectors of his own creation.

Let us first consider vectors for which we do not use the property component. For example, suppose I want to have a vector containing the two elements **baruch** and **atore**. I can create such a vector using the function **vector**:

> -> (setq x (vector 'baruch 'atore))
> vector[2]
> ->

Note that the vector is printed as **vector[length]**, where **length** refers to the number of elements in the vector.

We can access and change an element of a vector using the functions **vref** and **vset**, respectively. For example:

> -> (vref x 0)
> baruch
> -> (vref x 1)
> atore
> -> (vset x 1 'adonoi)
> adonoi
> -> (vref x 1)
> adonoi
> ->

18.6.1. Vectors as User-Defined Data Types

Suppose I want to have a special kind of vector. For example, I might want to store texts as vectors of words. I can do this by creating a vector just as I did above:

> -> (setq text1 (vector 'Mary 'had 'a 'little 'lamb))
> vector[5]
> ->

But for purposes of my own, I might want to be able to distinguish vectors that I am using to store text from those I am using to store other kinds of data. I can use the property component of a vector for this purpose. The property of a vector should be either a symbol or a list whose first element is a symbol. I can change the property of a vector using the functions **vsetprop** and **vputprop**. I can access this property using the function **vprop**. For example, I can change the property of the vector just created to **text**:

255

```
-> (vsetprop text1 'text)
text
-> text1
text[5]
-> (vprop text1)
text
->
```

Note that Franz prints out vectors with non-**nil** properties as **property[length]** rather than **vector[length]**. Other than print the vector in this manner, Franz will tend to ignore these properties; the user may exploit them to his own advantage. However, the symbols **fclosure** and **structure–value–argument** have a special meaning as vector properties. They are used by Franz to implement function closures. The user is advised against using them himself. In fact, there is no guarantee that other symbols will not be usurped for implementation purposes. Users are forewarned that they use non-**nil** vector properties at their own risk.

If the property of a vector is a list, LISP treats it as a disembodied property list. The first element of the list should be a symbol, and will be regarded as the distinguishing type of the vector. The rest of the list can be used for ordinary name-value associations, just like any other disembodied property list. See the section on disembodied property lists in the chapter on property lists to refresh your memory about how these work.

You can also create a vector using the function **new–vector**. This function takes three arguments, the latter two of which are optional. The first specifies the length of the vector; the second specifies a datum to which to initialize each element of the vector; the third becomes the vector's property. For example, I can create a text vector of three elements, all of whose elements are the symbol **word**, by doing the following:

```
-> (setq y (new-vector 3 'word 'text))
text[3]
-> (vref y 2)
word
->
```

18.6.2. Immediate-vectors

Immediate-vectors are just like vectors, except that they house binary data. As such, immediate-vectors are convenient for storing data for communicating with non-LISP functions. The data may be referenced as bytes, words (32 bit quantities), or longwords (64 bits).

Immediate-vectors can be created using the functions **vectori–byte**, **vectori–word**, and **vectori–long**. To create immediate-vectors specifying size, fill data, and a property, the functions **new–vectori–byte**, **new–vectori–word**, and **new–vectori–long** can be used. For example, suppose I create an immediate-vector to store a character string:

> −> (setq x (vectori–byte "a" "b" "c" "d"))
> vectori[4]
> −>

Now if I want the last character, say, I can access it directly:

> −> (vrefi–byte x 3)
> **100**
> −>

The value printed is the ASCII representation of the character, as it is stored in the array as binary data. We can use **maknam** to translate this into a more printable symbol:

> −> (maknam (list (vrefi–byte x 3)))
> **d**
> −>

18.7. VALUES

A *value* is a pointer to another LISP value. There is no convenient way to read in a value data type in Franz; when a value data type that points to **foo** is printed, it appears as **(ptr to)foo**.

The value data type exists only to address certain technical problems that arise in Franz LISP's implemention of arrays. As such, it is not of interest to the average programmer. The rationale for its existence is as follows: Recall that an array in Franz is a rather complex data structure. One of its components points to the block of contiguous storage where the array data are kept. In the case of Franz's MacLISP style arrays, this chunk of storage contains pointers to the actual data elements of the array. Thus if the first element of an array is the list **(a b c)**, the first location of the array's data space will contain a pointer to the representation of this list.

The internal array data access function used to implement MacLISP style arrays automatically follows these pointers, so the user never has to directly confront a pointer. However, should the user meddle with the internal components of these arrays, he may end up manipulating pointers himself.

Since these pointers do not correspond to any other Franz data type, a separate type has been created for them.

For example, the data portion of an array item may be accessed using the primitive function **arrayref**. This function takes an array name and an index, and returns the actual contents of the location of the array selected by that index. Since arrays are referenced by the function cell of the atom that is their namesake, we can access the array using **getd**. Then we can use **arrayref** to look at the actual data element:

```
-> (array foo t 3 4)
array[12]
-> (store (foo 0 0) '(a b c))
(a b c)
-> (setq x (arrayref (getd 'foo) 0))
(ptr to) (a b c)
-> (foo 0 0)
(a b c)
-> (type (getd 'foo))
array
-> (type x)
value
->
```

The call to **arrayref** references the first location of the storage for the array, which contains a pointer to the first data item of the array, i. e., the datum referenced by **(foo 0 0)**.

(In the original MacLISP language, arrays of fixnum data, i. e., those arrays created by calls of the form **(array foo fixnum x y)**, keep the actual data, rather than pointers to the data, in the array's data space. In this sort of implementation, evaluating **(setq x (foo i j))** results in the value of **x** and **(foo i j)** sharing the same storage location. Then changing the value of **(foo i j)** would change the value of **x** as well. The designers of Franz felt that this is dangerous. Thus in Franz, all MacLISP compatible arrays use pointers, except those specially designated as **block–fixnum** or **block– flonum** .)

You can create a value data object using the function **ptr**. **(ptr sexp)** will return a value data object which points to the value of **sexp**.

Pointers in Franz always evaluate to the data object at which they point. Thus we can follow pointers by using **eval**:

```
-> (setq x (ptr '(a b c)))
(ptr to) (a b c)
-> (eval x)
(a b c)
->
```

18.8. BINARY

Function definitions in LISP are usually stored as some sort of lambda form. However, not all function definitions in a LISP system will be written in LISP. The most primitive functions in LISP must be written in machine code; in addition, most common LISP functions are written in machine code for efficiency's sake. Most LISPs, including Franz, also let users compile functions written in LISP into machine code for efficiency. Finally, it is possible to write a function in another language, for example, C, to load this function into a LISP process, and use it as a function definition.

All these non-LISP functions are classified as **binary**. That is, if we use **getd** to get the definition of a machine coded function, it would return a datum of type **binary**. For example, **car** is coded in machine language:

```
-> (type (getd 'car))
binary
->
```

To apply any function, LISP needs to know where the body of the function is. It also needs to know how to deal with that function's arguments (e. g., should they be evaluated or not). Recall that the way in which a function deals with its arguments is called its *discipline*. Thus, binary data have two parts: a pointer to the beginning of the actual code that constitutes the function, and a symbol whose print name describes the function's argument discipline. For example, ordinary functions will have a discipline of either **lambda**, **macro**, or **nlambda**. Functions foreign to LISP will have disciplines that are strings of the form **"integer−function"**, **"double−c−function"**, **"subroutine"**, etc.

LISP prints out binarys by printing the code's starting address, hyphenated with the function's discipline:

```
-> (getd 'car)
#c376−lambda
->
```

You probably should have little reason to deal with these data types until you are a fairly accomplished LISP programmer.

18.9. SUMMARY

(1)   Most LISPs support several different types of data. The primitive data types known to Franz are **list** (i. e., dotted pairs), **symbol** (literal atoms), **fixnum** (small integers), **flonum** (double precision floating point numbers), **bignum** (arbitrarily large integers), **binary** (machine coded functions), **string** (character strings), **array** (blocks of contiguous functions with associated access functions), **hunk** (small vectors), **vector** (arbitrarily sized vectors with property lists), **vectori** (immediate vectors for binary data), **value** (pointers), **port** (I/O interfaces), and **other** (everything else).

(2)   The function **type** will return the type of a datum. Individual predicates exist which determine if a datum is of a particular data type, or combination of data types.

(3)   *Strings* are used mostly for efficiency. Most functions that work on atom names also work on strings, and conversely. Some useful string manipulation functions are **maknam**, **implode**, **getchar**, **concat**, **explode**, **get_pname**, **substring**, and **alphalessp**.

(4)   *Arrays* are blocks of data with associated accessing functions. Simple arrays, called *MacLISP style* arrays, can be created with the function **array**. Elements of these arrays are accessed by applying the array name to indices. They are changed using the function **store**. Franz LISP allows the user to supply completely arbitrary array accessing functions.

(5)   Hunks are small vectors whose length is always a power of 2. Accessing elements of a hunk is efficient, but it cannot be done as flexibly as with an array. Hunks are created using the functions **hunk** or **makhunk**. Their elements are accessed using the function **cxr**. The elements of a hunk can be changed using the function **rplacx**.

(6)   *Vectors* and *immediate-vectors* are experimental data types. They are arbitrarily sized vectors with associated properties. The properties are used to make vectors behave like user-defined data types. Vectors are created using the functions **vector** and **new—vector**. Elements are accessed using the function **vref**, and altered using the function **vset**. **vsetprop** and **vprop** set and get the property of a vector, respectively. The functions **vectori—byte**, **vectori—word**, and **vectori—long** create different types of immediate-vectors, as do **new—vectori—byte**,

new—vectori—word, and **new—vectori—long**. The elements of these data types are accessed by functions of the form **vrefi—byte**, etc.

(7)   *Values* are pointers to other LISP values. They are usually used only in the implementation of arrays.

(8)   *Binary* data refers to machine coded functions. These have a *discipline,* which refers to how LISP treats the function's arguments. They also have an address, at which location they reside in a LISP process.

Exercises

(1)   Use vectors, arrays, or hunks to implement your favorite hashing scheme. Note — LISP is particularly well-suited to implement a hash table with buckets.

(2)   Write a LISP function **matrix—multiply** that takes two arrays as input. **matrix—multiply** interprets these arrays as matrices and returns their matrix product.

(3)   Write a LISP function that interprets a vector as a point in n-dimensional space, and computes the distance between two of them.

19

Systems Functions

19.1. INTRODUCTION

LISP has a number of functions that reflect aspects of LISP as a system. This chapter describes such systems functions. Most of these functions are highly specific to Franz LISP and UNIX. However, functions analogous to many of these do exist in LISPs that run in other environments.

These functions fall into two categories: those that pertain to a process's interaction with the operating system, and those that refer to internal characteristics of the LISP interpreter. For example, finding out information about the current UNIX shell environment is an example of the former. Finding out how much time the interpreter has spent garbage collecting is an example of the latter. We present these functions in this order.

19.2. OPERATING SYSTEM FUNCTIONS

19.2.1. Cloning LISP

Suppose we have been interacting with the LISP interpreter for a while and now wish to test out an idea. However, our idea might be potentially dangerous. That is, it might destructively change some of the structures we have just spent hours setting up. What we would like is some way to save the current state of the LISP environment. Then if we test out our idea and it turns out to be a disaster, we can restore the world to its previous state and go on.

The function **fork** lets us do just this. A call to **fork** (with no arguments) causes the current LISP process to spawn an identical copy. Both processes continue running. Now the user can play with one of the processes. If it becomes unproductive, the user can kill that process and return to the other, which should still be in its virgin state.

However, the user must be careful that only one of the LISP processes interacts with the terminal after the fork. To do so, the system function **wait** can be used to make the original process wait for the spawned process to die off. **wait** causes the process in which it is called to wait until the next spawned process dies. Then **wait** returns **(processid . status)**, i. e., the UNIX process identification number dotted with a UNIX status code. To help tell the two processes apart, **fork** returns **nil** to the spawned process and the process number of the spawned process to the original process.

Here is an example of how to use **fork** and **wait** to temporarily duplicate the current LISP process. First, for demonstration purposes, I make some identifiable alteration in the current LISP process:

> **-> (setq proc 'parent)**
> **parent**

Now I spawn a duplicate child process:

> **-> (cond ((fork) (wait)))**
> **nil**

Fork always returns non-**nil** to the original process and **nil** to the child. Hence in the original, the **wait** is executed; in the spawned process, it is not. This results in the original process grimly waiting for the child to die. In the meantime, the child inherits the terminal. So we are talking to the spawned process now. In a real situation, I might do some potentially dangerous activity here. However, in this example, I will just do something to differentiate the child process from the parent:

> **−> (setq proc 'child)**
> **child**
> **−> proc**
> **child**

Now we kill the child process, which returns control to the parent:

> **−> (exit)**
> **(13605 . 0)**

As soon as the **exit** is complete, control returns to the parent, which takes over the terminal again. Remember, the parent was suspended in the **wait** above until this moment. Thus the dotted pair just printed was printed by the parent process. It constitutes the value of the **cond** that we began to execute above in the parent process. Just to be sure we are back in the right place, let us check the value of **proc**:

> **−> proc**
> **parent**

This testifies to the fact that we are in the original process.

19.2.2. Creating a Shell Subprocess

We can also fork off a new shell from LISP by typing **(shell)**. This function returns the exit code of the new shell when the new shell dies. For example:

> **−> (shell)**
> **% pwd**
> **/na/bair/wilensky/cs182**
> **% users**
> **arens baden chertok davis demmel despain despain despain**
> **diana fateman fujimoto jkf kateveni layer lisa markhill mayo**
> **ouster pattrsn salmon sequin stock tamir taylor wilensky**
> **% exit**
> **% 0**
> **−>**

19.2.3. Executing UNIX Commands

If we just want to execute a particular UNIX command, we can use the function **exec**. This function takes any number of arguments, concatenates them all together with spaces in between, and uses this string to fork off a process. For example, if I want to execute the UNIX command line **ls −l intro**, which gives me a long directory listing of my file **intro**, I can type the following:

> −> (**exec ls −l intro**)
> −rw−rw−r−− 1 **wilensky**   4556 Mar 28 14:17 intro
> **0**
> −>

We can also invoke a general UNIX process using the *process function. Applying *process to a single argument will cause it to fire up a UNIX process by that name, and wait for the process to die off before returning, e. g.:

> −> (***process 'uptime**)
> 3:42pm up 5:24, 41 users, load average: 6.55, 6.19, 5.74
> **0**
> −>

Used in this manner, *process returns the exit code of the process it creates, in this case, **0**. However, *process can also be used to fire up an arbitrary UNIX process that we can communicate with from LISP. This is done by supplying *process with optional arguments. If optional arguments are present, *process starts a process and returns a list that may contain I/O ports for communicating with the new process. If the first optional argument is non-**nil**, then a port will be created which the LISP process can use to send characters to the new process. The second argument works similarly with respect to reading from the new process. *process returns a list of the form (*readport writeport pid*) where *readport* and *writeport* are the ports created, or **nil** if the respective port was not requested. *pid* is the process id of the new process.

For example, suppose I want to use the UNIX command **wc** to count the number of characters in the list (**a bcd e fgh i**). Recall that **wc** reads an input source and outputs the number of lines, words, and characters, respectively, separated by spaces. I can get the number of characters by first setting up a **wc** process with an input and an output port. Then I can **print** the elements of the list to that port, and **read** in the result. First, let us set up the process and associated ports:

> −> (**setq ports (*process 'wc t t)**)
> (**%from−process %to−process 11727**)

The first two elements of value returned by *process are the ports we need to talk to the **wc** process. Now we can write to the process using the "to"

265

port:

> **—> (mapc '(lambda (x) (print x (cadr ports))) '(a bcd e fgh i))**
> **(a bcd e fgh i)**

Presumably, the process got what we sent it, has processed it, and is now ready to send back its result. We get the process's output by reading from the "from" port:

> **—> (setq lines (read (car ports)))**
> **0**

This returns **0** because there was no "newline" character in our input (i. e., **wc** counts this as 0 lines). Next, **wc** outputs the number of words. This is what our next **read** should tell us:

> **—> (setq words (read (car ports)))**
> **1**

We get only 1 word because we output no spaces to **wc** between each of the symbol names. Finally, we can **read** the number of characters:

> **—> (setq chars (read (car ports)))**
> **9**

This is the result we wanted. Now let us be good programmers and **close** the ports we no longer need:

> **—> (close (car ports))**
> **t**
> **—> (close (cadr ports))**
> **t**

Finally, we need to do one more thing because of a peculiarity of UNIX: Even though this process has finished and wants to die, UNIX will keep it around as a sort of zombie until someone asks about it. So we use **wait** to inquire about the process:

> **—> (wait)**
> **(613 . 0)**
> **—>**

wait returns immediately, as the process is ready to die. This enables UNIX to clean up the remnants of the process.

If only one port to the process is needed, the functions ***process—receive** and ***process—send** can be used. These each expect one argument, which should evaluate to a command. They fire up a background process, and return a port for either receiving from or sending to the new process. The process does its other I/O with **/dev/null**.

19.2.4. Overlaying the LISP Process

Instead of firing up a new subprocess, the user may want to replace altogether the current LISP process with another process. This can be done using the function **exece**. The argument to **exece** should evaluate to the name of a UNIX program (arguments to this program may occur as extra arguments to **exece**). LISP will try to fire up this process, and, if it is successful, the new process will replace the LISP process. If LISP fails to fire up this process for any reason, the LISP process will continue. In this case, **exece** will return the error code generated by the system.

For example, suppose I want to replace my current LISP process with the UNIX shell located in **/bin/sh**. I could use **exece** to do this as follows:

        —> (exece '/bin/sh)
        $ date
        Mon Apr 18 10:18:22 PST 1983
        $

Note that, in this example, I had to specify the full path name of the UNIX program I wanted to run. In our previous examples of LISP functions that started UNIX processes, we were able to supply the functions with only an abbreviated description of the process to be created (e. g., the name of the program), and let UNIX figure out where it is located. This is because the LISP functions used in these other examples call a UNIX shell process to do file name expansion on their arguments. **exece** does not do this expansion, so it needs to be supplied with the full path name.

19.2.5. Terminating the Current LISP Process

For completeness, we mention the function **exit** again in the current context. This is a function of no arguments that causes the current incarnation of LISP to die, and control to return to the parent process.

267

19.2.6. Saving the Current LISP Process

It is possible to save the current LISP process for subsequent use. This is done using the function **dumplisp**. **dumplisp** takes one argument, which should be a file name. The current LISP process is dumped into this file. When that file name is executed as a UNIX command, the resulting process will be identical to the original process when **dumplisp** was done.

dumplisp requires a fair amount of storage as it has to save an entire LISP core image. It may be more efficient, if you are compiling your code, to use the autorun option mentioned in the chapter on compiling. This requires more work to be done each time the process is run, but much less storage is required.

19.2.7. Changing the Current Directory

chdir sets the current directory to the value of its argument. The argument should evaluate to an atom name that conforms to the UNIX path conventions. **chdir** returns **t** if it succeeds; otherwise, it causes an error.

For example, if **foo** were a valid subdirectory in my current directory, I could change to this directory as follows:

        -> (chdir 'foo)
        t
        ->

Most UNIX shells accept as abbreviations a number of special symbols in directory names. For example, the symbol .. is an abbreviation for the parent of the current directory. We can supply such abbreviations as arguments to **chdir**, but we have to enclose them in symbol delimiters in order to get **read** to accept the input. Thus

        -> (chdir '|..|)
        t
        ->

would connect my process to the parent of the previously connected directory.

19.2.8. Obtaining Information about the UNIX Environment

The function **getenv** is useful for finding out information about the current UNIX environment. This function takes one argument, which it evaluates.

268

It treats the result as a UNIX environment variable and returns its value in the current environment. For example, **(getenv 'SHELL)** will return the value of the UNIX environment variable **SHELL** in the current environment. In my case, this returns the following:

> **−> (getenv 'SHELL)**
> **/bin/csh**
> **−>**

19.2.9. Catching Signals

There are a number of different *signals* that the UNIX operating system can send to a process. If these are sent to a LISP process, they will normally be handled in routine ways. For example, an *interrupt* signal might be sent to a LISP process by the user typing the interrupt character on the terminal. LISP normally intercepts this signal and treats it as a kind of error:

> **−> Interrupt:ˆc**
> **Break nil**
> **<1>:**

Here I typed my interrupt character, which is CTRL-c. LISP catches it, prints out a message, and enters the break package.

In Franz, the user program can handle some UNIX signals. To do this, the function **signal** is used to specify the function that the user would like to have executed should the process encounter a given signal. **signal** takes two arguments: The first should evaluate to a number that by convention designates the particular kind of signal to be caught. The second should evaluate to the name of the function that should handle the signal. This function should be a function of one argument, as UNIX will pass this function the code used to distinguish one sort of signal from another.

For example, the code for the signal *interrupt* is 2. If I want LISP to print out **boo** and then return to the top level upon receiving an *interrupt* signal, I would do the following:

> **−> (defun my−service−interrupt (x) (print 'boo) (reset))**
> **my−service−interrupt**
> **−> (signal 2 'my−service−interrupt)**
> **sys:int−serv**

Note **signal** returns as its value the old signal servicing function, which in this case was the default function **sys:int−serv**. Now I will type my

269

interrupt character. This will not appear on the screen. Instead, the function **my—interrupt—service** will be executed:

> $->$ **boo**
> [**Return to top level**]
> $->$

I typed my interrupt character, which caused my function to catch the interrupt, print out **boo**, and return to the top level.

Currently, only four UNIX signals are caught. These are the following, with associated code numbers: *interrupt (2), floating exception (8), alarm (14),* and *hang-up (1).*

19.3. INTERNAL LISP SYSTEMS FUNCTIONS

This section describes those LISP systems functions that we have not previously encountered.

19.3.1. Determining if an Atom Is Bound

boundp determines whether its argument, which should evaluate to a literal atom, is bound to a value. **boundp** returns **nil** if this atom is unbound; if its value is **val**, **boundp** returns **(nil . val)**.

19.3.2. Calling the Top Level Explicitly

top—level invokes the normal LISP top level. This is useful in that, if you redefine **top—level**, a subsequent **reset** will invoke the redefined top level.

19.3.3. Garbage Collection

gc forces a garbage collection. Normally, users do not call **gc** themselves, because garbage collection happens automatically when LISP runs out of free storage.

19.3.4. Timing

ptime is a function that returns a list of two elements. The first is the amount of processor time used by the LISP job so far; the second is the amount of time used by the garbage collector. Time is measured in 60ths of a second, with the first number including the second. However, the amount of time used by the garbage collector is not recorded until the first call to **ptime**. This prevents incurring overhead when the user is not interested in monitoring the time spent collecting garbage.

19.3.5. Obtaining On-Line Information about LISP

help is useful for obtaining on-line information about Franz. **help** causes a portion of the Franz LISP *Manual* to be printed on the terminal. Typing **(help fnc)** will start printing beginning with a description of the function **fnc**; **(help n)**, where **n** is a number, starts the printing at chapter **n**; **(help l)**, where l is the letter of an appendix, prints that appendix (currently works only for appendices **b** and **c**); finally, **(help tc)** prints a short table of contents.

help without any arguments prints a summary of its various commands.

19.3.6. Internal Options

Franz LISP has many internal options whose values can be queried and set through the use of the functions **status** and **sstatus**, respectively. The appendix should be consulted for information about these options, many of which are useful to the experienced LISP programmer but are not of great interest to us here.

19.4. SUMMARY

(1)   There are several ways to create new processes in LISP. **fork** creates a clone of the current LISP process. The function **wait** is useful in conjunction with **fork** to allow only one of these processes to access the terminal. **shell** creates a shell subprocess. **exec** executes a particular UNIX command. So does **process**, which also permits I/O between the LISP process and UNIX command. **exece** overlays the current LISP process with another UNIX process.

(2)   There are a number of functions for communicating between LISP and UNIX. **chdir** changes directories. **getenv** returns the value of a UNIX environment variable.

(3) The function **dumplisp** can be used to save the current LISP core image. The compiler's autorun option gives another way of doing this.

(4) The function **signal** lets the user program service UNIX signals on its own.

(5) Some miscellaneous LISP systems functions are **boundp**, **top–level**, **gc**, **ptime**, and **help**.

(6) Many internal options can be queried and set with the functions **status** and **sstatus**, respectively.

20

Compilation

20.1. INTRODUCTION TO LISP COMPILATION

As we discussed throughout this book, LISP code is usually interpreted. There are many advantages to interpretation. In particular, interpreted programs are easier to debug because the actual code is readily accessible. However, there is a price to pay for this convenience. Most LISP programs execute more slowly than they might if they were not interpreted. If the added flexibility of interpretation is outweighed by its cost, the user may wish to sacrifice the former for the latter.

This trade-off can be accommodated by *compiling* LISP code. Compiling in LISP is similar to compiling in other languages. A file of LISP code is passed through a program called a *compiler*. The output of the compiler is an *object* file. This file contains machine language versions of the original LISP code. When loaded into LISP, the compiled functions can be called just like ordinary LISP functions. The only differences are (1) the code will run much faster and (2) the original LISP code is no longer there to inspect.

Compiled code is much faster than interpreted code because it is possible to eliminate all sorts of overhead built in to the interpretation process. For example, to interpret a call to a function, LISP must first **cdr** down a list to reach the next s-expression. Then it must test to see if this form is an atom or a list. If it is a list, it must take its **car** to get its first element. This might be a symbol or a **lambda** form, etc., so LISP must check to see which it is. In any case LISP must examine its discipline to determine how to treat the arguments. Once the arguments are dealt with, the actual code of the function can be executed.

If the function were **car**, for example, the actual code might be a single machine instruction (all **car** has to do is follow a pointer). However, the LISP interpreter spent most of its time just getting to this instruction. If we translate this call into machine code, we could replace it by code that evaluates the argument and then executes the one machine instruction that is equivalent to **car**. The resulting code should therefore be enormously faster. And it is.

In this chapter we introduce *liszt,* a Franz LISP compiler. Liszt performs the transformation of LISP code into more efficient machine code. While the details of this compiler are specific to Franz, most of the considerations that have gone into its design are the same as those of other LISP compilers. We describe these special considerations that one must take into account to allow code to compile correctly. The use of this particular compiler is illustrated, and its various options given. We examine how compiled code can be loaded into a LISP process. Finally, some particular implementation issues are discussed.

20.2.   USING THE LISP COMPILER

The Franz LISP compiler is run as an ordinary UNIX command. For example, to compile the file **foo.l**, we would type the following:

> % **liszt foo**

This will compile the file **foo.l** and produce as output a file containing object code versions of its contents. This object file will be named **foo.o** (of course, other LISPs will use somewhat different conventions). Normally, the compiler prints the name of each function it compiles on the standard output. There are a number of options that may be given to the compiler, but we will not bother with these for now.

Once the object file has been produced by the compiler, the user may load it into a LISP process using the command **load**. This command is smart enough to know that files ending in **.o** are compiled code, and loads them accordingly. **load** uses the function **fasl** to do the actual work. The user may run **fasl** himself to load compiled code, but **load** is more convenient.

For example, suppose the code for **factorial** were in the file **f.l**:

```
% cat f.l
(defun factorial (n)
   (cond ((zerop n) 1)
         (t (times n (factorial (sub1 n))))))
%
```

We can run this source file through the compiler to produce an object file:

```
% liszt f
Compilation begins with Liszt vax version 8.36
source: f.l, result: f.o
factorial
%Note: f.l: Compilation complete
%Note: f.l:  Time: Real: 0:8, CPU: 0:0.38, GC: 0:0.00 for 0 gcs
%Note: f.l: Assembly begins
%Note: f.l: Assembly completed successfully
%
```

The compiler printed a number of messages on the terminal, marking its progress through the compilation. Noting that it has successfully completed its task, we are now ready to use its output within a LISP process:

```
% lisp
Franz Lisp, Opus 38.77
-> (load 'f.o)
[fasl f.o]
t
-> (factorial 8)
40320
->
```

Here we load the file **f.o**. This causes the function **factorial** to be defined, just as if we loaded a file of LISP code. However, although it is not obvious from this example, the code executed much faster than interpreted LISP code would have. Also, we can no longer examine the function's definition. For example, look what happens when I try to pretty-print **factorial**:

```
-> (pp factorial)

pp: function factorial is machine coded (bcd)

t
->
```

The function definition is opaque because it is no longer a chunk of LISP code. Rather, it is stored as executable but uninterpretable machine code.

20.2.1. Liszt Processing

As is true for virtually all LISP compilers, the main pass of Liszt is written primarily in LISP. This pass produces assembly code. When it is finished, the standard UNIX assembler is used to translate the assembly code into machine code.

Thus the compiler itself is essentially a big LISP program. When you run the compiler, you are really running an ordinary LISP process that happens to have the code for the compiler already loaded in. This is convenient because it means that the LISP compiler contains the entire LISP interpreter. This allows the user to communicate with the compiler in LISP when it is necessary to do so. Below we will describe some situations in which it is useful to take advantage of this feature.

20.3. COMPILER DECLARATIONS

LISP code to be compiled is virtually identical to code that is meant to be interpreted. However, there are a handful of considerations that one needs to take into account when writing code that is to be compiled. Not heeding these rules may result in code that will not compile or, even worse, code that compiles incorrectly.

While the details of this section are particular to Franz LISP, all LISP compilers are confronted with more or less the same problems. A very similar treatment of these problems will generally be found in other LISP systems.

Most compiler-specific considerations stem from the following fact: Everything the compiler needs to know to compile the next function in a file may not be available from what has been seen so far. For example, it is desirable to eliminate the overhead at runtime of determining how to treat arguments to a function call. Thus the compiler must know that a function is an expr or a fexpr, etc., in order to compile a call to it correctly. If it has already seen the function's definition, there is no problem. But the function definition may appear later on in the file in which it is referenced. Or it may appear in another file altogether. Thus some means of communicating information about a function to the compiler is necessary.

To address this problem, LISP lets you declare functions and variables to have certain properties. This is done using the function **declare**. This function will have no effect in interpreted code. However, it will supply the compiler with the information it needs to produce the correct object code. For example, to declare **foo** and **baz** to be fexprs, we can place the following code at the front of our source code file:

(declare (nlambda foo baz))

The keyword **nlambda** asserts that the functions following it are fexprs. The keyword **∗fexpr** is also permitted for the sake of MacLISP compatibility. It is also possible to declare a function to be a **lambda** or a **lexpr** (or an **∗expr** or **∗lexpr**, having the same effect). However, the compiler compiles exprs and lexprs the same way, and assumes undeclared functions are one of these kinds. So declaring something to be an expr or a lexpr is never really necessary. Declaring a function to be a fexpr is imperative if the fexpr will not have been seen by the compiler before a call to it is encountered. *Failure to do so may result in incorrectly compiled code that may be difficult to debug.*

20.3.1. Special Variables

Another use of **declare** involves the occurrence of what are called *special variables.* A symbol is a special variable when it is used free in a function. That is, it is referenced within a function but is not local to that function. For example, **var1** is special in the following code:

(defun foo (x) (cons var1 x))

Such variables are special to the compiler because, for the sake of efficiency, the compiler normally turns variable references into stack locations. This is in contrast to how the interpreter treats references to the value of a symbol, which is to use the value cell of that symbol. For example, if we called the LISP version of **foo** given above, LISP would stack the old value pointed to by the value cell of **x**. Then the body of **foo** would reference this value cell as the need arises. Upon exiting, the old value is restored. To speed things up, the compiler does not use the symbol **x** at all. Instead, it allocates a location for a value on the runtime stack. All references to **x** in the interpreted code will be translated into references to this stack location. Now the compiler does not have to bother with saving and restoring the old value of a symbol, because the actual symbol is never touched. And as long as **x** is strictly local to **foo**, no one will ever know the difference.

The problem comes in when some other function tries to reference this variable. For example, suppose we had a function with the following definition:

(defun caller (var1 var2) ... (foo 7) ...)

If we compiled this code as we suggested above, the **var**is would be turned into stack locations. But then when we tried to run **foo**, it would have no way of knowing which of these stack locations holds **var1**. For example, the arguments to **caller** could just as easily have been **(var2 var1)**. In this case, they would have been given different stack positions. In fact, **foo** might be called by some other function whose arguments appear in precisely this order. So it would not be possible for **foo** to reference the value of **var1** in any consistent manner.

The solution to this problem is to make sure that references to variables like **var1** are *not* compiled into stack locations when functions like **caller** are compiled. This gets tricky, though, because the compiler may not know at the time it compiles **caller** whether or not **var1** will be used free in some other function. So a declaration is useful here.

If you use a variable as a formal parameter to a function, or as a local variable in a **prog** or a **do**, and if some other function references it, then you must declare it to be special. Again, **declare** can be used for this purpose. For example, to declare **var1** and **var2** to be special, I can do the following:

(declare (special var1 var2))

In addition, **(declare (specials t))** declares *all* variables to be special.

Usually, a variable only needs to be considered special for some segment of code. For example, if I use **var1** in another function definition in which it is a strictly local variable, then I would not want it considered special. This can be achieved by the clause **(unspecial var1)** within a call to **declare**.

Remember, all variables used for communicating between functions must be declared special before they are seen by the compiler. *Failure to do so will result in incorrectly compiled code which may be extremely difficult to debug.*

20.3.2. Other Declarations

There are several other properties that can be declared. Doing so will enable the compiler to produce better code, although it will be able to produce correct code without these declarations.

Local Functions

A function can be declared *local to a file*. A local function's name is known only to the functions defined within the same file as that function. Declaring a function to be local has two advantages: First, it allows the same name to be used in another file without a conflict. Moreover, local functions can be entered and exited much faster than non-local functions.

The function **func** can be declared to be local to a file by including the following declaration in that file:

(declare (localf func))

Outputting Compiled Macro Code

Another useful declaration concerns how the compiler treats macro definitions. Normally, when the compiler encounters a macro definition, it simply evaluates its definition so that the macro is available within the current running of the LISP compiler. The compiler uses this definition to expand calls to a macro at compile time. The resulting expansion is compiled into machine code.

Thus the definition of the macro is not needed at runtime, and is normally not included in the output of the compiler. However, should you want the compiler to include the macro definition in its output anyway, you can insist that it do so. The compiler will comply by compiling the macro definition into machine code and including the compiled version in its output. Then the macro will be defined in the interpreter when the compiled object file is **load**ed.

You can declare that macro definitions be compiled as well as evaluated at compile time by issuing the declaration

(declare (macros t))

Compiling Fixnum Values

This declaration is concerned strictly with efficiency. The declaration **(declare (fixnum i j))** states that **i** and **j** are to be considered fixnums. Where possible, more efficient code will be generated for computations involving these variables.

Specifying the Number of Arguments to a Function

Franz also allows you to specify the range of the number of arguments to a function. This is useful if the compiler does not have enough information to figure this out by itself, but you would like an error message if the function is used incorrectly. You can declare the range of arguments by a call of the form (declare (*arginfo (*func min max*))). This asserts that the number of arguments to the function *func* must be between *min* and *max*. If one of these is **nil**, that bound is assumed to be unknown.

The General Call to DECLARE

You can include as many declarations as you like within a single call to **declare**. For example, the following usage of **declare** is valid:

```
(declare
   (nlambda func1 func2)
   (localf func2 func3)
   (special var1 var2 var3)
   (macros t))
```

20.3.3. Local Declarations

You can make a declaration local to a segment of code by placing the call to **declare** within a body of code rather than at the top level of a file. For example, a function definition of the form

```
(defun foo (a b)
   (declare (special a))
   ...)
```

will declare **a** to be special only for this function definition. The formal parameters of the function are included, e. g., the parameter **a** above would be special. Calls to **declare** can be placed at the beginning of a call to a **prog** or a **do** as well.

To declare the range of the number of arguments of the function being defined, you can use the form (declare (*args min max)). This is similar to the ***arginfo** declaration decribed above.

20.4. OTHER COMPILER-SPECIFIC FORMS

There are a number of forms that the Franz LISP compiler treats specially. These are fairly specific to this compiler, and are described below.

20.4.1. EVAL−WHEN

Suppose our code contains a call to a macro. As we mentioned above, the compiler expands macros when they are encountered and then compiles the expanded code. This requires that the macro definition be encountered by the compiler before a call to the macro is seen.

But even if this is done, there is another potential problem. Suppose our macro definition makes use of some utility function, say the expr **macro−utility**. Clearly, this function must also be defined before a call to the macro is encountered, since it is needed to do the macro expansion. However, just putting the definition of **macro−utility** in the file will not help. The compiler will treat this like any other expr and simply compile its definition. This is not what we want. Rather, we want the compiler to *evaluate* this definition, not compile it. But so far, we have no way of instructing the compiler to evaluate something rather than compile it.

To exercise more control over what the compiler does, the function **eval−when** may be used. A call to **eval−when** takes the form (**eval−when** *(-keywords-) -exps-*). The keywords may be any of **eval**, **compile**, or **load**. If the keyword **compile** is present, then the compiler will evaluate each of the subsequent expressions. If **load** is specified, then the compiler will compile each of the expressions (and the expression will subsequently be evaluated when it is loaded). The keyword **eval** is ignored by the compiler; its presence will cause the interpreter to evaluate the expressions, however.

Thus if we include the expression

>   (**eval−when (compile) (defun macro−utility ...)**)

in a file we are compiling, then the function **macro−utility** will be defined during the compilation. If we include the expression

>   (**eval−when (compile load) (defun macro−utility ...)**)

in the file, **macro−utility** will both be defined during the compilation and be compiled and included in the object file.

20.4.2. Including Other Files

The functions **include** and **includef** each take a file name as an argument; the latter evaluates its argument while the former does not. They each cause the specified file to be read in and compiled by the compiler. The result is just as if the included file were textually inserted into the original text. Nested inclusion is allowed.

20.4.3. Special PROGNs

When the compiler sees an expression of the form (**progn 'compile** -*exps*-) it compiles the expressions as if they were encountered on the top level. This is useful because it allows the user to write a macro that expands into more than one function definition. This is done by defining a macro that expands into one of these forms, where each expression is a function definition.

20.4.4. Function Definitions

When the compiler encounters a function definition of an expr, fexpr, or lexpr, it compiles it into machine code. The resulting code is included in the compiler's output file. Of course, it is to produce such code that we are compiling in the first place.

Whenever it is possible to do so, the compiler will expand the macros in these definitions. Thus all macro definitions must precede calls to those macros. As was mentioned above, function definitions of macros are themselves normally just evaluated rather than compiled. These will be compiled as well if a (**declare** (**macros t**)) declaration has been made.

20.4.5. Other Forms

All other forms are simply placed into the compiler's output file to be evaluated when that file is loaded into the intepreter.

20.5. SOME COMPILER-SPECIFIC PROGRAMMING
CONSIDERATIONS

The following sections describe some programming considerations that pertain to compiled code. In some cases, taking these considerations into account will prevent compiled code from behaving differently than interpreted code. In other cases, it will allow the programmer to produce better compiled code, or to produce it more easily.

20.5.1. A Problem with Lexprs

A function called within a compiled lexpr cannot use **arg** to reference the lexpr's arguments. That is, if **caller** is a lexpr and calls the function **callee**, then **callee** cannot use **arg** to reference **caller**'s arguments. This will work if both **caller** and **called** are interpreted, however. Be careful not to write such code if you plan to compile it later on.

20.5.2. A Problem with Literals

If a literal (i. e., **quote**d) s-expression appears in a compiled function definition, LISP will normally store the s-expression in something called *pure* program space. Pure space is storage for those things that should never change during the course of running a program. The garbage collector never looks at pure space, which reduces the amount of work it must do.

However, if your code uses some destructive functions, e. g., **rplaca**, to modify a literal, severe problems will result. Although it is not usually a good idea to write such code in the first place, there is a way around this problem. If the symbol **$purcopylits** is set to **nil**, LISP will not put literals into pure space. As a result, the compiled code is guaranteed to act just like interpreted code. The default value of **$purcopylits** is **t**.

20.5.3. Compiling Arithmetic Functions

The compiler will produce much more efficient code for functions that do arithmetic on fixnums only. **+**, **−**, *****, **/**, ****, **1+**, and **1−** are instances of such functions. Their use is recommended when possible.

20.5.4. Compiler-Only Macros

It is possible to have macros that are only used by the compiler. These are called *cmacros*. Cmacros are defined using the function **defcmacro**, which is otherwise identical to **defmacro**. Cmacros are stored on the property list of the function name, under the property **cmacro**. Thus a function can have both a normal macro definition and a cmacro definition.

20.5.5. Macro Autoloading

If Liszt encounters a symbol without a function definition, but with the property **macro−autoload** having a non-**nil** value, then it will interpret that value as a path name to a file. Liszt will load that file in hope of finding that function's definition. This allows the user to have symbols whose function definition will be loaded only on demand.

20.6. TRANSFER TABLES

When Franz LISP loads compiled code, it sets up something called a *transfer table*. (Note − This sort of thing varies greatly on a LISP to LISP basis.) A transfer table contains one entry for each function in the object file. It is used to transfer control to a compiled function. Depending on the value of a global flag, the interpreter may alter the transfer table at runtime to make calling a function more efficient. However, if this is done, there are two problems: No debugging information will be left on the stack when a call to a compiled function is made. This makes **showstack** and **baktrace** ineffectual. Also, if a compiled function is redefined, the previous version may still be called by old code.

The Franz LISP interpreter will behave as just described if the value of **(status translink)** is non-**nil**. The problems mentioned can be avoided by using the function **sstatus** to change the value of **translink**. A call of the form **(sstatus translink nil)** will clear all the transfer tables. This means that the next time the function is called, its current definition will be found. In addition, **showstack** and **baktrace** will work properly.

A call of the form **(sstatus translink on)** causes the LISP system to go through the transfer tables and reset all the appropriate links. The debugging functions will still not be useful, but transfer to the routines will be fast, and current function definitions at the time of the **sstatus** will be used. Doing a **(sstatus translink t)** will make compiled functions that are subsequently loaded have fast links, but it will not affect current linkages.

20.7. COMPILER OPTIONS

The compiler recognizes a number of options which are described below. The options are typed anywhere on the command line preceded by a minus sign. The entire command line is scanned and all options recorded before any action is taken. Thus the following are all equivalent:

```
% liszt −mx foo
% liszt −m −x foo
% liszt foo −mx
```

Before scanning the command line for options, Liszt looks in the UNIX environment for the variable **LISZT**. If found, Liszt scans its value as if it were a string of options.

The options are interpreted as follows:

C   The assembler language output of the compiler is commented.

e   The next argument on the command line should be a LISP s-expression surrounded by single quotes. It will be **eval**ed before compilation is started.

I   The next command line argument is taken as a filename, and loaded prior to compilation.

m   The file program is compiled in MacLISP mode.

o   The next argument is used as the name of the output file instead of the default practice of sticking **.o** on the name of the input file. If the previous option asked for an assembly language file to be generated, the name change will apply to that file.

p   Profiling code is placed at the beginning of each non-local function.

q   The names of functions being compiled and various messages are not printed.

Q   Compilation statistics and warnings of strange constructs are printed. This is the default.

r   Bootstrap code is placed at the beginning of the object file. The object file can then be executed. Doing so will cause a LISP process to be created and the object file loaded in. This is sometimes called *autorun*.

S   An assembler language file only is created. Its name will be the name of the input file with the characters **.s** appended.

T   The assembler language output is printed on the standard output file.

u   The file is compiled in UCI-LISP mode.

w   Warning messages are suppressed.

W   If a warning message is generated, the compiler will continue compiling but will not run the assembler on the assembly code generated.

x   A cross reference file is created. Its name is the name of the input file with the characters **.x** appended.

20.8. INITIALIZATION

Before Liszt starts compiling, it looks for an initialization file to load in. First it looks in the current directory, and then in the home directory. It looks for one of the following file names: **.lisztrc.o**, **.lisztrc.l**, **lisztrc.o**, or **lisztrc.o**. It loads the first one of these files that it finds.

20.9. SUMMARY

(1)   A LISP compiler translates LISP code into machine code. The resulting code is more efficient but harder to debug.

(2)   The Franz LISP compiler is called *liszt*. It is run by typing **liszt** *filename*. Liszt looks for an initialization file, and loads one if found. Then it compiles *filename*, and produces a file named *filename*.**o**. There are a number of options available to the compiler.

(3)   In writing code that is to be compiled, certain precautions need to be taken. These include having fexprs appear or be declared before they are used, having macro definitions appear before they are used, declaring *special* variables, making sure that functions within a lexpr do not refer to the lexpr's arguments using **arg**, and taking care not to put literals in pure space if they are going to be modified.

(4)   Properties of functions and variables can be specified using the function **declare**. Allowable declarations include **lambda**, **nlambda**, and **lexpr** (alternatively, **∗expr**, **∗fexpr**, and **∗lexpr**), which declare function types; **localf**, which declares a function local to a file; **special**, which declares a variable to be special; (**special t**), which declares all variables special; **unspecial**, which declares that a variable is no longer considered special; and (**macros t**), which declares that macro definitions should be compiled as well as evaluated.

(5)   A number of forms are handled specially by the compiler. In particular, **eval–when** allows for conditional evaluation during compilation. **include** and **includef** cause additional files to be read in and compiled. The form (**progn 'compile exp1 exp2 ...**) causes the expressions to be treated as if they were typed in at the top level. Macro function definitions are evaluated, and all others compiled. Everything else is just passed through to the output file.

(6)   A *transfer table* is used to enable transfer of control to compiled routines. The transfer table can be made to act in different ways depending on the status of **translink**.

Exercise

(1)   Compile the various functions you have written. Use the function **ptime** to compare the performance of compiled and interpreted code.

21

LISP Applications:
Pattern Matching

21.1. INTRODUCTION

Novice LISP programmers often know some other programming language. As a result, their code has more of the appearance of PASCAL or FORTRAN than would code written by more experienced LISP hands. To rectify this situation, the next two chapters present some complete LISP programs. The intent of these sample programs is to convey the flavor of writing in LISP.

We also take this opportunity to discuss two important applications of LISP. These are *pattern matching* and *associative, deductive data base management*. We first present a description of each task. Then we provide and discuss actual LISP programs that perform these tasks. Possible extensions and modifications of each program are discussed in the exercises.

21.2. PATTERN MATCHING

We begin with a LISP pattern matching program. Pattern matching is the process of comparing two expressions to see if one is similar to the other. Pattern matching has a number of important uses. For example, many

programs need to determine if a certain datum has one of a given set of properties. Often, these properties can be expressed as patterns. If so, we can
use our pattern matcher to classify the data by matching the data against
various patterns.

Another use of pattern matching is in artificial intelligence programs. Many
artificial intelligence programs need to perform some kind of reasoning
about the information they encounter. This reasoning typically requires
access to knowledge about the world. For example, a program trying to
understand a natural language text may encounter the sentence "John hit
Mary." To really understand this sentence, the program would need to realize that Mary may be hurt as a result of John's action. To deal with this
sentence appropriately, a program must have recourse to information about
the possible consequences of hitting someone.

Thus artificial intelligence programs need to have some sort of representation of facts about the world. They must then be able to access these facts
when they are applicable to the task at hand. And they must be able to
apply these facts to produce valid results.

Many artificial intelligence programs use pattern-like elements to represent
facts about the world. For example, we might use a pattern to denote the
general fact that hitting someone may hurt that person. Then if our program learned the particular fact that John hit Mary, it could use a form of
pattern matching to determine if it had any knowledge applicable to this
situation. If our program successfully matched the particular fact that John
hit Mary against a piece of the general pattern about the consequences of
hitting, our program could then conclude that Mary is apt to be hurt.

Of course, this description of the application of pattern matching to reasoning is necessarily vague at this stage. By the end of the next chapter, however, we will see how to write code that performs such operations.

21.3. A NOTION OF SIMILARITY

To build a pattern matcher, we first need to have some notion of when two
items are similar. Of course, there are many ways in which we might judge
similarity. The simplest way two expressions could be similar is if they are
identical. In addition, we might want to classify as similar those expressions
that are identical except in certain parts. For example, we might decide that
expressions are similar if they begin with the same three elements, or if they
are the same except for the second item, and so on.

Since we would like to build a general pattern matcher, we cannot decide in advance exactly what criteria we will use to judge similarity. Instead, we would like to provide a fairly general scheme. Then we could implement different criteria of similarity for different applications. One way to implement such a flexible pattern matching scheme is to allow patterns to contain *pattern matching variables*. When a pattern matching variable occurs in an item, the pattern matcher matches it against anything that appears in the corresponding position of the item being matched. Everything that is not a pattern matching variable is allowed to match only itself. We call items that are not variables *literals*.

For example, suppose we follow the standard practice and designate all our pattern matching variables by beginning their names with the character **?** (question mark). Then the following is a pattern:

(a b ?x d e)

This pattern should match any list beginning with the literals **a** and **b**, followed by any expression, which is in turn followed by the literals **d** and **e**. For example, this pattern should match the expressions

(a b c d e)

(a b (x y z) d e)

but not the expressions

(a b c d e f)

(a b c c d e)

(a b (c d e))

In a real program, patterns are more likely to reflect some content, in contrast to the patterns in the examples above. For example, we might represent a fact about the world with the following pattern:

(causes (hit ?x ?y) (hurt ?y))

This is supposed to mean that **?x** (i. e., someone) hitting **?y** (i. e., someone) causes **?y** (the person hit) to become hurt. Of course, our pattern matcher does not know this interpretation of the pattern, nor does it care about it. Rather, it will blindly match this pattern against any item that has the literals **causes**, **hit**, and **hurt** in the right place, and has anything where this pattern has variables. However, the matcher will make sure that whatever matches **?y** in one place matches it in the other. Other than that, it is up to us humans to use this pattern in some fashion so that it ends up acting like the fact it is supposed to represent.

Allowing variables in patterns does not give us complete flexibility in how we can represent similarity. For example, it does not provide us with a convenient way of talking about the length of a pattern. Nevertheless, it does provide a great deal of expressive power.

21.4. PATTERN MATCHING VARIABLE BINDINGS

When we match two expressions, we may want the result of a match to tell us more than just whether or not the expressions matched. For example, if we match **(a b ?x d e)** against **(a b c d e)**, we might like to know not only that they matched, but also that the variable **?x** matched the literal **c**. Similarly, if we have a pattern with more than one variable in it, we would like to know all the correspondences that need to be made for there to be a match. For example, if we match **(a ?x c ?y e)** against **(a b c d e)**, we would like to know that **?x** matches **b** and that **?y** matches **d**.

One way to do this is to have the result of the match return a list of *bindings*. A binding, in the context of pattern matching, is a correspondence of a pattern matching variable to an item made in the course of a match. We can represent a binding as a list of the variable and the item. Thus I can represent the fact that **?x** matches **b** in the above example by specifying the binding **(?x b)**.

We can represent the set of bindings that result from a match as a list. For example, the two bindings produced as a result of the previous example would be represented as the list **((?x b) (?y d))**.

Determining the bindings required for two items to match imposes some important constraints on the matcher. For example, suppose we want to know if the pattern **(a ?x ?x d)** matches **(a b c d)**. We would like the result to be negative, because there is no consistent binding of **?x** that makes this a valid match. This means that, during the course of a match, we need to check to see if the binding for a variable has already been assumed. If so, we need to make sure that subsequent bindings conform to this assumption.

Also, in the examples we have seen so far, we have assumed that we would be matching a pattern, which may contain variables, against a literal item, which does not. However, it may be desirable to match two patterns against each other. For example, we may want to ask if the following two items can be considered equivalent:

(a ?x c ?y e)

(a b ?z d e)

We would like the answer to be yes, if **?x** were bound to **b**, **?y** to **d**, and **?z** to **c**.

The meaning of a successful match between two patterns can be thought of this way: It yields a set of substitutions, which, if they are made in both patterns, will yield the same thing. Thus if **b**, **c**, and **d** were substituted for **?x**, **?z**, and **?y**, respectively, in both patterns, the result of both substitutions would be **(a b c d e)**.

Note that for this to work properly, we need to assume that the variables in different patterns are distinct from one another. We will make this assumption for the time being.

It should also be possible to match two items that have variables in the same place. For example, suppose we try to match the following together:

(a b ?x d e)

(a b ?y d e)

We would like the answer to be affirmative, with the proviso that **?x** is bound to **?y**. Intuitively, this would mean that the two items are the same whenever **?x** is the same as **?y**, or that the resulting expressions would be the same if we substituted **?y** for **?x** in the two patterns.

Similarly, we could allow variables to get bound to items that have variables in them. For example, suppose we match the following together:

(a b ?x d e)

(a b (1 ?y 3) d e)

We would like to know that these two can be the same if **?x** is bound to **(1 ?y 3)**.

This sort of match is actually very useful. For example, recall the representation shown above for the fact that hitting someone can hurt that person.

(causes (hit ?x ?y) (hurt ?y))

Suppose now that some program had just learned that John hit Mary. That is, suppose the program was given the input **(hit John Mary)**. Suppose further that this program wants to infer the consequences of this action. To do so, it might try to find some applicable knowledge about what might happen next. Since patterns that begin with **causes** encode such knowledge, our program might want to find those facts beginning with **causes** that are relevant to this input. This can be done by first building the following pattern:

(causes (hit John Mary) ?r)

This pattern can be interpreted as meaning "What is caused by John hitting Mary?" Now we can match this pattern against facts we know until we come to the fact about hitting. When we match these two items together, the match succeeds, and returns the following bindings:

((?x John) (?y Mary) (?r (hurt ?y)))

If we ask for the binding of **?r** in this result, and then substitute variables in the answer with their bindings, we get the item **(hurt Mary)**. Thus our program could conclude that Mary is likely to be hurt as a result of John hitting her.

Matching variables against items that contain variables has some important consequences for our matcher. For example, suppose I match together the following expressions:

(a ?x ?x)

(a ?y c)

If we bind **?x** to **?y**, we cannot also bind **?x** to **c**, because the same pattern matching variable cannot be bound to two different items. If we added no additional binding, the result would be erroneous: Just substituting **?y** for **?x** will not produce identical expressions. It also would be incorrect to call the match a failure, as the two expressions can be made identical. This happens whenever we substitute **c** for both variables.

To represent this condition of the match, **?y** must be bound to **c**. This binding is different from any we have seen so far. It binds a variable against an item that occurs in the same pattern as that variable. To come up with this binding, we need to be a bit cleverer than before. Whenever we match a variable against an item, we should first check to see if it already has a binding. If it does, we continue the match using the *binding* of the variable instead of the variable itself. In our example here, we would first bind **?x** to **?y**. Next, when we try to match **?x** against **c**, we check to see if **?x** has a binding. Since **?x** is bound to **?y**, we continue the match with **?y** instead of **?x**. This results in matching **?y** against **c**, which is exactly what we want.

Note that, in general, if we go about matching in different orders, we could come up with different sets of bindings. For example, in the case above, the matcher could just as well have bound **?y** to **?x** rather than the other way around. Then when it got around to matching **?x** to **c**, **?x** would have no binding and **c** could be assigned to it. We would then have the binding list **((?x c) (?y ?x))** rather than **((?y c) (?x ?y))**.

There is no real problem here. You just should be aware of the fact that there may be several different sets of bindings that constitute a valid result of a match.

21.5. UNIFICATION

If our matcher has the capability to match together two patterns in the manner just described, it is called a *unification pattern matcher.* This is a term from theorem proving. The intuition is that we "unify" two expressions by finding some appropriate bindings for their variables.

Matching two items with variables can lead to some rather nasty problems. For example, suppose we try to match the following expressions against one another:

   (a ?x ?x ?x)

   (a ?y ?y ?y)

As above, we begin by binding **?x** to **?y**. Then when we try to match **?x** against **?y** the second time, we recall the current binding of **?x** and match it against **?y**. Since the current binding of **?x** is **?y**, we end up matching **?y** against itself. Since **?y** has no previous binding, we might simply bind **?y** to **?y**, and add this to the current bindings.

But now look what happens. When we match **?x** against **?y** for the third time, we again get the current binding of **?x**, namely **?y**. And, as before, we match this against **?y**. But **?y** has just been given the binding **?y**. Now when we check to see if **?y** has a current binding, we find that it has the value **?y**. We continue the match with this value, first checking to see if it has a binding. Thus we keep on endlessly asking for the binding of **?y**.

The solution to this problem is to check to see if we are trying to match a variable against itself. If so, this is all right (after all, we want this match to succeed).   we had   not put the binding on the binding list in such an instance.

But an even worse problem can occur. Suppose we try to match the following:

> **(a ?x ?x)**

> **(a ?y (b ?y))**

As before, we end up matching **?y** against **(b ?y)**. Since **?y** has no previous binding, we might be tempted to bind **?y** to **(b ?y)** and say that the match succeeds. However, this cannot be right. If two patterns match, this means that we could substitute variables for their bindings and get identical expressions. But there is in fact no consistent binding of these variables that allows this to happen. If we try substituting **?y** for its value in **(b ?y)**, we would get the expression **(b (b ?y))**. We could now substitute the **?y** in this expression for its value, and so on ad infinitum.

Situations like this one are called *circularities*. To deal with circularities, a pattern matcher must explicitly check each variable against the item it is attempting to bind to it. If the item contains an instance of that same variable, we declare the match a failure. We have to be a bit careful while doing this, though. For example, in the course of some match, **?x** may get **?y** bound to it. Later on, if we try to match **?y** against **(b ?x)**, the match should fail, because the latter form implicitly contains **?y**.

21.6. THE MATCHER

The nasty situations described in the previous section occur infrequently in practice. We check for them in the algorithm given here for completeness and to demonstrate the LISP programming they require. Should you decide to implement your own version of a pattern matcher, you may decide to build one that is less complete, but perhaps a bit simpler.

First, we need to decide exactly what the input and output of our matcher will be. In our examples above, we expressed patterns as lists in which an atom beginning with a question mark denoted a variable. However, if the question mark is actually part of the atom's name, it is difficult to determine if something is a pattern matching variable as opposed to an ordinary atom. A better solution is to represent pattern matching variables as something like (*var* x), where *var* is some predetermined special symbol. Then we can check if something is a pattern matching variable simply by checking if it is a list beginning with the atom *var*.

We would still like to enjoy the convenience of the question mark notation, however. We can do so by making question mark a read macro. Question mark will read in the next s-expression, which should always be an atom, and return a list beginning with *var*, followed by the atom it has read. We can implement such a macro as follows:

(setsyntax '? 'vmacro '(lambda () (list '*var* (read))))

This defines **?** to be a read macro such that **?x** turns into (*var* x).

Now for the result of the match. Above we saw that we could represent the result of a match as a list of bindings. However, if we return a binding list as the result of a match, we would have an ambiguous situation. Presumably, if a match fails, we would like the matcher to return **nil**. But consider the case where we match an item against an identical item. We would not need any bindings to show that the two are equivalent. So if we return the binding list as the result, we could not tell whether the match failed, or whether it succeeded but without any bindings.

To represent the result of a match, we need to deal with three cases: (1) The match may fail altogether; (2) the match may succeed, and produce an associated list of bindings; or (3) the match may succeed, but not require any bindings. To handle these cases, we will have our matcher return a *list of a binding list* should it succeed, and **nil** if it fails. In this way we distinguish between the match failing, which should return **nil**, and the match succeeding with no bindings required, which should return (**nil**). If the match succeeds with the bindings ((?x b) (?y d)), say, the matcher will return the list (((?x b) (?y d))).

Our matcher will work by recursively matching one part of a pattern against another. The matcher will maintain a list of the bindings it has accumulated thus far. Each subsequent match will be done in the context of the previous bindings to make sure that we continue to bind variables consistently.

Thus the main burden of our matcher will be a routine called **match—with—bindings**. This will take as input two items to be matched, and a list of current bindings. **match—with—bindings** will conclude that the two items match if they do so in a way that is consistent with the list of current bindings. It will return the list of the binding list or **nil**, as described above.

We will interface to this routine through a routine called **match**. **match** simply calls **match—with—bindings**, passing it the two items to be matched and an empty list of current bindings.

As our matcher recursively descends both items, it checks to see if it has reached an atom or a pattern matching variable in either one. If it reaches an atom, it just needs to check if the atom is being matched against an **eq** atom. If it reaches a pattern matching variable, it will call the special routine **variable—match**. This routine checks to see if the variable can be bound to its corresponding item in the current context. This involves looking at the current binding of the variable, checking to see if the variable is being bound to itself or to an item that contains it. This latter check is done by the routine **contained—in**. If necessary, **variable—match** will add a new binding to the binding list. A list of the (possibly extended) binding list is returned as the value of **variable—match**.

Without further ado, here is the top-level matcher function:

```
(defun match (pattern1 pattern2)
   (match—with—bindings pattern1 pattern2 nil))
```

match—with—bindings does all the work:

```
(defun match—with—bindings (pattern1 pattern2 bindings)
   (cond [(pattern—var—p pattern1)
            (variable—match pattern1 pattern2 bindings)]
          [(pattern—var—p pattern2)
            (variable—match pattern2 pattern1 bindings)]
          [(atom pattern1)
            (if (eq pattern1 pattern2) (list bindings))]
          [(atom pattern2) nil]
          [t (let ((car—result
                      (match—with—bindings
                        (car pattern1) (car pattern2) bindings)))
               (and car—result
                  (match—with—bindings (cdr pattern1)
                                        (cdr pattern2)
                                        (car car—result))))]))
```

This routine uses the argument **bindings** to carry along the bindings that have been computed thus far in the match. First, the routine checks to see if either pattern is a pattern matching variable. To do so, it uses **pattern—var—p**, a predicate we define below that returns true when its argument is a pattern matching variable. When **match—with—bindings** runs into a pattern matching variable, it calls the routine **variable—match** to handle the matching. Otherwise, it checks if it has bottomed out on an atom. Note that if it succeeds, **match—with—bindings** returns the *list* of the value of **bindings**. As we agreed above, the pattern matcher always returns the list of the binding list as its result.

In the recursive step, we would like to match the **car** and the **cdr** of the patterns, and agree that the two patterns match if both of these submatches work. The difficulty here is that either submatch might return bindings that are inconsistent with those of the other. To prevent this from happening, we first match the **car**s of the two patterns and store the result in **car—result**. This will be either **nil** if this part of the match fails, or the list of a (possibly longer) binding list if it succeeds. We then use the binding list in **car—result** when we match the **cdr**s. This assures us that this half of the match will be consistent with the first half.

The major part left is dealing with the pattern variables. This is done by **variable—match**:

```
(defun variable—match (pattern—var item bindings)
  (if (equal pattern—var item) (list bindings)
    (let ((var—binding (get—binding pattern—var bindings)))
      (cond
        [var—binding
         (match—with—bindings var—binding item bindings)]
        [(not (contained—in pattern—var item bindings))
         (list (add—binding pattern—var item bindings))]))))
```

First, we check if we are matching a variable against itself. Doing so succeeds, but does not produce a new binding. Then we check to see if there is a binding of the variable on the current binding list. If so, we continue by matching this binding against the corresponding item. If there is no current binding, we check for circularities using the function **contained—in**. If the item does not contain the pattern variable, then we add a new binding to the current binding list and return the list of this list as the result.

The only complicated function left is **contained—in**:

```
(defun contained—in (pattern—var item bindings)
  (cond [(atom item) nil]
        [(pattern—var—p item)
         (or (equal pattern—var item)
             (contained—in
               pattern—var
               (get—binding item bindings)
               bindings))]
        [t (or (contained—in pattern—var (car item) bindings)
               (contained—in pattern—var (cdr item) bindings))]))
```

This function checks to see if the containing item is itself a variable. If so, it continues the search through that variable's binding. Otherwise it recursively descends through the item looking for an occurrence of the variable.

All that remains are a few utility functions: We add to a binding list by **cons**ing onto it a list of a variable name and the item bound to it:

> **(defun add—binding (pattern—var item bindings)**
>   **(cons (list pattern—var item) bindings))**

We determine if something is a pattern matching variable if it is a list beginning with ***var***:

> **(defun pattern—var—p (item)**
>   **(and (listp item) (eq '*var* (car item))))**

We get a binding by doing an **assoc**, and then taking a **cadr**. Note that the **cadr** of **nil** in Franz is **nil**, so this is safe to do even if there is no binding:

> **(defun get—binding (pattern—var bindings)**
>   **(cadr (assoc pattern—var bindings)))**

Having gone to all this trouble, let us see how the matcher actually works:

> **—> (match '(a b c) '(a b c))**
> **(nil)**
> **—>**

Here we succeed in matching two identical objects. This is indicated by the list of the empty binding list as the result.

Let us try some expressions with variables. First we match two patterns with variables in different places:

> **—> (match '(a ?x c ?y e) '(a b ?z d e))**
> **((((*var* y) d) ((*var* z) c) ((*var* x) b)))**

The result is the correct list of bindings for the variables in both patterns. Note that the result is hard to read because it contains pattern matching variables in their internal representation rather than in the more convenient input form.

Now let us do an example in which the same variable occurs more than once in a pattern:

```
-> (match '(a ?x ?x) '(a ?y b))
((((*var* y) b) ((*var* x) (*var* y))))
```

As we can see, a consistent set of bindings is found, including the binding of **?y** to **b**.

Here are some more complicated matches:

```
-> (match '(a ?x (c ?y)) '(a (b ?z) (?w ?z)))
(((((*var* y) (*var* z)) ((*var* w) c) ((*var* x) (b (*var* z)))))
-> (match '(causes (hit John Mary) ?r)
          '(causes (hit ?x ?y) (hurt ?y)) )
(((((*var* r) (hurt (*var* y)))
   ((*var* y) Mary)
   ((*var* x) John)))
->
```

Finally, let us test some of the pathological cases we described above:

```
-> (match '(a ?x ?x ?x) '(a ?y ?y ?y))
((((*var* x) (*var* y))))
-> (match '(a ?x ?x) '(a (b ?y) ?y))
nil
->
```

As the examples demonstrate, the matcher correctly handles the cases of matching variables against themselves and of matching a variable against an item that contains that variable.

21.7. SUMMARY

(1) Pattern matching is a way of judging the similarity of LISP objects.

(2) A *pattern* is an s-expression that may contain *pattern matching variables*. A pattern matching variable will get bound to that part of the s-expression against which it is matched.

(3) *Unification* is a kind of pattern matching in which variables are allowed in both objects being matched. A unification pattern matcher tries to find some consistent set of bindings for the variables in both objects. If it is successful, then the substitution of variables by their bindings in each object will result in identical expressions.

(4)   A unification pattern matcher is complicated by the need to check for a number of anomalous situations. In particular, it must detect *circularities,* i. e., circumstances in which the matcher is compelled to bind a variable against an expression containing that variable.

(5)   A unification pattern matcher can be implemented by a modest amount of LISP code. The implementation is recursive in nature.

Exercises

(1)   Modify the pattern matcher to use dotted pairs instead of lists to represent bindings.

(2)   The result of a pattern match is rather messy. This is the case because the result contains the internal representation of pattern matching variables. The function **print** just prints these out as ordinary lists.

Write a version of **print** that prints out pattern matching variables using the question mark notation (i. e., **?x** rather than **(∗var∗ x)**). Now install your print function in your own **read-eval-print** loop so that the result of a match is displayed more legibly.

(3)   The scheme we used to represent bindings is rather inefficient. The first element of a binding is always a pattern matching variable, so there is no reason to store the representation of the entire pattern matching variable. That is, instead of representing the binding of **?x** to **(a b c)** as **((∗var∗ x) (a b c))**, we can simply use **(x (a b c))** without introducing any ambiguity.

Write a version of the pattern matcher which stores binding lists using this more economical representation.

(4)   We could represent pattern matching variables as "marked" atoms instead of as lists beginning with a unique atom. That is, instead of internally representing **?x** as **(∗var∗ x)**, we could represent this variable by setting the **pattern−matching−variable** property of **x** to **t**. Modify the pattern matcher to use this representation of pattern matching variables.

Note that a disadvantage of this representation is that pattern matching variables are no longer obvious when we print out a pattern. Write a function **pattern−print** which causes pattern matching variables to be printed preceded by a question mark.

(5) Suppose we want to specify a pattern that would match only those items that have *numbers* in a certain position. We currently have no way to do this, as we cannot constrain a match so that a variable will match only items of a certain type.

One way to implement this feature is to allow the user to attach an arbitrary predicate as a property of a pattern matching variable. Then when the matcher tries to match a variable against an item, it checks the attached predicate, if one exists. It allows the match only if the item satisfies the attached predicate.

Add a facility to attach arbitrary predicates to pattern matching variables. Then modify the matcher so that variables will be bound only to those items that satisfy their predicates.

22

LISP Applications:
Associative Data Base Management

22.1. INTRODUCTION

Having implemented a pattern matcher in the previous chapter, we are now
in a position to maintain an *associative data base* of facts. An associative
data base is a collection of facts that are retrievable by their content. This is
in contrast to a data base in which you can only ask to see the nth element.
For example, I might ask an associative data base to tell me all the objects it
knows about that happen to be animals, or all the events in which John hit
someone, or whether Fido is a dog.

In this chapter, we describe and implement a simple associative data base
system. We then extend it to handle large data bases more efficiently.
Finally, we add to our system the ability to do automatic deduction. This
will enable the system to "retrieve" facts that are implied by items in the
data base, but which are not literally present.

22.2. AN ASSOCIATIVE DATA BASE IMPLEMENTATION

One way to implement an associative data base is to represent all facts as
patterns. Simple facts may be represented as literal items, and more

complex facts as items that contain variables. For example, we can represent the simple fact that Fido is a dog by the literal item **(dog Fido)**. We can represent the more complex fact that all dogs are animals by an item of the form **(implies (dog ?x) (animal ?x))**. This pattern is meant to denote the idea that being a dog implies being an animal. Now if we want to know which elements in our data base happen to be dogs, we can run through the collection of facts in the data base looking for all those that match the pattern **(dog ?x)**. Or if we want to know if it is true that Fido is a dog, we can check to see if the literal pattern **(dog Fido)** matches anything in our data base. Similarly, if we want to know what is implied by being a dog, we can look for all items that match the pattern **(implies (dog ?x) ?what)**. We will call a pattern that we use to interrogate a data base a *request*.

Of course, for this scheme to work, we need to have some uniform way of representing facts as patterns. Exactly how to do this is a topic of active research in artificial intelligence. It is referred to as the problem of *knowledge representation*. We will not examine or endorse any of the prevailing theories of knowledge representation here. Instead, we shall assume that some simple scheme exists which allows us to represent an individual fact by an individual pattern. The techniques demonstrated here will apply to any such scheme. It makes no difference whether you choose to represent "John loves Mary" as **(loves John Mary)** or **(John loves Mary)**, or **(mumble frump gezork)**, as long as you do so consistently.

22.2.1. Some Implementation Considerations

To build an associative data base, we first need to store all facts in some fashion. In the version shown here, the data base will be a simple list. We will add to that data base by **cons**ing onto it, and look for items in the data base by marching down the list. This is rather inefficient for large data bases, but we will not be concerned with such matters for now.

When we retrieve facts from any associative data base, however, we must be careful that the variables in our request pattern do not clash with those in the patterns in the data base. For example, suppose we represent the fact that everybody loves Mary as **(loves ?x Mary)**. Now suppose we want to know who John loves. We would eventually match the request **(loves John ?x)** against the previous pattern. But rather than succeeding, the match will fail. This happens only because we happened to use the same variable name in one pattern as in the other: After binding **?x** to **John**, the matcher finds that it cannot also match **?x** against **Mary**, so the match fails. Had the request pattern been **(loves John ?z)**, we would have had no problem.

To guard against such difficulties, we can do one' of two things. The matcher can be designed so as to remember which variables are associated with which pattern. Alternatively, it can automatically generate new names for variables in patterns. The solution we will use is a variant of the latter. We will rename all variables in a pattern when the pattern is added to the data base. This is better than renaming the variables in the request pattern, because programs making the request may make assumptions about the names of variables in requests they generate.

Our matcher will return all the items in the data base it finds that match a given request. So in general, the result of querying the data base will be a (possibly empty) list of answers. Each answer will be the form of a binding list. For example, suppose we had a data base that contained the items **(loves ?z ?z)**, **(loves John Mary)**, and **(loves John Sue)**. Then if we queried the data base with the pattern **(loves John ?x)**, we would get the following answer:

> ((((*var* x) Mary))
> (((*var* x) Sue))
> (((*var* z) John) ((*var* x) (*var* z))))

This answer indicates three matches. The first binding list says that the request matched an item in the data base with **?x** bound to **Mary**; the second that it matched an item with **?x** bound to **Sue**; and the third that it matched an item with **?z** bound to **John** and **?x** bound to **?z**. The last binding list is a somewhat convoluted way of saying that the request matches an item with **?x** bound to **John**.

Note that if we query our data base with a literal item, we will get a list of at most one answer. This answer will not have bindings. For example, if we queried our sample data base with the request **(loves John Mary)**, we would get the answer **(nil)**. As in the case of pattern matching, this result indicates a successful operation with no associated bindings. Failure to match anything in the data base will be represented by returning **nil**.

22.2.2. The Manager

We will call our code for dealing with associative data bases a *data base manager*. It consists of two routines. One adds an item to a data base; the other searches through the data base matching each item against the specified request.

First we define **add—to—data—base**, the routine that adds an item to a given data base. We will normally store a data base as the value of an atom. It is therefore useful to pass **add—to—data—base** an unevaluated atom, and change its value to store the updated data base. In addition, patterns usually are known in advance rather than produced on the fly. So we will want our data base updater not to evaluate the item we pass it. We can accomplish these desirata by making **add—to—data—base** a macro.

Also, we must remember to replace with new names the pattern matching variables in the item being added. We will call the routine that does this replacement **replace—variables**. Thus we have the following:

```
(defmacro add—to—data—base (item d—b—name)
  '(setq ,d—b—name
         (cons (replace—variables (quote ,item)) ,d—b—name)))
```

We use the backquote character macro to facilitate the writing of this macro. Other than that, the code is straightforward.

Writing the routine **replace—variables** is a bit trickier. This routine can use **newsym** to create new names for variables. But it must be sure to use consistently the variables it creates. That is, if it replaces the first **?x** in **(loves ?x ?x)** with **?var3**, then it must be sure to replace the second occurrence of **?x** with **?var3**. To do this, **replace—variables** will maintain a list of bindings that associate old variables with their new replacements. Then if it encounters those variables again, it can use the same replacements it used for them last time.

replace—variables will do a normal recursive pass through an item with one twist. A name created for substitution while descending through the **car** of an item needs to be available when we descend through **cdr** of that item. Thus we need to store bindings in some location where they are available to both parts of the recursion. In our pattern matcher we were able to solve a similar problem simply by returning the bindings as the result of a recursive step. But here the result is used to rebuild the new edition of the item. So we need to have an alternative means of communication.

We achieve the needed communication by having **replace—variables** initialize a variable called **!bindings** (the exclamation mark is used as a spelling convention to indicate that the variable is free in some function). **replace—variables** will then call another routine called **replace—variables—with—bindings**. This routine does the actual recursive step, referring to the free variable **!bindings** as needed. Since this variable is free in **replace—variables—with—bindings**, its value will still be available after each recursive step finishes and returns:

```
(defun replace-variables (item)
  (let ((!bindings nil))
    (replace-variables-with-bindings item)))

(defun replace-variables-with-bindings (item)
  (cond [(atom item) item]
        [(pattern-var-p item)
         (let ((var-binding (get-binding item !bindings)))
           (cond [var-binding]
                 [t (let ((newvar (makevar (newsym 'var))))
                      (setq !bindings
                        (add-binding item newvar !bindings))
                      newvar)]))]
        [t (cons (replace-variables-with-bindings (car item))
                 (replace-variables-with-bindings (cdr item)))]))

(defun makevar (atom)
  (list '*var* atom))
```

Let us exercise these functions a bit before going on. First, let us test **replace-variables** on some typical patterns. It should leave literal expressions alone:

```
-> (replace-variables '(loves John Mary))
(loves John Mary)
->
```

It should replace different variables with new, different variables:

```
-> (replace-variables '(loves ?x ?y))
(loves (*var* var0) (*var* var1))
->
```

And it should replace the same variable consistently:

```
-> (replace-variables '(loves ?x ?x))
(loves (*var* var2) (*var* var2))
->
```

Now let us add a few expressions to a test data base. I will call this data base **!d-b!** to indicate that it is a global variable. I will begin by initiating it:

```
-> (setq !d-b! nil)
nil
->
```

We can now use **add-to-data-base** to update **!d-b!**:

```
-> (add-to-data-base (loves John Mary) !d-b!)
((loves John Mary))
-> (add-to-data-base (loves ?x ?x) !d-b!)
((loves (*var* var3) (*var* var3)) (loves John Mary))
-> (add-to-data-base (dog Fido) !d-b!)
((dog Fido)
 (loves (*var* var3) (*var* var3))
 (loves John Mary))
->
```

All that remains is to write a routine that retrieves all items from a data base that match a given pattern. We will call this routine **query**. **query** will simply march through the data base, matching each item against the specified pattern. Since **match** always returns a list of a binding list, we can get the result we want by **nconc**ing together the result of the matches. The function **mapcan** does all this for us, so our retriever is quite simple:

```
(defun query (request data-base)
   (mapcan (function (lambda (item) (match item request)))
          data-base))
```

Let us test out our retriever on the data base **!d-b!** created above. First, let us check to see whether some literal propositions are known to be true:

```
-> (query '(loves John Mary) !d-b!)
(nil)
->
```

The result is a list of one element. This means that we found one item in the data base that matched the request. The one element in our result is **nil**, which means that the item that matched did so without requiring any variable bindings. That is, the request was **equal** to something in the data base. Now let us try the retriever on something we do not know is true:

```
-> (query '(loves John Sue) !d-b!)
nil
->
```

The retriever does not find any expression in the data base that matches this one. It returns **nil** to indicate failure.

We now ask the question "Who does John love?":

> $->$ **(query '(loves John ?x) !d-b!)**
> **((((*var* x) John) ((*var* var3) John))**
> **(((*var* x) Mary)))**
> $->$

The result is a list of two elements, meaning that we found two matches.
The first is a binding list that has **?x** bound to **John**, and **?var3** bound to
John. So this is a baroque way of saying that John loves himself. The
second element shows **?x** bound to **Mary**, meaning that John loves Mary
too.

Note that our simple retriever has a fair amount of power. In particular, we
can query on any part of an item. Thus we can ask questions like "Who
loves Mary?" as well as "Who does John love?":

> $->$ **(query '(loves ?x Mary) !d-b!)**
> **((((*var* x) Mary) ((*var* var3) (*var* x)))**
> **(((*var* x) John)))**
> $->$

We can even ask what relationships exist between John and Mary:

> $->$ **(query '(?r John Mary) !d-b!)**
> **((((*var* r) loves)))**
> $->$

Or who loves whom:

> $->$ **(query '(loves ?x ?y) !d-b!)**
> **((((*var* x) (*var* y)) ((*var* var3) (*var* x)))**
> **(((*var* y) Mary) ((*var* x) John)))**
> $->$

Note that we can get an affirmative answer to a literal query that is not actually in the data base. For example, suppose I asked the question, "Does
John love himself?" We would like to conclude that he does, as our data
base knows that everyone loves himself. In fact, our data base retriever
makes exactly this conclusion:

```
-> (query '(loves John John) !d-b!)
((((*var* var3) John)))
->
```

The result indicates that the query is true, although the answer is a bit cryptic.

In fact, we have observed several other cases in which the results of a query contain distracting references to variables that occur in items in the data base rather than in items in the request. We could modify our retriever to examine each result of the matcher, and eliminate such references. This is left as an exercise to the reader.

22.3. Indexing

As noted above, our retriever will be rather inefficient on large data bases. We could speed it up considerably if we had some clever way to select good candidates for matching rather than looking at every item in the data base. There are a variety of techniques to do so, all of which involve some sort of *indexing*. Indexing means organizing data in some manner so as to facilitate subsequent retrieval of that data. For example, sorting a list is a form of indexing, since sorting makes subsequent look-up amenable to efficient binary search.

Indexing patterns is more difficult than indexing many other forms of data. Patterns have a great deal of structure to them, so it is not obvious exactly how to organize them. Also, patterns may contain variables. The appearance of variables tends to throw a wrench into most simple schemes. For example, it is not clear where patterns with variables should be placed if we tried sorting a data base of facts.

There are a variety of techniques that have been developed to index patterns in a data base. Most of these would take us well beyond the scope of this book. However, we shall look at one simple idea here. The idea takes advantage of LISP property lists to break up a large data base into several small ones. When we add an item to a data base in this scheme, we shall look to see if its **car** is an atom. If so, we will store the item on a list under some property name of that atom. Then, when we try to retrieve a request, we will examine its **car** for a property of this name. Then we need only look down the resulting value to find candidates with which to unify the request.

Since we may want to support several data bases at the same time, we can use the name of the data base as the name of the property to index under.

For example, suppose I want to add **(loves John Mary)** to the data base **!d—b!** using this scheme. I do so by adding this item to the list stored under the **!d—b!** property of the atom **loves**. When fetching a request like **(loves ?x ?y)** from this data base, I first get the list under the **!d—b!** property of **loves**. Then I search this list in the usual fashion.

There are two problems with this scheme, however. First, we may want to store items in the data base that begin with either variables or lists. Such cases are rare in practice. In an actual retriever, we might be willing not to allow such patterns in a data base at all. However, we allow them here for completeness. The solution is simple in any case. Anytime we are asked to add an item to the data base that begins with a list, we stick it on the property list of some special atom, say ***list***. When we add an item that begins with a pattern matching variable, we will put it under a property of the atom ***var***. When we retrieve an item beginning with a list, we will look under ***list***. We will look under ***var*** for every request, however. We need to do this because an item in the data base beginning with a variable might match a request beginning with anything.

The second problem is a bit trickier. Suppose we try to retrieve a request that begins with a variable. We do not want to look solely at the list under ***var***. After all, the request could match items that begin with anything. So we need to search the whole data base in such cases. Again, we could constrain our system not to handle such requests, but we will allow them here.

The reason this is a problem is that we do not have the data base in any one place. We know what is in the data base only via the property lists of a number of atoms. But we have not been keeping track of which atoms we have been using. To do so, we will place on a list each atom which we use to index an item. We will keep this list under a property of the data base name, say ***keys***. Now whenever we need to search the entire data base, we can do so through this property.

We will call our new routine to build up a data base **index**. **index** will determine if the **car** of the item to be added is an atom. If so, it will store the item under a property of that atom. If the item begins with a list, it will be stored under the corresponding property of the symbol ***list***; if it begins with a pattern matching variable, it will be stored under a property of the atom ***var***. **index** will also add the atom name it used to index the entry to a list kept under the ***keys*** property of the name of the data base. To make sure that the name is not added twice, **index** uses a routine called **enter** to update this list:

```
(defun index (item data-base)
  (let ((place (cond [(atom (car item)) (car item)]
                     [(pattern-var-p (car item)) '*var*]
                     [t '*list*])))
    (putprop place
             (cons (replace-variables item) (get place data-base))
             data-base)
    (putprop data-base
             (enter place (get data-base '*keys*))
             '*keys*)))
```

enter adds an atom to a list only if it is not already there:

```
(defun enter (e l)
  (cond [(not (memq e l)) (cons e l)] [t l]))
```

We can use **index** to add some items to a test data base:

```
-> (index '(loves John Mary) '!d-b!)
(loves)
-> (index '(loves ?x ?x) '!d-b!)
(loves)
-> (index '(person John) '!d-b!)
(person loves)
-> (index '((a b c)) '!d-b!)
(*list* person loves)
-> (get 'loves '!d-b!)
((loves (*var* var4) (*var* var4)) (loves John Mary))
-> (get 'person '!d-b!)
((person John))
-> (get '*list* '!d-b!)
(((a b c)))
->
```

Note that unlike **add-to-data-base**, **index** requires its arguments to be quoted. It also returns a list of atom names used to index items rather than the entire data base. These are fairly arbitrary design decisions. In addition, **index** does not require initialization of a data base. Do you see why? It might be useful to have a routine to initialize a data base, however, if we want to start over from scratch.

Now we will define **fast-query**, our data base retrieval function that accesses an indexed data base. If the request to **fast-query** begins with a pattern matching variable, **fast-query** will search the entire data base starting from the *keys* property of the data base name. Of course, in this case, the retrieval is no faster than in our original scheme. If the request begins with anything else, **fast−query** will get the data base list either from the **car** of the request or from *list*, depending upon whether the request begins with an item or a list. It will then search this list using **query**. In these cases, **fast−query** will also search the list under *var*, as the request may also match some item in the data base that begins with a variable:

```
(defun fast−query (request data−base)
  (cond [(pattern−var−p (car request))
         (mapcan
           (function
             (lambda (key)
               (query request (get key data−base))))
           (get data−base '*keys*))]
        [t (nconc
             (query request (get (cond [(atom (car request))
                                        (car request)]
                                       [t '*list*])
                                  data−base))
             (query request (get '*var* data−base)))])))
```

Let us test **fast−retrieve** on the test data base **!d−b!** we created with **index**:

```
−> (fast−query '(loves John ?x) '!d−b!)
((((*var* x) John) ((*var* var4) John)) (((*var* x) Mary)))
−> (fast−query '(?r John Mary) '!d−b!)
((((*var* r) loves)))
−>
```

Note that we cannot tell **fast−query** from **query** insofar as these examples are concerned. This is just what we want, of course, provided that **fast−query** is actually faster than **query** when the data base is large.

22.4. A Deductive Retriever

We noted above that our retriever does a simple form of deduction. Namely, it will conclude that a particular fact is true if the data base contains a more general version of that fact. In an example above, we saw our retriever conclude that John loves himself because the data base contains the fact that everyone loves himself.

It is possible to add a great deal more deductive power to a retriever. For example, suppose our data base contains the fact that dogs are mammals. That is, suppose it contains the pattern **(implies (dog ?x) (mammal ?x))**.

Suppose it also contains the item **(implies (poodle ?x) (dog ?x))**, meaning that poodles are dogs. Suppose further that we know that Fido is a poodle, i. e., that our data base contains the item **(poodle Fido)**. Now we would like to be able to ask our retriever the question "Is Fido a mammal?" and get an affirmative reply. That is, we would like to query the data base with the request **(mammal Fido)**, and have the retriever *deduce* that this it true, even though this fact is not literally in the data base.

When a retriever has such capabilities, it is called, naturally enough, a *deductive data base retriever*. We can think of deductive retrievers as implementing a kind of "virtual" data base. A deductive retriever may tell us that an item is in the data base if the item can be inferred from other items in the data base, even though the item itself is not explicitly present.

Many artificial intelligence systems use some form of deductive retriever. In some systems, the inferential mechanism of the retriever does the main part of the system's computation. Other systems use deductive retrievers merely as a convenience. In the latter case, the deductive retriever is used to handle many details of the computation. In this way, the rest of the program, which does the interesting part of the work, need not be concerned about bookkeeping tasks.

22.4.1. Backward Chaining

We can implement a form of deduction through a technique called *backward chaining*. In backward chaining, we store implications in the data base in the form (<− *consequent antecedent*). This means that *antecedent* being true implies that *consequent* is true. Then, when we want to know if some item *request* is true, in addition to our normal querying process, we do the following. We fetch all items in the data base of the form (<− *request antecedent*). If we find any, we recursively query the data base to see if *antecedent* is true. If so, then we can conclude that *request* is true, even if it is not explicitly present in the data base.

Note that the process of querying the data base to see if *antecedent* is true might result in the consultation of another "backward" implication rule. In general, we may chain through any number of such rules to make a deduction. From this process, the name of the technique is derived.

Let us look at an example. In the case of our Fido example above, our data base will contain the backward chaining rules (<− **(mammal ?x) (dog ?x)**) and (<− **(dog ?x) (poodle ?x)**), in addition to the fact **(poodle Fido)**. Now when we retrieve the request **(mammal Fido)**, the retriever accesses the first of these rules. This causes it to recursively retrieve on **(dog Fido)**. Doing so will result in accessing the second rule, and thereby retrieving on **(poodle Fido)**. This is known to be true, so the query succeeds.

22.4.2. A Deductive Retriever Implementation

Building such a deductive retriever is simple. All we need to do is supplement our normal querying operation with a component that chases down backward implications. This component will query the data base with the pattern **(<− *request* ?antecedent)**. This request will match all the backward implications that can imply the original request. Then we need only get the binding of **?antecedent** in the result of each match. This binding represents a fact, which, if true, implies the original request. We determine if this fact is true simply by trying to retrieve it using the deductive retriever.

We will call our deductive retriever **retrieve**. The only complication in it is that the binding of **?antecedent** may contain variables whose bindings are known. For example, if we unify **(<− (mammal Fido) ?antecedent)** with **(<− (mammal ?x) (dog ?x))**, the binding of **?antecedent** would be **(dog ?x)**. We do not want to continue the search using this pattern, though, but with **(dog Fido)**. So we need to substitute all variables in the binding of **antecedent** with their values, if they have any, before doing the recursive step of the retrieval. **retrieve** relies on the routine **substitute−vars** to do this:

```
(defun retrieve (request data−base)
  (nconc
      (fast−query request data−base)
      (mapcan
          '(lambda (bindings)
            (mapcar
              '(lambda (rbindings) (append rbindings bindings))
              (retrieve
                  (substitute−vars
                      (get−binding '?antecedent bindings)
                      bindings)
                  data−base)))
          (fast−query '(<− ,request ?antecedent) data−base]
```

Note that we use **fast−query** to do the explicit interrogation of the data base. Also, it is safe to **nconc** together the results of the explicit and deductive parts, because both generate fresh s-expressions as their results.

Finally, we indiscriminately collect together the results of the deductive component; as a result, some of our answers will have bindings for variables that did not occur in the request. (See Exercise 1.)

Now for **substitute–vars**. This is a fairly standard recursive function that goes down an s-expression until it finds a pattern matching variable. When it finds one, it returns the binding if there is one. The only thing to be careful about is that the binding of the variable may itself contain substitutable variables. For example, suppose our binding list is

> **((?antecedent (loves John ?y)) (?y ?z) (?z Mary))**

If we substitute variables in the binding of **?antecedent**, we will get **(loves John ?z)**. However, we do not want to retrieve on this, but on **(loves John Mary)**.

Fortunately, the difficulty is easy to overcome. We merely call **substitute–vars** recursively on the variable's binding. Here is the complete function:

```
(defun substitute–vars (item bindings)
  (cond [(atom item) item]
        [(pattern–var–p item)
         (let ((binding (get–binding item bindings)))
           (cond [binding (substitute–vars binding bindings)]
                 [t item]))]
        [t (cons (substitute–vars (car item) bindings)
                 (substitute–vars (cdr item) bindings))]))
```

Now let us test **retrieve** on the example used to motivate it above. First, let us load up a data base:

```
-> (index '(<– (mammal ?x) (dog ?x)) '!d–b!)
(<–)
-> (index '(<– (dog ?x) (poodle ?x)) '!d–b!)
(<–)
-> (index '(poodle Fido) '!d–b!)
(poodle <–)
->
```

A literal examination of the data base using **fast–query** should show that the item **(mammal Fido)** is not present:

```
-> (fast–query '(mammal Fido) '!d–b!)
nil
->
```

315

Now let us see if our deductive retriever can infer the answer:

> (retrieve '(mammal Fido) '!d−b!)
((((*var* antecedent) (poodle (*var* var6))) ((*var* var6) fido)
 ((*var* antecedent) (dog (*var* var5))) ((*var* var5) fido)))

The result shows that the request is true, with no bindings required. This is just what we would expect **fast−query** to return if the fact were literally present.

While deductive data base management is an attractive technique, the programmer is advised to use it cautiously. An unbounded amount of computation may be triggered by a simple query. Thus the convenience of hiding all the details of a computation may result in hiding a lot of computation one would rather not perform.

22.5. SUMMARY

(1)   Associative data base management involves updating and accessing a collection of s-expressions in a flexible fashion.

(2)   We can use pattern matching as the basis for an associative data base system. Facts are represented as patterns; patterns are also used to query the data base. Patterns used in the latter fashion are called *requests*. The retriever will return all items in the data base that can be unified with the specified request.

(3)   We can make accessing an associative data base faster by using *indexing*.

(4)   We can extend a data base manager to do automatic deduction. A *deductive retriever* is one which can infer items not explicitly present in the data base.

(5)   A technique used to implement deduction is called *backward chaining*. With this technique, implications are stored as facts in the data base. When a request is retrieved, these implications are used to suggest items that may imply the request. These items are then recursively retrieved from the data base. If one of them turns out to be true, this confirms the original request.

Exercises

(1)   Modify the retriever so that its answers do not contain references to variables that do not occur in requests.

316

(2)   An alternative means of efficient storage for a data base is to keep the data base as a hash table with buckets. You can use arrays for this purpose. Each array represents a data base, with each element of the array pointing to a bucket. You must compute some hash key based on some aspect of an item or request, and translate this into a number (the function **maknum** is useful here). Then the corresponding bucket of the array is searched or updated.

Implement a version of **fast–query** that uses this storage scheme.

(3)   While backward chaining has its uses, it may be inefficient. For example, suppose the data base contains many items of the form

$\quad\quad\quad$ **(<– (mammal ?x) (dog ?x))**

$\quad\quad\quad$ **(<– (mammal ?x) (cat ?x))**

$\quad\quad\quad$ **(<– (mammal ?x) (horse ?x))**

Now when we retrieve on **(mammal Fido)**, a deductive retriever will look for *all* backward implications that might be useful. So our retriever will try to deduce that Fido is a cat and that he is a horse. Both efforts will fail, of course, but only after a potentially arbitrary amount of effort.

It may be more efficient in such cases to have explicitly in the data base the fact that Fido is a mammal. However, we would like to avoid the effort of explicitly adding the proposition that something is a mammal whenever we add one asserting that something is a dog.

We can accomplish this through a technique called *forward chaining*. In forward chaining, we use implication rules to add new information to the data base upon *learning* a fact; this is in contrast to backward chaining, in which we use implications to deduce something upon *retrieving* a request.

We implement forward chaining using "forward" implications. For example, we could represent the forward implication that dogs are mammals as **(–> (dog ?x) (mammal ?x))**. Now whenever we add an item to our data base, we will check to see if we can unify it with the left-hand side of any forward implication. If so, then we will add the right-hand side to the data base. Thus if the above rule were in the data base, and we add the proposition **(dog Fido)**, the data base manager will automatically add the assertion **(mammal Fido)**.

Modify the data base manager to allow forward chaining. Be sure that your code really *chains* forward. That is, adding an item to a data base may entail adding another item, and adding that one may entail adding yet another item, and so on.

(4)   We currently have no easy way to answer questions like "Who is a famous movie actress who is also a political activist?" We could represent this logically as an expression of the form **(and (actress ?x) (activist ?x))**. However, if we merely queried a data base with this request, it would fail even if **(actress JaneFonda)** and **(activist JaneFonda)** were both in the data base. Why?.

Requests of this form are sometimes called *conjunctive requests,* or *conjunctive subgoals.* Write a version of the retriever that handles conjunctive requests properly.

Appendix A

Summary of Franz LISP Functions

For each Franz LISP function, we present a typical instance of a call to that function. Generic arguments are shown in italics, where the argument name suggests the type of the corresponding formal parameter. For example, (**member** *exp list*) indicates that **member** takes two arguments, the first of which can be any expression, and the second of which must be a list. Optional arguments are surrounded by square brackets — *[* and *]*. Indefinite repetition is indicated by forms surrounded by hyphens. For example, *-fixnums-* means that an indefinite sequence of fixnum-type arguments is permitted. Arguments are normally assumed to be evaluated, unless they are shown enclosed in double quotes.

1. DATA STRUCTURE ACCESS AND MANIPULATION FUNCTIONS

The following functions allow one to create, access, and manipulate the various types of LISP data structures.

1.1. General Data Structure Predicates

1.1.1. *Data Type Determination Functions*

(arrayp *exp*)
> Returns **t** if *exp* is an array.

(atom *exp*)
> Returns **t** if *exp* is not a list or hunk object. **(atom nil)** returns **t**.

(bcdp *exp*)
> Returns **t** if *exp* is of type binary.

(bigp *exp*)
> Returns **t** if *exp* is a bignum.

(dtpr *exp*)
> Returns **t** if *exp* is a list cell. **(dtpr nil)** is **nil**.

(fixp *exp*)
> Returns **t** if *exp* is a fixnum or bignum.

(floatp *exp*)
> Returns **t** if *exp* is a flonum.

(hunkp *exp*)
> Returns **t** if *exp* is a hunk.

(listp *exp*)
> Returns **t** if *exp* is a list object or **nil**.

(litatom *exp*)
> Returns **t** if *exp* is an atom, but not a number.

(numbp *exp*)
(numberp *exp*)
> Returns **t** if *exp* is a number.

(portp *exp*)
> Returns **t** if *exp* is a port.

(purep *exp*)
> Returns **t** if the object *exp* is in pure space (i. e., is non-changing, non-garbage-collected data).

320

(stringp *exp***)**
> Returns **t** if *exp* is a string.

(symbolp *exp***)**
> Returns **t** if *exp* is a symbol.

(valuep *exp***)**
> Returns **t** if *exp* is a value cell.

(vectorp *exp***)**
> Returns **t** if *exp* is a vector.

(vectorip *exp***)**
> Returns **t** if *exp* is an immediate-vector.

(type *exp***)**
(typep *exp***)**
> Return the type of *exp*.

1.1.2. *Data Structure Comparison Functions*

(eq *exp1 exp2***)**
> Returns **t** if *exp1* and *exp2* are the same LISP object.

(equal *exp1 exp2***)**
(eqstr *exp1 exp2***)**
> Return **t** if *exp1* and *exp2* have the same structure.

(neq *exp1 exp2***)**
> Returns **t** if *exp1* is not **eq** to *exp2*.

(nequal *exp1 exp2***)**
> Returns **t** if *exp1* is not **equal** to *exp2*.

(not *exp***)**
(null *exp***)**
> Return **t** if *exp* is **nil**.

1.2. Lists

1.2.1. *List Creation Functions*

(append *-lists-***)**
> Returns the list formed by joining the elements of the lists together.

(append1 *list exp***)**
> Equivalent to **(append** *list* **(list** *exp***))**.

(cons *exp1 exp2***)**
> Returns a list whose **car** is *exp1* and whose **cdr** is *exp2*.

(copy *exp***)**
> Returns a structure **equal** to *exp* but made of new **cons** cells.

(list *-exps-***)**
> Returns a list of the expressions.

(ncons *exp***)**
> Equivalent to **(cons** *exp* **nil)**.

(quote! *-exps-***)**
> **quote!** works like the backquote read macro. It returns a list consisting of the expressions. If one of the expressions is the symbol **!**, then the value of the next expression is used. If it is the symbol **!!**, then the value of the next is spliced into the result. Otherwise the argument is literally inserted in the result. Thus **(quote! a ! b !! c)** is equivalent to **'(a ,b ,@b)**.

(xcons *exp1 exp2***)**
> Equivalent to **(cons** *exp2 exp1***)**.

1.2.2. *List Predicates*

(member *exp list***)**
(memq *exp list***)**
> Return the sublist of *list* beginning with the first occurrence of *exp*. If *exp* is not in the top level of *list*, these functions return **nil**. **member** tests for equality using **equal**, while **memq** uses **eq**.

(tailp *list1 list2***)**
> Returns *list1* if a **cons** cell **eq** to *list1* is found by **cdr**ing down *list2* zero or more times, and **nil** otherwise.

322

1.2.3. *List Accessing Functions*

(car *list***)**
> Returns the first element of *list*.

(cdr *list***)**
> Returns the sublist of *list* after its first element.

(c...r *list***)**
> Here the **...** represents any number of **a**'s and **d**'s. This is the equivalent to applying the corresponding sequence of **cars** and **cdrs**. For example, **(cadar x)** is equivalent to **(car (cdr (car x)))**.

(last *list***)**
> Returns the last **cons** cell in *list*.

(ldiff *list1 list2***)**
> Returns a list of all elements in *list1* that are not in *list2*. *list2* must be a "tail" of *list1*, that is, **eq** to some sublist of *list1*. The value returned is always new list structure, unless *list2* is **nil**. In this case the result is *list1*.

(length *list***)**
> Returns the number of elements on the top level of *list*.

(nth *number list***)**
> Returns the *number*-th element of *list*, assuming zero-based index. Thus **(nth 0 l)** is equivalent to **(car l)**.

(nthcdr *number list***)**
> Returns the result of **cdr**ing down *list number* times. If *number* is less than 0, **(cons nil** *list***)** is returned.

(nthelem *number list***)**
> Like **nth**, but the indexing begins at 1 rather than 0.

1.2.4. *List Manipulation Functions*

(attach *exp list***)**
> *exp* is actually made into the first element of *list*, and the resulting value returned. All items that formerly pointed to *list* now point to a list whose **car** is *exp*.

(delete *exp list [number]*)

The first *number* occurrences of *exp* are destructively removed from the top level of *list*. If *number* is not given, all occurrences of *exp* are removed. The resulting modified list is returned. Note — **delete** uses **equal** to make its comparisons.

(delq *exp list [number]*)
(dremove *exp list [number]*)

These are just like **delete** except that they use **eq** rather than **equal** to make comparisons.

(dsubst *exp1 exp2 list*)

Like **subst**, except that **dsubst** modifies *list*.

(insert *exp list function flag*)

insert destructively inserts *exp* into *list* at a point determined by the ordering function *function*. If *function* is **nil**, alphabetical order is used. If *flag* is non-**nil**, *exp* will not be inserted if an **equal** element is already there. The modified list is returned as the result. For example, **(insert 'c '(a b d e) nil nil)** returns **(a b c d e)**.

(lsubst *list1 exp list2*)

A copy of *list1* is returned with *list2* spliced into it in place of all occurrences of *exp* at all levels.

(merge *list1 list2 function*)

merge assumes that *list1* and *list2* are sorted, and then merges them using the comparison function *function*. The resulting value is returned. If *function* is **nil**, alphabetical order is used. **merge** destructively changes both its arguments.

(nconc *-lists-*)

nconc is like **append**, except that it destructively changes the last cell of each of the lists to point to the next list.

(nreconc *list exp*)

Equivalent to **(nconc (nreverse** *list*) *exp*).

(nreverse *list*)

Like **reverse**, but does the reversal in place, that is, it modifies its argument.

(remove *exp list [number]***)**
(remq *exp list [number]***)**

> **remove** and **remq** are just like **delete** and **delq**, respectively, except that the former create new lists while the latter modify the old ones.

(reverse *list***)**

> Returns *list* with the top level elements in reverse order. **reverse** creates a new list, while **nreverse** modifies its argument.

(rplaca *list exp***)**

> The **car** of *list* is actually changed to *exp,* and the resulting value returned.

(rplacd *list exp***)**

> The **cdr** of *list* is actually changed to *exp,* and the resulting value returned.

(subpair *list1 list2 list3***)**

> *list3* is returned with each element of *list1* replaced by the corresponding element of *list2*. For example, **(subpair '(a d) '(1 2) '(a b c d))** returns **(1 b c 2)**.

(subst *exp1 exp2 list***)**

> All **equal** occurrences of *exp2* are replaced by *exp1* at all levels of *list*. **subst** creates a new list, while **dsubst** modifies *list*.

1.3. Symbols and Strings

1.3.1. *Symbol and String Creation Functions*

(allsym *exp***)**

> If *exp* has the form (*symbol fixnum*), **allsym** will return the list of all **newsym**ed symbols beginning with *symbol* from the *fixnum*-th one on. If *exp* is a symbol, all **newsym**ed symbols beginning with that symbol are returned.

(ascii *number***)**

> Returns a symbol whose print name is the single character whose fixnum representation is *number*.

(character—index *string char***)**
 Returns the position of the character *char* in *string,* or **nil** if *char* does not occur in *string.* The position of the first character is 1. *char* can be either an atom or a string, in which case the first character is used. Alternatively, *char* can be the fixnum value of a character.

(concat *-atoms-***)**
 Returns a symbol whose print name is the result of concatenating the names of the atoms. **concat** interns its result on the oblist, while **uconcat** does not.

(concatl *list***)**
 Equivalent to **(apply 'concat** *list***)**.

(copysymbol *atom flag***)**
 Returns an uninterned symbol with the same print name as *atom.* If *flag* is non-**nil**, then the value, function binding, and property list of the new symbol are made **eq** to those of *atom.*

(gensym *["atom"]***)**
 Returns a new uninterned atom beginning with the first character of *atom*'s pname, or beginning with **g** if *atom* is not given. The symbol looks like **x0nnnnn**, where **x** is *atom*'s first character and **nnnnn** is the number of times **gensym** has been called.

(implode *list-of-atoms***)**
 Returns the symbol whose print name is the result of concatenating the first characters of the print names of the items in *list-of-atoms.* **implode** interns the symbol it creates, while **maknam** does not.

(initsym *-lists-***)**
 The lists should be of the form (*symbol fixnum*). **initsym** returns a list of interned symbols whose name is the symbol and fixnum appended together. If a symbol appears in place of a list, the symbol is suffixed with **0**. The function **newsym** will continue a symbol series started at the point declared by **initsym**.

(intern *atom***)**
 atom is put on the oblist if it is not already there. The interned symbol is returned.

(maknam *list-of-atoms***)**
 Just like **implode**, except that **maknam** does not intern its result on the oblist.

326

(newsym *symbol***)**

> Returns a new interned symbol whose name begins with *symbol* and ends in an integer. The integer will be one more than the last integer used to number a symbol in this series, or 0 if the symbol has not been used in a series or initialized by **initsym**.

(oldsym *symbol***)**

> Returns the last symbol generated in the **newsym** series for *symbol*, or *symbol* if *symbol* has not been used before.

(rematom *atom***)**

> *atom* is put on the free atoms list, meaning that the garbage collector will reclaim it at the first opportunity. **rematom** returns **t** if *atom* is in fact an atom.

(remob *atom***)**

> *atom* is removed from the oblist. The value *atom* is returned.

(remsym *-lists-***)**

> The lists should be of the form (*symbol fixnum*). Removes from the oblist all **newsym**ed symbols beginning with the name *symbol* and starting at number *fixnum*. If a symbol occurs as an argument instead of a list, all the elements of that series are removed from the oblist.

(symstat *-symbols-***)**

> Returns that list of each symbol paired with its current **newsym** counter. If the symbol has not been used in a series, the symbol will be followed by **nil**.

(uconcat *-atoms-***)**

> Like **concat**, but does not intern its result on the oblist.

1.3.2. *Symbol and String Predicates*

(alphalessp *string1 string2***)**

> Returns **t** if *string1* is alphabetically less than *string2*. If atoms are supplied, then their print names are used.

(boundp *atom***)**

> Returns **nil** if *atom* is unbound. If *atom* has the value **val**, then **(nil . val)** is returned.

1.3.3. *Symbol and String Accessing Functions*

(getchar *symbol number***)**
(getcharn *symbol number***)**
(nthchar *symbol number***)**
> Return the character of the print name of *symbol* designated by *number*. These functions return **nil** if *number* is less than 1 or greater than the length of *symbol*'s print name. **getchar** and **nthchar** return a symbol with a single character print name, while **getcharn** returns the fixnum representation of the character.

(getd *symbol***)**
> Returns the function definition of *symbol* or **nil** if there is no function definition.

(get_pname *symbol***)**
> Returns the string that is the print name of *symbol*.

(plist *symbol***)**
> Returns the property list of *symbol*.

(substring *string number1 [number2]***)**
(substringn *string number1 [number2]***)**
> Return a string of length at most *number2* starting at the *number1*-th character in the string. If *number2* is not given, all of the characters from *number1* to the end of the string are returned. If *number1* is negative, the string begins at the *number1*-th character from the end. If *number1* is out of bounds, **nil** is returned. **substring** returns a list of symbols, while **substringn** returns a list of fixnums. If *number2* is 0, then a single fixnum corresponding to the *number1*-th character is returned.

(symeval *symbol***)**
> Returns the value of *symbol*. This function has the same effect as **eval**, but is more efficient.

1.3.4. *Symbol and String Manipulation Functions*

(aexplode *symbol***)**
(explode *exp***)**
(aexplodec *symbol***)**
(explodec *exp***)**
(aexploden *symbol***)**
(exploden *exp***)**

These functions return a list of the characters used to print out *symbol* or *exp*. The functions beginning with **a** are internal functions that work only on symbol arguments. The functions **aexplode** and **explode** return a list of characters which **print** would use to print the argument, including all necessary escape characters. The functions **aexplodec** and **explodec** return a list of characters which **patom** would use to print the argument (that is, without escape characters). The functions **aexploden** and **exploden** are like **aexplodec** and **explodec** except that the former return a list of fixnum representations of the characters.

(defv *exp1 exp2***)**

Equivalent to **(set** *exp1 exp2***)**.

(desetq *exp1 exp2 [...]***)**

If the *expi* are atoms, this acts just like **setq**. Otherwise *exp1* and *exp2* should have the same list structure. The elements of *exp1* are then set to the corresponding elements of *exp2*. For example, **(desetq (a (b) (c . d) e) '(1 (2) (3 4 5) 6))** sets **a** to **1**, **b** to **2**, **c** to **3**, **d** to **(4 5)** and **e** to **6**.

(makunbound *symbol***)**

symbol is unbound from any previous value.

(set *symbol exp***)**

The value of *symbol* is set to *exp,* and that value is returned.

(setplist *symbol list***)**

The property list of *symbol* is set to *list*.

(setq-["*symbol*" *exp*]-)

symbol, which is not evaluated, is set to the value of *exp*. **setq** allows any number of *symbol-exp* pairs. For example, **(setq x 'a y 'b)** sets **x** to **a** and **y** to **b**. The value of the last expression is returned as the value of the call to **setq**. If no arguments are supplied, **setq** returns **nil**.

1.4. Vectors

1.4.1. *Vector Creation Functions*

(new—vector *number [exp1 [exp2]]***)**

Returns a vector of length *number*. Each data element is initialized to *exp1,* or to **nil**, if *exp1* is not given. The vector's property is set to *exp2,* or to **nil**, by default.

(new−vectori−byte *number [exp1 [exp2]]***)**
(new−vectori−long *number [exp1 [exp2]]***)**
(new−vectori−word *number [exp1 [exp2]]***)**
> These are just like **new−vector**, except that they return immediate-vectors. The actual memory requirement is two long words + *number**n bytes, where n is 1 for **new−vectori−byte**, 2 for **new−vectori−word**, or 4 for **new−vectori−long**. Each data element is initialized to zero, if the argument **exp1** is not given.

(vector *-exps-***)**
> Returns a vector, with as many data elements as there are arguments. The vector's property will be null.

(vectori−byte *-fixnums-***)**
(vectori−long *-fixnums-***)**
(vectori−word *-fixnums-***)**
> Return an immediate-vector, with as many data elements as there are arguments. Only the low order byte or word is used in the case of **vectori−byte** and **vectori−word**. The vector's property will be null.

1.4.2. *Vector Access Functions*

(vget *vector exp***)**
> Returns the value of property name *exp* if *vector* has a real property list associated with it.

(vprop *vector***)**
> Returns the property associated with a vector.

(vref *vector index***)**
(vrefi−byte *vectori index***)**
(vrefi−long *vectori index***)**
(vrefi−word *vectori index***)**
> Return the desired data element from a vector. The indices must be fixnums. Indexing is zero-based. The **vrefi** functions sign-extend the data.

(vsize *vector***)**
(vsize−byte *vector***)**
(vsize−word *vector***)**
> Return the number of data elements in the vector. The functions **vsize−byte** and **vsize−word** return the number of data elements in terms of bytes and words, respectively.

1.4.3. *Vector Manipulation Functions*

(vset *vector number exp*)
(vseti—byte *vector number exp*)
(vseti—long *vector number exp*)
(vseti—word *vector number exp*)

> The *number*-th element of *vector* is set to *exp*. For **vseti—word** and **vseti—byte**, *number* is interpreted as the number of the data element within the vector. For those two functions, the low order byte or word of the argument is stored.

(vputprop *vector exp1 exp2*)

> If the property list of *vector* is a disembodied property list, then **vputprop** adds the value *exp1* under the property name *exp2*. Otherwise, a disembodied property list is created, and the old vector property is made the first element of the list.

(vsetprop *vector exp*)

> The property list of *vector* is set to *exp*. *exp* should be either a symbol that identifies the type of the vector, or a disembodied property list whose **car** is a symbol that identifies the type.

1.5. Arrays

1.5.1. *Array Creation Functions*

(*array *symbol flag -numbers-*)
(array *"symbol" "flag" -numbers-*)

> These functions turn *symbol* into a usable array. Following the MacLISP convention, *flag* designates the type of the elements of the array, and may be either **t, nil, fixnum, flonum, fixnum—block,** or **flonum—block.** However, in Franz, the flags **t, nil, fixnum,** and **flonum** are equivalent, and allow the array to be filled with arbitrary s-expressions. Fixnum—block and flonum—block arrays are restricted to fixnums and flonums respectively. They are used mainly to communicate with foreign functions. The numbers indicate the size of each dimension of the array. ***array** evaluates all its arguments, while **array** does not evaluate the first two.

(marray *block function exp fixnum1 fixnum2*)

> This is the basic array defining function in Franz LISP. *block* designates a block of contiguous storage, *function* an access function, *exp* goes into an auxiliary cell that the user can use for any purpose, *fixnum1* designates the number of elements in *block,* and *fixnum2* the

number of bytes in each element of *block*. A call to **marray** sets up an array with the specified arguments.

The access function *function* should be a lexpr. When LISP sees an array access of the form (**array–name a b**), it calls the access function of **array—name**, passing the name of the array following the arguments **a** and **b.** When a call of the form (**store (array–name a b) c**) occurs, LISP simply expands this into (**array–name c a b**). In this case, the array accessing function will get called with one more argument. The array accessing function may treat its arguments anyway it likes—it is up to it to realize that a call with an extra argument is a store.

1.5.2. *Array Accessing Functions*

(**arraycall** *flag array -numbers-*)
> This is a MacLISP compatible function. It returns the element of *array* selected by using the numbers as indices. *flag* is ignored by **arraycall** and is included only for compatibility with MacLISP.

(**arraydims** *array*)
> Returns a list of the type and bounds of *array*.

(**arrayref** *array number*)
> Returns the *number*-th element of the array object *array,* with zero accessing the first element.

(**getaccess** *array*)
(**getaux** *array*)
(**getdelta** *array*)
(**getdata** *array*)
(**getlength** *array*)
> Each function returns the respective field of *array*.

(**listarray** *array [number]*)
> Returns a list of all of the elements in *array*. If *number* is given, then only the first *number* elements are returned.

1.5.3. *Array Manipulation Functions*

(fillarray *array list*)
> This fills *array* with elements from *list*. If there are not enough elements in *list* to fill the entire array, then the last element of *list* is used repeatedly to fill the remainder of the array.

(putaccess *array function*)
(putaux *array exp*)
(putdata *array exp*)
(putdelta *array number*)
(putlength *array number*)
> These functions replace the field of *array* by the designated argument.

(store *array-exp exp*)
> *array-exp* should be an array reference. The array location which *array-exp* references is changed to contain *exp*.

1.6. Hunks

1.6.1. *Hunk Creation Functions*

(hunk *-exps-*)
> Returns a hunk whose elements are initialized to the expressions.

(makhunk *exp*)
> Returns a hunk of length *exp* initialized to all **nil**s if *exp* is a fixnum. If *exp* is a list, then **makhunk** returns a hunk initialized to the elements in *exp*.

(∗makhunk *number*)
> Returns a hunk of size 2^{number} initialized to the special symbol **EMPTY**. **∗makhunk** is an internal function used by **hunk** and **makhunk** to create hunks for users. Users are cautioned against using **∗makhunk** themselves.

1.6.2. *Hunk Accessing Functions*

(cxr *number hunk*)
> Returns the *number*-th element (starting at 0) of *hunk*.

(hunk—to—list *hunk*)
   Returns a list consisting of the elements of *hunk*.

1.6.3. *Hunk Manipulation Functions*

(hunksize *hunk*)
   Returns the size of *hunk*.

(rplacx *number hunk exp*)
(∗rplacx *number hunk exp*)
   The *number*-th element of *hunk* is set to *exp*. **rplacx** will not modify
   an element filled with the distinguished value **EMPTY**, whereas
   ∗rplacx will.

1.7. Binary Coded Data

(getdisc *bcd-function*)
   Returns the discipline of *bcd-function,* which should be a binary-coded
   function.

(mfunction *code discipline*)
   Returns an object of type binary composed of *code* and *discipline*. *code*
   should be a pointer to the machine code for a function, and *discipline*
   should be the function's discipline.

(putdisc *bcd-function discipline*)
   Sets the discipline field of the binary-coded function *bcd-function* to
   discipline.

1.8. Structures

This section describes functions that operate on three structures constructed
out of **cons** cells: assoc lists, property lists, and tconc structures.

1.8.1. *Assoc List Functions*

An *assoc list* is a list of the form
         ((*key1* . *value1*) (*key2* . *value2*) ... (*keyn* . *valuen*))

(assoc *exp assoc-list*)
(assq *exp assoc-list*)
> Return the first top level element of *assoc-list* whose **car** matches *exp*. **assoc** uses **equal** to perform the match, while **assq** uses **eq**.

(sassoc *exp assoc-list function*)
(sassq *exp assoc-list function*)
> Return the result of applying *function* to **nil** if (**assoc** *exp assoc-list*) (or in the case of **sassq**, (**assq** *exp assoc-list*)) returns non-**nil**.

(sublis *assoc-list list*)
> Returns *list* with every occurrence of a key in *assoc-list* replaced by its corresponding value.

1.8.2. *Property List Functions*

(defprop *"symbol" "exp1" "exp2"*)
> Like **putprop** but does not evaluate its arguments.

(get *symbol exp*)
> Returns the value associated with property name *exp* in *symbol*'s property list. If *symbol* is a list rather than a symbol, **get** treats it as a disembodied property list, and ignores the first element.

(getl *symbol list*)
> Returns the property list of *symbol* beginning at the first property name which is a member of *list*, or **nil** if none of the elements in *list* is on *symbol*'s property list. If *symbol* is a list rather than a symbol, **getl** assumes it is a disembodied property list and ignores the first element.

(plist *symbol*)
> Returns the property list of *symbol*.

(putprop *symbol exp1 exp2*)
> Adds to the property list of *symbol* the value *exp1* associated with the property name *exp2*. **putprop** evaluates it arguments, while **defprop** does not. *symbol* may be a disembodied property list.

(remprop *symbol exp*)
> The property name *exp* and its associated value are removed from the property list of *symbol*. The sublist of *symbol*'s property list beginning with the property under *exp* is returned. *symbol* may be a disembodied property list.

(setplist *symbol list***)**
>   Sets the property list of *symbol* to *list*.

1.8.3. *Tconc Structure Functions*

(lconc *tconc-str list***)**
>   Returns *tconc-str* with *list* spliced in at the end.

(tconc *tconc-str exp***)**
>   Returns *tconc-str* with *exp* added to the end.

1.8.4. *Fclosure Functions*

(fclosure *list function***)**
>   *list* should be a list of variables. This returns a vector which is the fclosure of *function* with respect to these variables.

(fclosure—alist *fclosure***)**
>   Returns an association list representing the variables in *fclosure*.

(fclosure—function *fclosure***)**
>   Returns the function component of *fclosure*.

(fclosure–list -[*list function*]-**)**
>   Any number of *list-function* pairs may be supplied. A list of the closures of each function with respect to the variables in its list is returned. A variable appearing in more than one list will be shared by the associated functions.

(fclosurep *fclosure***)**
>   Returns **t** if the argument is an fclosure.

(set—in—fclosure *fclosure symbol exp***)**
>   *symbol* is bound in *fclosure* to *exp*.

(symeval—in—fclosure *fclosure symbol***)**
>   Returns the current binding of *symbol* in *fclosure*.

1.9. Miscellaneous Data Structure Functions

(bcdad *function***)**
>   If *function* is a machine coded function, then **bcdad** returns a fixnum representing the memory location where *function* begins. Otherwise, **bcdad** returns **nil**.

(copyint∗ *fixnum***)**

> Returns a fixnum with the same value as *fixnum* but in a new storage location.

(cpy1 *exp***)**

> Returns a new item of the same type as *exp* and having the same value.

(getaddress *symbol1 symbol2 discipline [... ... ...]***)**

> This function is relevant primarily to **cfasl** users. **getaddress** examines in the process's symbol table for a symbol of the name *symbol1*. It creates a binary object whose entry field points to *symbol1* and whose discipline is *discipline*. This object is stored in the function field of *symbol2*. If *discipline* is **nil**, then **subroutine** is used as the default.

(kwote *exp***)**

> Returns **(list (quote quote)** *exp***)**.

(macroexpand *list***)**

> Returns *list* with all macros in it expanded. **macroexpand** does not work on expressions that cannot be evaluated, nor does it handle nlambdas such as **cond** and **do**.

(ptr *exp***)**

> Returns a value cell initialized to point to *exp*.

(purcopy *exp***)**

> Returns a copy of *exp* with new pure cells (i. e., non-changing, non-garbage-collected data) allocated wherever possible.

(quote *"exp"***)**

> Returns *exp*.

(replace *exp1 exp2***)**

> The fields of *exp1*'s structure are made **eq** to the corresponding fields of *exp2*'s structure. For example, if **x** and **y** have lists as values, then the effect of **(replace x y)** is the same as **(rplaca x (car y))** and **(rplacd x (cdr y))**.

> For fixnum and flonum arguments, **replace** changes the value in the cell in which the fixnum lives. For example, if **(setq y x)** is evaluated, and then **(replace x 12345)** is evaluated, **y** will also have the value **12345**.

> Note − The fixnums between −1024 and 1023 are stored in a read-

only area. Attempts to replace them will result in an illegal memory reference.

(setf *refer-exp exp***)**

    setf stores into the location referred to by *refer-exp* the value *exp*.

(sort *list function***)**

    Returns a list of the elements of *list* ordered by the comparison function *function*. *list* is modified in the process. If *function* is **nil**, alphabetical order will be used.

(sortcar *list function***)**

    Returns a list of the elements of *list* with the **cars** ordered by the sort function *function*. *list* is modified in the process. If *function* is **nil**, alphabetical order will be used.

2. ARITHMETIC FUNCTIONS

For most arithmetic functions, if the size of a partial result exceeds the limit of a fixnum, the partial resultis converted to a bignum. If any of the arguments are flonums, the partial result is converted to a flonum and the result is a flonum. Having to convert a bignum into a flonum generates an error.

2.1. Simple Arithmetic Functions

(add *-numbers-***)**
(plus *-numbers-***)**
(sum *-numbers-***)**
(+ *-fixnums-***)**

    Return the sum of the arguments. If no arguments are given, **0** is returned.

(add1 *number***)**
(1+ *fixnum***)**

    Return the argument plus 1.

(diff *-numbers-***)**
(difference *-numbers-***)**
(− *-fixnums-***)**

    Return the result of subtracting from the first argument all subsequent arguments. If no arguments are given, **0** is returned.

(Divide *integer1 integer2*)
> Returns a list whose **car** is the quotient and whose **cadr** is the remainder of the division of *integer1* by *integer2*.

(Emuldiv *fixnum1 fixnum2 fixnum3 fixnum4*)
> *fixnum1* is multiplied by *fixnum2*. *fixnum3*'s sign is extended and added to this product. The result is then divided by *fixnum4* and the resulting value returned. This function is used to help implement bignum arithmetic.

(minus *number*)
> Returns zero minus *number*.

(product *-numbers-*)
(times *-numbers-*)
(∗ *-fixnums-*)
> Return the product of all of the arguments. **1** is returned if no arguments are given.

(quotient *-numbers-*)
(/ *-fixnums-*)
> Return the result of dividing the first argument by succeeding ones. If there are no arguments, **1** is returned. A division by zero causes a floating exception interrupt.

(∗quo *integer1 integer2*)
> Returns the integer part of *integer1* divided by *integer2*.

(sub1 *number*)
(1− *fixnum*)
> Return the argument minus 1.

2.2. Arithmetic Predicates

(evenp *fixnum*)
> Returns **t** if *fixnum* is even.

(greaterp *-numbers-*)
(> *number1 number2*)
(>& *fixnum1 fixnum2*)
> Return **t** if the arguments are in a strictly decreasing order. The functions **greaterp** and **>** use **difference** to compare adjacent values. The arguments to **>** must both be fixnums or both be flonums. The arguments to **>&** must both be fixnums.

(**> =** -*numbers*-)
(**> =&** *fixnum1 fixnum2*)

Ta These are macros that expand into (**not** (**<** -*numbers*-)) and (**not** (**<&** *fixnum1 fixnum2*)), respectively.

(**lessp** -*numbers*-)
(**<** *number1 number2*)
(**<&** *fixnum1 fixnum2*)

Ta Return **t** if the arguments are in a strictly increasing order. **lessp** and **<** use **difference** to compare adjacent values. The arguments to **<** may be either fixnums or flonums but must be the same type. The arguments to **<&** must be fixnums.

(**< =** -*numbers*-)
(**< =&** *fixnum1 fixnum2*)

Ta These are macros that expand into (**not** (**>** -*numbers*-)) and (**not** (**>&** *fixnum1 fixnum2*)), respectively.

(**minusp** *exp*)

Ta Returns **t** if *exp* is a negative number.

(**oddp** *fixnum*)

Ta Returns **t** if *fixnum* is odd.

(**onep** *exp*)

Ta Returns **t** if *exp* is a number equal to **1**.

(**plusp** *number*)

Ta Returns **t** if *number* is greater than zero.

(**signp** *test exp*)

Ta Returns **t** if *exp* is a number and the test indicated by *test* applied to *exp* returns true. The permitted values for *test* are **l**, **le**, **e**, **n ge**, and **g**; their associated meanings are to test *exp* to see if it is $\leqslant$, $=$, $\neq$, $\geqslant$, and $>$ than 0, respectively.

(**zerop** *exp*)

Ta Returns **t** if *exp* is a number equal to 0.

(**=** *number1 number2*)
(**=&** *fixnum1 fixnum2*)

Ta Return **t** if the arguments have the same value. The arguments to **=** must be either both fixnums or both flonums. The arguments to **=&** must be fixnums.

2.3. Trigonometric Functions

(acos *number***)**
> Returns the arc cosine of *number* in the range 0 to π.

(asin *number***)**
> Returns the arc sine of *number* in the range $-\pi/2$ to $\pi/2$.

(atan *number1 number2***)**
> Returns the arc tangent of *number1* divided by *number2* in the range $-\pi$ to π.

(cos *number***)**
> Returns the cosine of *number. number* is assumed to be in radians.

(sin *number***)**
> Returns the sine of *number. number* is assumed to be in radians.

2.4. Bignum Functions

(bignum—leftshift *"integer" "fixnum"***)**
> Returns *integer* shifted left by *fixnum*. If *fixnum* is negative, *integer* is shifted right by $-fixnum$ and rounded to the nearest even number.

(haipart *"number" "fixnum"***)**
> If *fixnum* is positive, **haipart** returns an integer which contains the *fixnum* high bits of the absolute value of *number*. Otherwise it returns $-fixnum$ low bits of the absolute value of *number*.

(haulong *"integer"***)**
> Returns the number of significant bits in *integer*. The result is equal to the least integer greater than or equal to the base two logarithm of one plus the absolute value of *integer*.

(sticky—bignum—leftshift *integer fixnum***)**
> Returns *integer* shifted left by *fixnum*. If *fixnum* is negative, *integer* is shifted right by $-fixnum$ and rounded. After shifting, the low order bit is changed to 1 if any 1's were shifted off to the right.

2.5. Bit Manipulation

341

(boole *key fixnum1 fixnum2 ...***)**

Returns the result of the bitwise boolean operation indicated by *key*. If there are more than 3 arguments, then evaluation proceeds from left to right. The possible values of *key* are 0 through 15, and designate a particular operation as described below. Here $*$ represents bitwise *and,* $+$ represents bitwise *or,* and $\oplus$ represents bitwise *xor.* $\neg$ represents bitwise negation and has the highest precedence: $0 \Rightarrow 0$ (i. e., the result is always 0), $1 \Rightarrow x*y$, $2 \Rightarrow \neg x*y$, $3 \Rightarrow y$, $4 \Rightarrow x*\neg y$, $5 \Rightarrow x$, $6 \Rightarrow x \oplus y$, $7 \Rightarrow x+y$, $8 \Rightarrow \neg(x+y)$, $9 \Rightarrow \neg(x \oplus y)$, $10 \Rightarrow \neg x$, $11 \Rightarrow \neg x+y$, $12 \Rightarrow \neg y$, $13 \Rightarrow x+\neg y$, $14 \Rightarrow \neg x+\neg y$, $15 \Rightarrow -1$.

(lsh *fixnum1 fixnum2***)**

Returns *fixnum1* shifted left by *fixnum2* if *fixnum2* is positive. If *fixnum2* is negative, then **lsh** returns *fixnum1* shifted right by $-fixnum2$. A fixnum is returned even when the result is large enough to be converted to a bignum. Some bits may be lost in this process.

(rot *fixnum1 fixnum2***)**

Returns *fixnum1* rotated left by *fixnum2* if *fixnum2* is positive. If *fixnum2* is negative, then *fixnum1* is rotated right by $-fixnum2$.

2.6. Other Arithmetic Functions

(abs *number***)**
(absval *number***)**

Returns the absolute value of *number*.

(bignum—to—list *bignum***)**

Returns a list of the fixnums which are used to represent *bignum*.

(exp *number***)**

Returns *e* raised to the *number* power. **exp** always returns a flonum.

(expt *number1 number2***)**

Returns *number1* raised to the *number2* power. If either of the arguments are flonums, the calculation is done using **log** and **exp**.

(fact *fixnum***)**

Returns *fixnum* factorial.

(fix *number*)

Returns a fixnum as close as possible to *number*. **fix** rounds down.

(float *number*)

Returns a flonum as close as possible to *number*.

(frexp *flonum*)

Returns a **cons** cell of the form (*exponent* . *mantissa*) which represents *flonum*. *exponent* will be a fixnum, and *mantissa* a 56 bit bignum. The binary point is assumed to occur right after the high order bit of *mantissa*, so *flonum* $= 2^{exponent} * mantissa$.

(list−to−bignum *list-of-fixnums*)

Returns a bignum constructed of the given fixnums.

(log *number*)

Returns the natural logarithm of *number*.

(max *-numbers-*)

Returns the maximum of the numbers.

(min *-numbers-*)

Returns the minimum of the numbers.

(mod *integer1 integer2*)
(remainder *integer1 integer2*)

Return the remainder when *integer1* is divided by *integer2*. The result has the same sign as *number1*.

(*mod *fixnum1 fixnum2*)

Returns the "balanced" representation of *fixnum1* modulo *fixnum2*. The balanced representation is guaranteed to be in the range between abs(*fixnum2*)/2 and (abs(*fixnum2*)/2) $-$ *fixnum2* $+$ 1.

(random *[fixnum]*)

Returns a fixnum between 0 and *fixnum*−1, if *fixnum* is given. If *fixnum* is not given, any fixnum may be returned.

(scons *fixnum bignum*)

Returns a bignum which begins with *fixnum* and whose higher order parts are from *bignum*.

(sqrt *number***)**
> Returns the square root of *number*.

3. INPUT/OUTPUT FUNCTIONS

The following functions are used to read from and write to external devices, files, and other processes.

(add—syntax—class *symbol list***)**

> Defines a syntax class called *symbol* that has the properties in *list*. The syntax class of a character determines how **read** interprets that character. There are three kinds of properties: *character class*, which tells **read** what to do when it sees this character; *separator,* which tells whether the character indicates the termination of a number or symbol name; and *escape*, which tells the printer when to put escape characters around a character. There are the following character classes: **ccharacter, cnumber, csign, cleft—paren, cright—paren, cleft—bracket, cright—bracket, cperiod, cseparator, csingle—quote, csymbol—delimiter, cescape, cstring—delimiter, csingle—character—symbol, cmacro, csplicing—macro, csingle—macro, csingle—splicing—macro, cinfix—macro, csingle—infix—macro,** and **cillegal.** There are three escape types: **escape—always, escape—when—unique** (i. e., when the character name is one long), and **escape—when—first** (i. e., when the character is the first of a symbol). There are the following predefined syntax classes: **vcharacter, vnumber, vsign, vleft—paren, vright—paren, vleft—bracket, vright—bracket, vperiod, vseparator, vsingle—quote, vsymbol—delimiter, vescape, vstring—delimiter, vsingle—character—symbol, vmacro, vsplicing—macro, vsingle—macro, vsingle—splicing—macro, vinfix—macro, vsingle—infix—macro,** and **villegal.**

(cfasl *filename name function [discipline [libraryname]]***)**
> **cfasl** is used to load the output of the assembler, C compiler, FORTRAN compiler, and PASCAL compiler. The object file *filename* is loaded into the LISP system. *name* should be an entry point in the file just loaded. The function binding of the symbol *function* is set to point to *name,* so that when the LISP function *function* is called, *name* will be run. *discipline* is the discipline to be given to *function* (defaults to **subroutine** if it is not given or if it is given as **nil**). If *libraryname* is non-null, then after *filename* is loaded, the libraries given in *libraryname* are searched to resolve external references. The form of *libraryname* should be something like −lS −lm. The C library (i. e., −lc) is always searched. For FORTRAN files, −lF77 should be

specified, and if the code does any I/O, the library entry should be −ll77 −lF77. For PASCAL programs, −lpc is required. If a file has more than one entry point, then **getaddress** must be used to locate and set up other foreign functions. It is an error to load in a file which has a global entry point of the same name as a global entry point in the current LISP process. The same file cannot be **cfasl**ed twice unless **removeaddress** is used to change global entry points to local entry points.

(close *port***)**

The specified port is **drain**ed and closed, releasing the port.

(cprintf *string atom [port]***)**

The UNIX formatted output function **printf** is called with arguments *string* and *atom*. If *atom* is a symbol then its print name is passed to **printf**. *string* may contain literal text as well as special formatting commands preceded by a percent sign, as described in the UNIX manual.

(drain *[port]***)**

If the port is an output port, then the characters in the output buffer are all sent to the device. If it is an input port, then all pending characters are flushed. The default output port is used as the default port.

(ex *["filename"]***)**
(vi *["filename"]***)**
(exl *["filename"]***)**
(vil *["filename"]***)**

LISP starts up an editor on the file *filename*. It will try appending **.l** to the name if it cannot find *filename*. The functions **exl** and **vil** load the file after it is edited. These functions remember the name of the file edited for subsequent invocations.

(fasl *filename1 [filename2 [flag]]***)**

This function is designed to load in an object file generated by the LISP compiler. It will append **.o** to *filename1* if it is not already present. If *filename2* is non-**nil**, then it is used as the name of the map file created. **fasl** writes in the map file the names and addresses of the functions it loads and defines. If *flag* is non-**nil** and if a function is loaded which is already defined, then a warning message is printed. **fasl** looks only in the current directory for the file to load.

(ffasl *filename name function [discipline [libraryname]]***)**

The FORTRAN object file *filename* is loaded. *name* should be an entry point in the file just loaded. A binary object is created and its entry field is set to point to *name*. The discipline field of the binary is set to *discipline* or **subroutine** by default. If *libraryname* is present and non-null, then after *filename* is loaded, the libraries given in *libraryname* are searched to resolve external references. The form of *libraryname* should be something like −lS −ltermcap. The standard FORTRAN libraries are also searched to resolve external references. Note: In F77 on UNIX, the entry point for the FORTRAN function **foo** is named **_foo_**.

(fileopen *filename mode***)**

Returns a port for reading or writing *filename,* depending on *mode. mode* may be **r** for read, **w** for write, and **a** for append ; **r+**, **w+**, and **a+** permit both reading and writing on a port provided that **fseek** is done between changes in direction. The file *filename* is opened (or created if opened for writing and it does not yet exist). **fileopen** does not look through a search path for a given file.

(filepos *port [fixnum]***)**

If *fixnum* is given, the next byte to be read or written to the port will be at position *fixnum*. The current position in the file is returned if *fixnum* is not given, and *fixnum* is returned otherwise.

(filestat *filename name***)**

Returns a vector containing various numbers which UNIX assigns to files. The individual entries can be accessed by functions of the form **filestat:***field* where field may be any of **atime**, **ctime**, **dev**, **gid**, **ino**, **mode**, **mtime**, **nlink**, **rdev**, **size**, **type**, or **uid**. See the UNIX programmer's manual for a more detailed description of these items.

(flatc *exp [fixnum]***)**

Returns the number of characters required to print *exp* using **patom**. If *fixnum* is given, and if **flatc** determines that it will return a value greater than *fixnum,* then it stops and returns the value it has computed thus far.

(flatsize *exp [fixnum]***)**

Returns the number of characters required to print **exp** using **print**. *fixnum* is interpreted here as it is for **flatc**.

(fseek *port fixnum flag*)

If *flag* is **0**, then the file's read/write pointer is set to *fixnum* bytes from the beginning of the file. If *flag* is **1**, then the pointer is set to *fixnum* bytes from the current location in the file. If *flag* is **2**, then the pointer is set to *fixnum* bytes from the end of the file. The new position in the file is returned.

(getsyntax *symbol*)

symbol should have a print name that is one character long. The syntax class of that character is returned. The syntax class determines how **read** interprets a character.

(infile *filename*)

Returns a port ready to read *filename*.

(lineread *[port [flag]]*)

reads and returns a list consisting of s-expressions on a line from *port*. If an s-expression takes more than one line, or a line terminates in a space or tab, then **lineread** continues **read**ing until an expression ends at the end of a line. If *flag* evaluates to **t**, then if the first character on a line is a "newline" character, **lineread** performs a **tyi** and returns **nil**. If *flag* is **nil** or not present, **lineread** does a **read**, skipping over any blank lines to make sure that an s-expression is read in.

(load *filename [filename2 [flag]]*)

load **read**s in the file *filename* as follows: If *filename* ends with **.l** or **.o**, then **load** looks only for a file named *filename*. Otherwise, **load** first looks for *filename*.**o**, then *filename*.**l**, and finally *filename*. If it ends up reading a file whose name ends in **.o**, **load** assumes that it is a LISP object file (i. e., compiled code) and reads it in using **fasl** (the optional arguments *filename2* and *flag* are passed to **fasl** should **fasl** be called). Otherwise, it assumes that it is a source file, which is loaded by reading and evaluating each form in the file. The search path which **load** uses is the value of **(status load−search−path)**. The default is **(|.| /usr/lib/lisp)**, which means to look in the current directory first and then check **/usr/lib/lisp**. **load** normally prints a message for each file that it reads, unless the value of the flag **$ldprint** is **nil**. If the flag **load−most−recent** is non-**nil**, and *filename* does not end in **.o** or **.l**, then the most recently modified of *filename.o* or *filename.l* is loaded.

(makereadtable *[flag]*)

If *flag* is non-null, returns a readtable equal to the original readtable. Otherwise it returns a readtable equal to the current readtable.

(msg -*"exps"*-**)**

This is a message-printing function. If an expression is an ordinary s-expression, it is evaluated and then passed to **patom**. The following forms are interpreted specially: **(P** *port*) causes subsequent output to go to *port,* **B** prints a single blank, **(B** *number*) prints *number* blanks, **N** prints a "newline" character, **(N** *number*) prints *number* "newlines," and **D** drains the current port.

(nwritn *[port]*)

Returns the number of characters in the buffer of the given port but not yet written out to the file or device.

(outfile *filename [mode]*)

Opens a port to write *filename*. If *mode* is a symbol or string whose name begins with **a**, then the file is opened in append mode. Otherwise, the file opened is truncated if it existed beforehand.

(patom *exp [port]*)

If *exp* is a symbol or string, the print name is printed without without symbol delimitors, even if it contains special characters. If *exp* is a list then this is equivalent to **print**. **patom** returns *exp*.

(pntlen *atom*)

Returns the number of characters needed to **print** *atom*.

(pp *[option] symbol* ...**)**

The function binding of *symbol* is pretty-printed, if it is non-**nil**. Otherwise, if *symbol* has a value, then the value is pretty-printed. **pp** uses **pp—form** to do the pretty-printing. The options allow the user to redirect output: **(F** *filename*) directs future printing to *filename,* **(P** *port*) causes output to go to *port,* and **(E** *exp*) causes *exp* to be evaluated, but not printed.

(pp—form *exp [port [integer]]*)

This is the basic pretty-printing function of Franz LISP. *exp* is pretty-printed to the port *port* (or **poport** if *port* is not given). If **pp—form** is also supplied with *integer,* then *integer* is used as the left margin setting (0 is the default). **pp—form** pretty-prints any s-expression; functions like **pp** use **pp—form** to do the work of printing function definitions, etc. Some programmers use **pp—form** as a top level printer so that long values are printed intelligibly.

(princ *exp [port]*)

Equivalent to **patom**, but always returns **t**.

(print *exp [port]*)

Prints *exp* on the port *port* or on the default port, and returns **nil**.

(probef *filename*)

Returns **t** if the file *filename* exists.

(ratom *[port [exp]]*)

Returns the next atom read from the given or default port. On end of file, **exp** is returned. This defaults to **nil**.

(read *[port [exp]]*)

Returns the next LISP expression read from the given or default port. On end of file, *exp* is returned. The default **nil** is used if *exp* is unspecified.

(readc *[port [exp]]*)

Returns the next character read from the given or default port. On end of file, *exp* is returned. The default **nil** is used if *exp* is unspecified.

(readlist *list*)

Returns the LISP expression "read" from the list of characters in *list*.

(removeaddress *-symbols-*)

The entries for the symbols in the LISP process's symbol table are removed.

(resetio)

All ports are closed except the standard input, output, and error ports.

(setsyntax *symbol syntaxclass [function]*)

symbol should have a print name of only one character. The syntax class of that character is set to *syntaxclass* in the current readtable. The syntax class determines how **read** interprets a character. If *syntaxclass* is **macro** or **splicing** then *function* is made the associated function definition.

(sload *-files-*)

The files are opened for reading; each form is read, optionally printed, and evaluated. Printing is controlled by the special atom **$sldprint**. If **$sldprint** is **t** (the default), then if a form is recognizable as a function definition, only the function name is printed; otherwise the whole form is printed. If **$sldprint** is **eq** to the particular atom **value**, then the result of each form's evaluation is also printed. The printing of the forms' values can be controlled by setting the special atom **sload–print** equal to the name of the function to be called. **sload** determines the name of the function that is being defined by looking at the **sloadprintarg** property of the function defining function. The value of the **sloadprintarg** property should be the number of the argument at which the name of the function appears. For the standard Franz LISP functions, these properties are already set; the default is **1**.

(tab *fixnum* *[port]*)

Enough spaces are output to move the cursor to column *fixnum*. If the cursor is beyond *fixnum* initially, a **terpr** is done first.

(terpr *[port]*)
(terpri *[port]*)

A "newline" character is sent to *port*, and the port is drained.

(tilde–expand *filename*)

Returns a symbol whose name is the UNIX tilde-expansion of *filename*. If *filename*. does not begin with a tilde, *filename* is returned.

(truename *port*)

Returns the name of the file associated with *port*, or **nil** if there is none.

(tyi *[port [exp]]*)

Returns the fixnum representation of the next character read. On end of file, *exp* (default −**1**) is returned.

(tyipeek *[port]*)

Returns the fixnum representation of the next character to be read. **tyipeek** does not actually read the character, but just peeks at it, i. e., a subsequent **read** will input that character.

(tyo *fixnum* *[port]*)

The character whose fixnum representation is *fixnum* is printed on *port* (or default output port).

(untyi *fixnum* *[port]*)

The character designated by *fixnum* is put back in the input buffer so that a subsequent **tyi** or **read** will read it next. Only one character may be put back in the input stream.

(username—to—dir *name***)**

> Returns the home directory of user *name*.

(zapline)

> All characters up to and including the "newline" character are discarded from the last port used for input. **nil** is returned. This is used as the read macro function definition of the semicolon comment character.

4. SYSTEMS FUNCTIONS

The following functions are used to interact with internal components of LISP and UNIX.

(allocate *type fixnum***)**

> Attempts to allocate *fixnum* pages of data type *type*. The storage allocated is added to the free storage list of type *type*.

(argv *fixnum***)**

> Returns a symbol whose name is the *fixnum*-th argument (starting from 0) on the command line which started the current LISP process. If *fixnum* is less than zero, a fixnum whose value is the number of arguments on the command line is returned.

(chdir *pathname***)**

> The current directory is set to *pathname*. **chdir** follows the standard UNIX conventions: if *pathname* does not begin with a slash, the default path is changed to the current path with *pathname* appended; tilde-expansion is employed.

(command—line—args)

> Returns a list of the arguments typed on the command line, either to the LISP interpreter, or saved LISP dump, or application compiled with the autorun option, i. e., **liszt —r**.

(cvttointlisp)

> **read** is modified to conform with the Interlisp syntax. The character % is made the escape character. The special interpretation of comma, backquote, and backslash will no longer be made. **read** will subsequently convert uppercase to lowercase.

(cvttofranzlisp)

read is modified to conform with Franz's default syntax. Backslash is made the escape character, and superparentheses are made to work. **read** will subsequently distinguish between uppercase and lowercase.

(cvttomaclisp)

read is modified to conform with MacLISP syntax. The character / is made the escape character. The special interpretations for backslash and left and right bracket are no longer recognized. **read** will subsequently not distinguish lower case from upper case.

(cvttoucilisp)

read is modified to conform with UCI-LISP syntax. The character / is made the escape character, tilde is made the comment character, exclamation point becomes the unquote read macro in place of comma. Backslash, comma, and semicolon no longer have a special interpretation. **read** will subsequently not distinguish lower case from upper case.

(deref *fixnum*)

Returns the contents of *fixnum* interpreted as a longword memory location.

(dumplisp *"filename"*)

The current LISP process is dumped to the named file. When *filename* is executed, the resulting process will be in the same state as when the **dumplisp** was done.

(exec -*"symbols"*-)

Returns the result of forking and executing the command string created by concatenating the symbols together with spaces in between.

(exece *symbol [(-argumentsymbols-) [(-environmentsymbols-)]])*

The LISP process is overlaid by the process obtained by executing the command *symbol* with the specified arguments and environment. If the command cannot be executed, the system error code is returned.

(exit *[fixnum]*)

The LISP process dies with exit code *fixnum* (0 is the default).

(fake *fixnum*)

Returns the LISP object at address *fixnum*.

(fork)

A copy of the current LISP process is created and both processes are run. **nil** is returned to the child process and the process number of the child to the parent.

(gc)

Causes a garbage collection.

(gcafter *"type"***)**

After a garbage collection caused by running out of data type *type*, **gcafter** is called. It allocates more space of the appropriate type if necessary.

(getenv *symbol***)**

Returns a symbol whose name is the value of *symbol* in the current UNIX environment.

(hashtabstat)

Returns a list of fixnums representing the number of symbols in each bucket of the oblist.

(help *["atom"]***)**

If *atom* is a symbol, then the section of the LISP manual describing *atom* is printed. If *atom* is a fixnum or the name of one of the appendices, that chapter or appendix is printed. If no argument is provided, **help** prints the options that it recognizes.

(include *"filename"***)**

The given filename is **load**ed into LISP. **include** is treated specially by the compiler, as described in Chapter 20.

(include–if *exp "filename"***)**

This has the same effect as **include**, except that *filename* is read in only if *exp* is non-**nil**.

(includef *filename***)**

Same as **include** except the argument is evaluated.

(includef–if *exp "filename"***)**

Same as **include–if** except the argument is evaluated.

(maknum *exp***)**

Returns the address of *exp* converted into a fixnum.

(monitor *[atom]***)**

> If *atom* is **t** then profiling of the entire LISP process is begun. If it is a fixnum, then profiling is done only up to address *atom*. If *atom* is not given, then profiling is stopped and the data obtained are written to the file **mon.out**.

(oblist)

> Returns a list of all symbols on the oblist.

(opval *symbol [exp]***)**

> If *exp* is specified, the value associated with *symbol* is changed to *exp*. If *symbol* is the name of a LISP data type, then **opval** returns a list of three fixnums representing the number of items of that type in use, the number of pages allocated, and the number of items of that type per page. If *symbol* is **pagelimit**, then **opval** returns the maximum amount of LISP data pages it will allocate. If *exp* is specified, the value associated with *symbol* is changed to **opval**.

(*process *command [readflag [writeflag]]***)**

> Starts another process by passing *command* to the shell. If only one argument is given, ***process** waits for the new process to die and then returns the exit code of the new process. If two or three arguments are given, ***process** starts the process and then returns a list which may contain I/O ports for communcating with the new process. If *writeflag* is non-null, then a port is created for the LISP process to use to send characters to the new process. Similarly for *readflag*. The value returned by ***process** is (*readport writeport pid*) where *readport* and *writeport* are the ports created, or **nil** if the respective port was not requested. *pid* is the process id of the new process.

(*process—receive *command***)**

> The command *command* is given to the shell and it is started running in the background. The output of that command is available for reading via the port returned as the value of this function. The input of the command process is set to **/dev/null**.

(*process—send *command***)**

> The command *command* is given to the shell and it is started running in the background. The LISP process can provide input for that command by sending characters to the port returned by this function. The output of the command process is set to **/dev/null**.

(process *"command" ["symbol1" "symbol2"]***)**

> (This command is obsolete. Use one of the ∗**process** commands given above instead.) If *symbol1* and *symbol2* are given, they are bound to ports which direct characters from the LISP process to the new process and to the LISP process from the new process, respectively. **process** waits for the new process to die iff there no port arguments are given.

(ptime)

> Returns a list of two elements: The first is the amount of processor time used by the LISP system so far, and the second is the amount of time used by the garbage collector so far. The time is measured in those units used by the **times** UNIX system call, usually 60ths of a second. The first number includes the second number. The amount of time used by garbage collection is not recorded until the first call to **ptime**.

(reset)

> The LISP runtime stack is cleared and the system restarts at the top level by executing a **(funcall top–level nil)**.

(restorelisp *filename***)**

> The file *filename* (which should have been created by **savelisp**) is read and a **(reset)** is issued. This is only needed on VMS systems where **dumplisp** cannot be used.

(savelisp *filename***)**

> The current LISP process is saved in the file *filename*. It can be read in by **restorelisp**. This is only needed on VMS systems where **dumplisp** cannot be used.

(segment *type fixnum***)**

> Returns a segment of contiguous LISP values of type *type*. **segment** always allocates new space in 512 byte chunks. Use **small–segment** to allocate space more efficiently.

(shell)

> Forks a new shell and returns the exit code of the shell when it dies.

(signal *fixnum function***)**

> Declares that *function* will handle the signal number *fixnum*. If *function* is **nil**, the signal is ignored. Only four UNIX signals are caught. They are indicated by the following numbers: *interrupt(2), floating exception(8), alarm(14), and hang-up(1).*

(sizeof *exp*)

Returns the number of bytes required to store one object of type *exp*.

(sleep *fixnum*)

Causes the LISP process to sleep for *fixnum* seconds.

(small−segment *type fixnum*)

Returns a segment of *fixnum* data objects of type *type,* which may be either **fixnum**, **flonum**, or **value**. **small−segment** uses **segment** to allocate new space but first tries to fill the request on a page already allocated.

(sstatus *"symbol" "exp"*)

If *symbol* is not one of the special codes described below, **sstatus** sets *exp* as the value of status type *symbol* in the system status property list. The following values of *symbol* have a special interpretation:

appendmap − If *exp* is non-null when **fasl** creates a load map, it appends to the file name given in the **fasl** command, rather than create a new map file. The initial status has value **nil**.

automatic−reset − If *exp* is non-null when an error occurs, a **reset** is done instead of entering a break loop. The initial value is **t**.

chainatom − If *exp* is non-**nil** and a **car** or **cdr** of a symbol is done, then **nil** is returned. Otherwise doing so would cause an error. This does not affect the compiler. The initial value is **nil**.

dumpcore − If *exp* is **nil**, then a segmentation violation or bus error will cause a core dump. If *exp* is non-**nil** then Franz will catch those errors and print a message advising the user to reset. The initial value is **nil** The user is advised never to change it.

dumpmode − All subsequent **dumplisp**'s will be done in mode *exp,* which may be either **413** or **410** (decimal). The initial value is **413**, which has the advantage that the dumped LISP can be demand paged in when first started.

evalhook − *exp* being non-**nil** enables the evalhook and funcallhook traps in the evaluator.

feature − *exp* is added to the list **(status features)** returns.

gcstrings − If *exp* is non-null, and if string garbage collection was enabled when the LISP system was compiled, string space will be garbage-collected. The default value is **nil**.

ignoreeof − If *exp* is non-null, an end-of-file is ignored by the standard top-level interpreter; normally it would cause the LISP process to exit. This has no effect if the standard input is a file or pipe. The initial value is **nil**.

nofeature − *exp* is removed from the status features list if it was present.

translink − If *exp* is **nil** then all transfer table entries are cleared. In addition, further calls through the transfer table will not cause fast links to be set up. If *exp* is the special symbol **on**, then transfer table entries are linked and a flag is set to cause fast links to be set up subsequently. Otherwise only the flag to cause fast links to be set up dynamically is set. The initial value is **nil**.

uctolc − If *exp* is not **nil** then all unescaped capital letters in symbols read by the reader are converted to lowercase.

(status *"type"*)

Returns the value associated with the status code *type* if *type* is not one of the special cases described below. Otherwise it does the following:

ctime − Returns a symbol whose print name is the current time and date. (This has been made obsolete by the function **time−string**.)

feature − Returns **t** if *exp* is in the status features list.

features − Returns a list of features present in the system.

isatty − Returns **t** if the standard input is a terminal.

localtime − Returns a list of fixnums representing the current time with the following interpretation: **(46 36 14 25 11 83 0 358 0)** means 46th second, 36th minute, 14th hour, 25th day, 11th month **(0 −> January)**, 83st year **(0 −> 1900)**, 0th day of the week **(0 −> Sunday)**, 358th day of the year, and daylight savings time is not in effect.

undeffunc − Returns a list of all undefined functions that are pointed to by transfer table entries.

version − Returns a string which is the current LISP version name.

(syscall *fixnum -atoms-*)

Returns the result of issuing the UNIX system call number *fixnum* using the atoms as arguments.

(sys:access *filename mode*)
(sys:chmod *filename mode*)
(sys:gethostname)
(sys:getpid)
(sys:getpwnam *username*)
(sys:link *oldfilename newfilename*)
(sys:nice *fixnum*)
(sys:time)
(sys:unlink *filename*)

As the actual system call numbers may vary among different UNIX systems, users may wish to use this group of functions rather than **syscall**. Another advantage of these functions is that tilde-expansion is performed on all filename arguments. These functions do what is described in the system call section of the UNIX manual.

(time–string *[fixnum]***)**

    Returns a string giving the time and date that is *fixnum* seconds after UNIX's idea of creation (Midnight, Jan 1, 1970 GMT). If no argument is given, the current date is returned.

(top–level)

    This function is the top level **read-eval-print** loop. If it is redefined, and a **(reset)** is issued, then the new top level will be invoked. The default top level for Franz allows one to specify his own printing and reading functions by binding the symbols **top–level–printer** and **top–level–reader**. Also, one can bind the symbol **user–top–level** to a routine that concerns itself only with the **read-eval-print** loop. This leaves the default top level to contend with catching errors, etc.

(wait)

    Returns a dotted pair (*processid . status*) when the next child process dies.

5. FLOW OF CONTROL FUNCTIONS

(and *-"exps"-***)**

    The expressions are evaluated left to right. Evaluation ceases when the first **nil** is computed. The value of the last expression evaluated is returned. **and** returns **t** if called with no arguments.

(caseq *exp -"(key -exps-) "-***)**

    key is either a symbol, a small fixnum, or a list of small fixnums or symbols. Each list is examined until a *key* is found consistent with the *exp*. (If *key* is a symbol or a fixnum, the two must be **eq**. If it is list, then *key* must be **eq** to some element of the list. The symbol **t** is special: it matches anything.) Having matched a key in a list, **caseq** evaluates each expression within the list and returns the value of the last one. If no match occurs, **nil** is returned.

(catch *"exp" ["tag"]***)**

    Equivalent to (***catch** *tag exp*). If *tag* is not given, it is assumed to be **nil**.

(*catch *tag exp***)**

    This is the internal function used to implement **catch**. *tag* is either a symbol or a list of symbols. ***catch** evaluates *exp*. If it evaluates normally, its value is returned. If, however, a call to **throw** occurs during the evaluation of *exp,* then ***catch** returns with the value passed to **throw** if the **throw** is made to the tag *tag,* or to a member of *tag* if *tag* is a list, or if *tag* is **nil**.

(cond - *"(test -exps-) "*-**)**

    cond is the basic LISP structure for conditional evaluation of s-expressions. The tests are evaluated in order until one returns non-**nil**. Then the expressions following that test are evaluated, and the value of the last one returned. If no test returns non-**nil**, **nil** is returned.

(do (- *"(symbol [exp1 [exp2]])"* -) *"test"* - *"exps"*-**)**
(do *"symbol"* *"exp1"* *"exp2"* *"test"* - *"exps"*-**)**

    These are more structured iterative forms. The symbols are initialized to *exp1* and reset to *exp2* each time through the loop. In the more elaborate version, *test* has the form of a **cond** clause (or else is **nil**). Its **car** is evaluated, and, if the result is non-null, the rest of its elements are evaluated and the value of the last one is returned as the value of the **do**. If the **cdr** of *test* is **nil**, then **nil** is returned. If the test does not pan out, the expressions are evaluated. In the simpler version of **do**, *test* is just an expression that is evaluated, and the function exits with **nil** if *test* evaluates to non-**nil**. The expressions of the **do** are treated just like **prog** expressions, meaning that they may contain labels and the function **go** and **return** are legal here.

(err *[symbol [nil]]***)**

    err causes an error to be generated. If the error is caught by an **errset** then that **errset** returns **symbol** instead of **nil**. The second argument exists only for the sake of MacLISP compatibilility, and must be **nil**.

(error *[symbol1 [symbol2]]***)**

    The symbols are printed using **patom** and then **err** is called with no arguments.

(errset *"exp"* *["flag"]***)**

    errset evaluates *exp;* if no error occurs during this evaluation, the list of the value of *exp* is returned. If an error occurs during the evaluation of *exp,* the **errset** returns immediately with value **nil**. If the error is explicitly generated by a call to **err**, then the value of the argument to **err** is returned. *flag* is evaluated before *exp;* if it is not given, it is assumed to be **t**. If an error occurs during the evaluation of *exp* and *flag* evaluated to a non-null value, then the error message associated with the error is printed before control returns to **errset**.

(go *"exp'*)

    exp is either a symbol or an expression. If it is an expression, that expression is evaluated and should result in a symbol. Control is transferred to just after the symbol *exp* in the current **prog** or **do** body. This is only valid in the context of a **prog** or **do** body. The compiler does not allow *exp* to be a non-atomic expression.

(if *exp1 exp2*)

    This is a macro that expands into a **cond**. **(if a b)** equivalent to **(cond (a b))**; **(if a b c ...)** is equivalent to **(cond (a b) (t c ...))**; and

> **(if a then b c**
>   **elseif d then e f**
>   **elseif g thenret**
>   **else h i))**

is equivalent to

> **(cond (a b c)**
>   **(d e f)**
>   **(g)**
>   **(t h i))**

(map *function -lists-*)

    The function *function* is applied to successive sublists of the lists, which should all have the same length. The first argument list is returned.

(mapc *function -lists-*)

    function is applied to successive elements of the lists. All of the lists should have the same length. The first argument list is returned.

(mapcan *function -lists-*)

    function is applied to successive elements of the argument lists, and the resulting values are **nconc**ed together and returned.

(mapcar *function -lists-*)

    function is applied to successive elements of the argument lists. The list of the resulting values is returned.

(mapcon *function -lists-*)

    function is applied to successive sublists of the argument lists. The resulting values are **nconc**ed together.

(maplist *function -lists-*)

    function is applied to successive sublists of the arguments lists. The list of the resulting values is returned.

(or *-"exps"-*)

    Evaluation proceeds left to right and stops as soon as one of the arguments evaluates to a non-null value. This value is returned.

(prog (*-"symbols"-*) *-"exps"-*)

    The symbols are lambda-bound to **nil** and the expressions are evaluated from left to right. Atomic expressions are treated as labels. The functions **return** and **go** are allowed. The old values of the symbols are restored when the **prog** is exited.

(prog1 *exp1 -exps-*)

    The expressions are evaluated from left to right and the value of *exp1* is returned.

(prog2 *exp1 exp2 -exps-*)

    The expressions are evaluated from left to right and the value of *exp2* is returned.

(progn *-exps-*)

    The expressions are evaluated from left to right and the value of the last expression is returned.

(progv (*-symbols-*) (*-exps-*) *-exps-*)

    The expressions in the second argument are bound to the symbols in the first. If there are too few expressions, the missing values are assumed to be **nil**. If there are too many, the extra ones are evaluated but otherwise ignored. Then the second group of expressions is evaluated left to right. The previous values of the symbols are restored upon exiting, and the value of the last expression evaluated is returned.

(return *[exp]*)

    Returns *exp* from the enclosing **prog** or **do** body. If *exp* is missing it is assumed to be **nil**.

(selectq *exp -"(key -exps-) "-*)

    Like **caseq**, except that the symbol **otherwise** has the same semantics as the symbol **t** when used as a key.

(throw *exp [tag]***)**

> Returns the value of **(∗throw** *tag exp***)**. *tag* defaults to **nil** if it is not specified.

(∗throw *tag exp***)**

> *exp* is returned from the first enclosing **catch** that has either no tag or the tag *tag*.

(unwind—protect *"exp" - "exps"*-**)**

> *exp* is evaluated and its value saved; then the expressions are evaluated and the saved value of *exp* is returned. If, during the evaluation of *exp* control is caused to pass through *exp* and thus through the call to **unwind—protect**, the expressions will still be evaluated. The expressions are usually used to cleaned up something if *exp* is not completely evaluated.

6. EVALUATION CONTROL FUNCTIONS

(apply *function list***)**

> Returns the result of applying function *function* to the arguments in the list *list*.

(environment *[when-list what-list ...]***)**
(environment—maclisp *[when-list what-list ...]***)**
(environment—lmlisp *[when-list what-list ...]***)**

> These are used mainly to control when the compiler or the interpreter evaluates a form. The *when-lists* are sublists of the list **(eval compile load)**; the interpreter only pays attention to *what-lists* that are preceded by *when-lists* that contain the atom **eval**. The *what-lists* are of either the form **(file** -*"file-names"*-**)** or the form **(syntax** *type***)**, where *type* is one of **maclisp**, **intlisp**, **ucilisp**, or **franzlisp**. If they are of the former variety, this ensures that the named files are loaded. To see if a file is loaded, LISP looks for a **version** property under that file name's property list. Thus putting **(putprop 'myfile t 'version)** at the end of the file **myfile.l** prevents multiple loadings of that file. If a *what-list* is of the latter form, the corresponding syntax is set up. **environment—maclisp** sets the MacLISP environment and **environment—lmlisp** sets up the LISP machine environment. The latter is like MacLISP with some additional macros. For these specialized environments, the only *what-list* clauses that are useful are those containing file specifications.

(eval *exp [number]*)

Returns the result of evaluating *exp*. If a *number* is given, it is interpreted as the length of the variable binding stack at a certain point, and the bindings of symbols are interpreted with respect to this point on the stack.

(evalframe *number*)

Returns an *evalframe descriptor* for the evaluation frame just before *number*, or just before the current call to **evalframe** if *number* is **nil**. An evalframe descriptor describes a call to **eval**, **apply**, or **funcall**. A descriptor is of the form (*type pdl-pointer expression bind-pointer np-index lbot-index*) where *type* is **eval**, **apply**, or **funcall**, depending on the function that caused the evaluation to happen. *pdl-pointer* is a number which can be used to refer to the context of this call. It can be passed to **evalframe** to obtain the next descriptor and to **freturn** to cause a return from this context. *bind-pointer* is the size of variable binding stack when this evaluation began; if passed as a second argument to **eval**, the bindings of symbols in the s-expression being evaluated will be taken from this context. If *type* is **eval**, then *expression* has the form (*function-name arg1* ...); if *type* is **apply**, then *expression* has the form (*function-name (arg1* ...)). *np-index* and *lbot-index* are pointers into the "namestack array" at the time of call. *lbot-index* points to the first argument; *np-index* points one beyond the last argument. **(*rset t)** must have been called for **evalframe** to work properly (this is the default)

(evalhook *exp function1 [function2]*)

The symbol **evalhook** is bound to *function1*, and, if *function2* is given, **funcallhook** is bound to *function2*. Then *exp* is evaluated. When **eval** is called, and if the symbol **evalhook** is non-**nil**, **eval** binds **evalhook** and **funcallhook** to **nil** and calls the function that was the value of **evalhook**, passing it the expression passed to **eval** as an argument. It is this function's responsibility to evaluate the expression. (Normally, this is a user function that calls the function **evalhook** to do the evaluation. This allows the evaluation process to advance one step at a time, subject to the control of the user's function.) In order for this to work, **(*rset t)** and **(sstatus evalhook t)** must be the current state of affairs (this is the default).

(eval–when *(-"keywords"-) -"exps"-*)

The keywords may be **eval**, **load**, or **compile**. If the keywords include **eval**, then the expressions are evaluated by the interpreter. The other keywords are meaningful only to the LISP compiler. **compile** means that the compiler will evaluate each of the expressions. **load** means that the compiler will compile each of the expressions.

(freturn *pdl-pointer exp***)**

Returns *exp* from the context given by *pdl-pointer,* where the latter refers to some expression currently being evaluated. The pdl-pointer for a given expression can be obtained from **evalframe.**

(funcall *function [-exps-]***)**

Returns the value of applying function *function* to the expressions. If *function* is a macro then that result is evaluated. For lamdbda, lexprs, and arrays, as many expressions are supplied to **funcall** as *function* requires. To **funcall** an nlambda or a macro, only one expression is supplied. In the case of an nlambda, the expression should be a list of all actual arguments; in the case of a macro, the expression should be the entire call to the macro.

(funcallhook *list function1 [function2]***)**

The symbol **funcallhook** is bound to *function1* and, if it is given, **evalhook** is bound to *function2.* Then **funcall** is used to apply the **car** of *list* to the already evaluated arguments in the **cdr** of *list.* If **funcall** is called recursively in the process, and if *function1* is non-null, then the arguments to **funcall** will be given to *function1* to be **funcall**ed. In order for this to work, **(∗rset t)** and **(sstatus evalhook t)** must have been done previously (this is the default), and *function1* must be a lexpr.

(function *"function"***)**

Returns the function binding of *function* if it is a symbol that has a function binding; otherwise *function* is returned.

(let *"list" - "exps"-***)**

list is a (possibly empty) list of objects of the form (*symbol expression*). When a **let** is entered, all of the *expression*s are evaluated and then simultaneously bound to the corresponding symbols. Next, the *exps* are evaluated and the symbols restored to their previous values. If *list* contains an element that is just a symbol, the expression corresponding to that symbol is assumed to be **nil.** If it contains an element whose first element is another list, then that list is assumed to be a set of bindings and **let** applies **desetq** to it.

(let∗ *"list" - "exps"-***)**

This is just like **let** except that the expressions in *list* are evaluated and bound sequentially instead of in parallel.

(lexpr—funcall *function [-exps-] list***)**

The expressions and the elements of *exp* are stacked. Then *function* is **funcall**ed. The last expression must be a (possibly empty) list.

(∗rset *flag***)**

If *flag* is non-**nil** then LISP maintains the information about calls to **eval** and **funcall** that is required for the functions **evalhook, funcallhook,** and **evalframe** to work. Evaluation is slowed down somewhat as a consequence.

7. DEBUGGING FUNCTIONS

(baktrace)

The names of the functions currently in execution are printed, the most recently active appearing first. **(sstatus translink nil)** needs to be done to trace compiled code. Even so, **baktrace** occasionally misses the names of compiled LISP functions.

(break *[exp1 [exp2]]***)**

Returns the value of **(∗break** *exp1 exp2***)**. If *exp1* is not given it is assumed to be the null string; if *exp2* is not given it is assumed to be **t.**

(∗break *exp1 exp2***)**

If *exp1* evaluates to non-null, the interpreter stops and prints out **Break** followed by *exp2*. Then it enters the break **read-eval-print** loop. **return, retbrk,** and **reset** are valid here.

(debug *[message]***)**

Enters the debugger. If an argument is given, it is treated as a message to be printed before the debug loop is entered. Once in the loop, the following special commands are recognized:

top − go to top of stack (latest expression)
bot − go to bottom of stack (first expression)
p − show current expression (with ellipsis)
pp − show current expression in full
where − give current stack position
help − list the recognized debugger commands
dn − move down the stack
u − move up the stack
ok − continue after an error or debug loop
redo − restart the computation with the current stack frame
redo *f* − restart the computation with the last call to function *f*
step − restart the computation at the current stack frame, turning on

365

stepping mode.

return *e* − return from the current position in the computation with the value *e*.

bk − print a backtrace. The **bk** command may be suffixed by one or more of the following modifiers: **f** − show function names instead of expressions, **a** − show all functions/expressions, not just user-written ones, **v** − show variable bindings as well as functions/expressions, **e** − show the expression without using ellipsis, **c** − go no further than the current position on the stack

bk.. *n* − show only *n* levels of the stack (starting at the top)

bk.. *f* − show stack down to first call of function *f*

bk.. *n f* − show stack down to *nth* call of function *f*

(debugging *exp*)

If *exp* is non-null, Franz makes some internal changes that facilitate debugging. These include unlinking the transfer tables, doing a (**∗rset t**), and setting the flag **ER%all** to be **debug−err−handler.** If *exp* is **nil**, all of these changes are undone.

(retbrk *[fixnum]*)

If *fixnum* is negative, **retbrk** moves up *fixnum* levels, or goes to the top level if there are not enough. If *fixnum* is non-negative, **retbrk** moves to the *fixnum*-th level. If *fixnum* is not present, the value −**1** is assumed.

(retrace)

This ensures that all functions that should be traced are being traced. If a function is being traced, and then a file containing that function definition is loaded, calling **retrace** will make sure that that function is still being traced.

(showstack *-flags-*)

All s-expressions currently being evaluated are printed, beginning with the most recently attempted evaluation. If **showstack** is given an argument of **t**, it will print some forms on the stack that are normally not of interest. Given a numeric argument of n, it will only print the first n items on the stack. A call of the form (**showstack lev n)** will abbreviate expressions of more than **n** levels; a call of the form (**showstack len n)** will abbreviate expressions of more than **n** elements.

(trace *-specialforms-*)

The functions indicated by the special forms are traced. If no argument is given, the list of functions currently being traced is returned. The special forms are interpreted as follows:

function — the function *function* is to be traced.

(*function* **break**) — LISP breaks upon entering *function*.

(*function* **if** *exp*) — trace if *exp* is non-null.

(*function* **ifnot** *exp*) — trace if *exp* is **nil**.

(*function* **evalin** *exp*) — trace and evaluate *exp* after *function* is entered.

(*function* **evalout** *exp*) — trace and evaluate *exp* when *function* exits.

(*function* **evalinout** *exp*) — trace and evaluate *exp* when *function* is entered and when it exits.

(*function* **lprint**) — trace and use the level printer to print the arguments to *function*.

(*function1* **traceenter** *function2*) — causes *function2* to be called when *function1* is entered. *function2* should be a function of two arguments, and will be applied to *function1* and the list of its actual arguments.

(*function1* **traceexit** *function2*) — similar to the previous form but *function2* is called upon exiting.

(*function* **evfcn** *exp*) — causes *exp* to be evaluated to get the value of *function* applied to its arguemnts.

(*function1* **printargs** *function2*) — causes *function2* to be used to print the arguments to *function1*.

(*function1* **printres** *function2*) — causes *function2* to be used to print the result of applying *function1* to its arguments.

(traceargs *"function"* [*"fixnum"*]**)**

The arguments to the *fixnum*-th call to the traced function *function* are returned. *fixnum* defaults to **1**.

(tracedump)

The currently active trace frames are printed on the terminal.

(untrace -*"functions"*-**)**

The specified functions are untraced. If no argument is given, all functions are untraced.

8. FUNCTION DEFINITION FUNCTIONS

(def *"symbol"* *"function-form"***)**

Makes *function-form* the function definition of *symbol*. *function-form* must be either a **lambda**, **nlambda**, **macro**, or **lexpr** form. The keywords **&optional**, **&rest**, and **&aux** may appear in the formal parameter list. These have the same interpretation that they have in **defun**.

(defmacro *"symbol"* *"(-symbols-)"* -*"exps"*-**)**
(defcmacro *"symbol"* *"(-symbols-)"* -*"exps"*-**)**

Define the macro *symbol*. The symbols get bound to the actual arguments and the expressions are evaluated to produce the macro expansion. **defcmacro** defines macros that are only used by the compiler.

These are stored on the property list of *symbol* under the property name **cmacro**. Ordinary macros are stored in the function cell of a symbol.

The symbols designating formal parameters need not appear in a list. Instead, an s-expression of any structure may appear in the formal parameter list position. The resulting macro will expect the actual arguments to appear in this format and will bind them to the corresponding symbols. The keywords **&optional,&rest**, and **& aux** may also appear. These have the same interpretation that they have in **defun**.

(**defun** *"symbol"* [*"type"*] *"list" -exps-*)

Defines *symbol* to be a function of type *type,* where this is either **fexpr**, **expr**. or **macro**. The default is **expr**. If *list* is a non-**nil** symbol, then the type is assumed to be lexpr. Otherwise *list* is interpreted as a list of formal parameters. There are three keywords that can occur in *list:* **&optional** declares that the objects following it correspond to optional arguments. If the object is a symbol, it will be bound to an actual argument if given, or to **nil** otherwise. If the object is a list, the first element will be bound to the optional argument if given, or to the value of the second element otherwise. If a third element appears, it will be bound to **t** if the optional argument is supplied, and to **nil** otherwise. **&rest** declares that all actual arguments not accounted for by previous parameters are to be bound to the symbol following it. **&aux** declares that the objects following it specify local variables. If they are symbols, they are lambda-bound to **nil**; if they are lists, then the first element is the local variable and it is lambda-bound to the value of the second.

If any of these keywords appear, they must appear in the order **&optional &rest &aux**.

(**putd** *symbol function*)

Sets the function binding of *symbol* to *function*.

9. MISCELLANEOUS FUNCTIONS

9.1. Lexpr Functions

(**arg** [*fixnum*])

The *fixnum*-th argument to the enclosing lexpr is returned. If *fixnum* is not specified, then this returns the number of arguments to the enclosing lexpr.

(listify *fixnum***)**

>   Returns a list of *fixnum* of the arguments to the current lexpr. If *fixnum* is negative then a list of last −*fixnum* arguments is returned.

(setarg *fixnum exp***)**

>   The current lexpr's *fixnum*-th argument is set to *exp.*

9.2. Declaration Functions

(declare *-"exps"-***)**

>   This is a no-op to the interpreter. **declare** tells the compiler that certain symbols are to be treated specially. See Chapter 20 for more detail.

(defvar *"symbol" [exp]***)**

>   This is useful primarily with respect to compiled code, where it occurs on the top level of a file. It declares *symbol* to be special. If *exp* is present, and *symbol* is unbound when the file is read in, *symbol* is set to the value of *exp.*

9.3. Other

(comment *[-exps-]***)**

>   This does nothing except cause its arguments to be evaluated and return the symbol **comment**.

Appendix B

Special Franz LISP Symbols

A number of symbols are used as global variables by Franz LISP. Many of them have unusual names to avoid clashing with user symbols. Various Franz LISP internal functions inspect the value of one or more of these symbols, and adapt their behavior accordingly. Other functions set the value of a symbol to allow the user access to certain information. These symbols and their associated interpretations are as follows:

ER%all — Its value is the function that LISP uses to handle errors.

ER%brk — Its value is the function that handles the error signal generated by the function **break**.

ER%err — Its value is the function that handles the error signal generated by the function **err**.

ER%misc — Its value is the function that handles the error signal generated by an unclassified error. Most errors are currently unclassified.

ER%tpl — Its value is the function that is called when an error has occurred that has not been handled otherwise.

ER%undef — Its value is the function that handles the error signal generated by a call to an undefined function.

defmacro—for—compiling − During compilation, if its value is non-null, macros defined by **defmacro** are compiled and included in the object file.

environment − Its value is the UNIX environment in **assoc** list form.

errlist − When **reset** is executed, the value of **errlist** is saved. After control is transferred to the top level, **eval** is mapped over the saved value.

errport − Its value is a port initially bound to the standard error file.

evalhook − If this symbol is bound, its value is the function that handles evalhook traps.

float—format − Its value is a string that describes the format to be used by **print** to print flonums. See the UNIX documentation on **printf** for a list of allowable formats.

funcallhook − If this symbol is bound, its value is the function that handles funcallhook traps.

$gccount$ − Set to the number of garbage collections that have occurred.

gcdisable − If its value is non-**nil**, then garbage collections are not done automatically when a collectable data type runs out of storage.

$gcprint − If its value is non-**nil**, then a summary of storage allocation is printed after each garbage collection and subsequent storage allocation.

ibase − Its value is the input radix used by **read**. This value may be either eight or ten. Numbers with a decimal point are assumed to be decimal regardless of the value of **ibase**.

$ldprint − If its value is non-**nil**, then during each **fasl** or **cfasl** a diagnostic message is printed.

linel − Its value is the line length used by the pretty-printer, **pp**.

nil − This symbol designates the empty list. Its value is always **nil**. An attempt to change its value results in an error.

piport − Its value is a port initially bound to the standard input (usually the keyboard). A **read** with no arguments reads from **piport**.

poport − Its value is a port initially bound to the standard output (usually the terminal). A **print** with no second argument sends its output to

poport.

prinlength — If its value is a positive fixnum, then **print** prints no more than **prinlength** elements of a list or hunk. Additional elements are abbreviated as **....** **prinlength** is **nil** initially.

prinlevel — If its value is a positive fixnum, then **print** prints only **prinlevel** levels of nested lists or hunks. Lists below this level are abbreviated by **&**; hunks below this level are abbreviated by **%**. **prinlevel** is **nil** initially.

ptport — If its value is a port, then all output sent to the standard output is also sent to this port (as long as this port is not also the standard output). Initially bound to **nil**.

$purcopylits — If its value is non-**nil** (the default), literals are put into pure space; otherwise, they are not.

readtable — Its value is an array representing the current readtable. (Note — The elements of the value of **readtable** should not be changed using array functions. Instead, use **setsyntax** to change these values. **(status syntax ...)** may be used to read these values.)

$sldprint — Used by **sload** to determine how to print forms.

sload-print — Used by **sload** to determine the printing function used to print forms.

sloadprintarg — This is the property name used by **sload** to determine where the name of a function being defined appears in a call to a function definition function.

t — This symbol is used as a default non-**nil** value. **t** has the value **t**.

top-level — If **/usr/lib/lisp/toplevel.l** is not loaded, then, after a **reset**, the value of **top-level** is **funcalled** if it is non-**nil**. If **/usr/lib/lisp/toplevel.l** is loaded, **top-level** is set to **franz-top-level**. In this case, **reset** is changed so that once **franz-top-level** starts, it cannot be replaced by changing **top-level**. **franz-top-level** provides its own mechanism for changing the top level, via the symbol **user-top-level**.

top-level-print — If its value is non-**nil**, then that value is used by the top level to print out the result of each evaluation.

top-level-read — If its value is non-**nil**, then that value is used by the top level to read forms for evaluation.

user-top-level — If this symbol is bound, then, after a **reset**, instead of

372

entering a **read-eval-print** loop, the value of this symbol is **funcall**ed.

ˆ**w** — If its value is non-**nil**, output to the standard output port (i. e., **poport**) is not printed. Instead, the output is simply thrown away. For the sake of MacLISP compatibility, system error handlers bind ˆ**w** to **nil** to assure that error messages are not lost. ˆ**w** is a two character symbol, not a control character.

Bibliography

Allen, John. (1978). *Anatomy of LISP.* McGraw-Hill, New York.

Charniak, E., Riesbeck, C., and McDermott, D. (1979). *Artificial Intelligence Programming Techniques.* Lawrence Erlbaum Associates, Hillsdale, New Jersey.

Church, Alonzo. (1941). "The Calculi of Lambda-Conversion." In *Annals of Mathematical Studies,* Vol. 6. Princeton University Press, New Jersey.

Foderaro, John. (1985). "The Franz LISP Manual." Franz, Inc., Alameda, California.

McCarthy, John. (1960). "Recursive Functions of Symbolic Expressions and their Computation by Machine, Part I." In *Communications of the ACM,* Vol. 3, No. 4, pp. 185-195, April 1960.

McCarthy, J., Abrahams, P. W., Edwards, D. J., Hart, T. P., and Levin, M. I. (1962). *LISP 1.5 Programmer's Manual.* MIT Press, Cambridge, Massachusetts.

Meehan, J. R. (1979). *The New UCI LISP Manual.* Lawrence Erlbaum Associates, Hillsdale, New Jersey.

Moon, David. (1974). *MACLISP Reference Manual,* Version 0. Laboratory for Computer Science, MIT, Cambridge, Massachusetts, April 1974.

Rich, Elaine. (1983). *Artificial Intelligence.* McGraw-Hill, New York.

374

Siklossy, Laurent. (1976). *Let's Talk LISP.* Prentice-Hall, Englewood Cliffs, New Jersey.

Sussman, G., and Abelson, H. (1983). *The Structure and Interpretation of Computer Programs.* MIT Press, Cambridge, Massachusetts.

Teitelman, Warren. (1974). *INTERLISP Reference Manual.* Xerox Corporation, Palo Alto Research Center, Palo Alto, California, and Bolt Beranek and Newman, Cambridge, Massachusetts.

Touretzky, David S. (1983). *LISP: A Gentle Introduction to Symbolic Computation.* Harper and Row, New York.

Weinreb, Daniel L., and Moon, David. (1978). *LISP Machine Manual.* Artificial Intelligence Laboratory, MIT, Cambridge, Massachusetts.

Winston, P. H. (1977). *Artificial Intelligence.* Addison-Wesley, Reading, Massachusetts.

Winston, P. H., and Horn, B. H. (1981). *LISP.* Addison-Wesley, Reading, Massachusetts.

Index

Entries whose names begin with non-alphabetic characters are found under the first alphabetic character in their name. For example, *rset appears as if it were **rset**. Entries without alphabetic characters in their names appear at the end of this index. Page numbers in italics refer to the descriptions of functions given in Appendix A.

Index

378

Index

Index

384